HOLISTIX

CAROLE CAPLIN
AND SYLVIA CAPLIN

Cartoons by Gray Jolliffe

SIDGWICK & JACKSON

LONDON

The publishers would like to thank the following for all their hard work:
Design: Hammond Hammond
Freelance editing: Karen Hurrell
Exercise drawings: Rick Sullivan

First published in Great Britain in 1990 by
Sidgwick & Jackson Ltd
1 Tavistock Chambers, Bloomsbury Way
London WC1A 2SG

Reprinted September 1990

ISBN 0 283 06040 9

Photoset in Linotron Century Old Style by
Rowland Phototypesetting Ltd,
Bury St Edmunds, Suffolk

Printed in Great Britain by
Butler and Tanner Ltd, Frome and London

Contents

Acknowledgements

First of all, my profound thanks to all the top experts who have helped me to create Holistix and write this book:

Ron Clubley, practitioner in ortho-bionomy, and his wife, Sheila Clubley, of the Natural Healing Centre. Life simply has not been the same since I met you and I have a feeling that this is going to escalate. Your wisdom and dedication are awesome and I am honoured to have met you in this life; Professor John W.T. Dickerson, Professor of Human Nutrition, University of Surrey, Guildford. Thank you for being so generous with your astounding knowledge and guidance; Keith Edmunds FRCOG, FRACOG, eminent gynaecologist. Thank you for your care and the amount of time you have spent with us; Caroline Guy BSc (Hons), MRODO, and Melanie Coutinho BSc (Hons), MRODO, cranial osteopaths, who have been at the end of the phone or on my doorstep in the blink of an eye, for invaluable advice; Sally Goss EDH, DDHE, secretary and director of the Consumer Services for the British Dental Health Foundation; Clare Harvey-Thompson, Bach's remedy practitioner, and Eliana Harvey, Shen Tao therapist. Thank you both for taking such good care of the people who come into contact with you; Pamela Hornby, colour consultant. Thank you for adding something special; Dr Elizabeth Lee MB, BS, GP; Dr George Lewith MA, MRCP, MRCGP; Phillip Hynd and Anni Nicholls B.Soc.Sci., Dip.Th.Psy., MSAPP, of Harley Young Associates, consultant trainers in the private, public and corporate bodies in communication, personal management and future planning, who have been there as teachers and friends and who have shared every joy and heartache. Their advice has been invaluable to this book; Karin Reece, a special thank you for help on nutrition; Denise Sedar DTHD, dietary therapist. You opened my eyes and set me on a road of learning that I will be eternally grateful for; Bharti Vyas MBA, BTAC, CIDESCO, paramedical beauty therapist. Thank you for being the one person who believed in me and backed Holistix right from the beginning. Your own work has always been a true inspiration and learning ground for me and all those who have come into contact with you; Margaret Balfour, beautician.

Secondly, I would like to acknowledge the following people who have left a stamp on my heart:

Pearl Reed, who stuck by my side and is a constant inspiration to me.
Rose Shepherd of the *Sunday Times*, whose quiet care and brilliant writing inspires me to carry on. Heather McGlone of the *Daily Express*, who was responsible for a centre-spread article that resulted in the Holistix book and video coming to life. Karen Robinson, who wrote the first-ever article on Holistix and set a precedent for the quality of our press ever since. Kim and Robert, who gave life to the idea of Holistix. Mandy Pearson, who was responsible for marrying me to Sidgwick & Jackson. Pete Sofroniou and Nancy Bravo: thank you for all your personal care and wisdom, and for the inspirational cooking that stopped me reverting to junk food. Gemma Craven and David Beamish: not a day goes by when I don't think about you with a grin. Thank you for your constant support and friendship. Katie Orchard and J.J. Caruth, for hours of labour typing up my scribble. Stella Risner, my grandmother. At eighty-eight years of age she plays tennis, drives everywhere and runs rings around me. Thank you for being such an example of the generosity of life itself. My father and stepmother, Michael and Rosemary Caplin: thank you for providing me with the backbone and much-needed prodding to do what I do. Beryl Shackleton: thank you for being my fairy godmother at a time when I desperately needed one. Michael Shackleton: without your crucial presence in my life I would have never known how to be calm and patient. I can't imagine life without you looking over my shoulder. Thank you for entering into the lion's den with such trust and love, for being there for me to lean on, and for providing me with a sanctuary when my whole world was going mad. Barbara Townsend MBE, B' Geipel, Sarah McClean, Brigitte Jaquillard of Educom International, and Kate Owen, for your continued support and encouragement. Simon Kemp: your courage and love saw me through all this, and I cherish you for everything you taught me. You are in my heart forever. Diane Rule, who is my right arm and leg. Thank you for aspiring beyond all my expectations to every challenge and demand I have thrown at you, and for being there at my side injecting ideas and inspiration whenever I was falling down. Your input into this book has been invaluable. Caroline Shott: quite simply my saviour. Where you go I go. My editor and constant support throughout this project, Gill Paul. Thank you for your faith, your invaluable input and expertise, and, of course, patience. Peter Robinson, my literary agent. Your energy, belief and constant encouragement for the book has been a guiding force from the beginning to the end. Thank you.

I dedicate this book with all my heart to Sylvia, my mother, who is the first and foremost inspiration in every area covered within. Her courage and determination have shown that anything is possible. Thank you for giving birth to my dream.

Foreword

IT TOOK TEN years to bring together all the ideas that were to become Holistix – and a lot of trial and error along the way. I got things abysmally wrong over and over again, from my eating habits to my career and my relationships, and a lot of the information in this book was learned the hard way!

I was lucky to be involved over the years in many diverse forms of education, business and communication, and in time I realized that what seemed to be lacking in most people's lives was a comprehensive health and fitness plan that guided them in *everything* they needed to know in that area. No one had ever brought together all the strands of knowledge about nutrition, exercise, relationships, good health, and so on, and demonstrated how they interlink and affect each other – as, of course, they do.

The idea for Holistix was born out of a desire to provide people with a way of looking at the whole picture of themselves, and to explore the hidden aspects that stop them from getting what they want out of life. The information that I have put together in this book has been gleaned over the years from the top experts in each field – osteopaths, nutritionists, orthodox and alternative practitioners, gynaecologists, paramedical beauticians, aromatherapists and many, many more – and most important of all, thousands of people's real-life experiences. Each tip has been tried and tested by the Holistix team, so we recommend them with complete confidence.

I have chosen a vast mixture of subjects – some well-known, like nutrition and exercise, where we can address the real nitty-gritty, and some interesting ideas that haven't been touched on before in the modern world of health and fitness. Holistix is not about imposing the same old boring routine upon everyone, but about educating and guiding the individual so that they can make informed choices about their own lives which will suit their lifestyles as well as their physical and psychological makeup. We recognize that no two people are the same and that everyone will have different needs, and invite you to discover the ideal solution for you.

I am not a specialist in all the subjects covered within – but I know the people who are! I have given everything I can to write a book that is both realistic and thorough. What I passionately want is that by the end of this book *you* will have the energy and the determination to take responsibility for yourself – for your life, your body and your health.

CAROLE CAPLIN
AUGUST 1990

It was real-life experience that was the starting block for Holistix, and the net result is that we have developed ways to make healthy living immensely pleasurable and very practical.

ONE

Introducing Holistix

WE LIVE IN a world where people don't communicate with each other, a world where doctors give you just a few minutes to discuss your health – and very often a prescription to get you out of the surgery. It's a world where most people are not entirely happy with their self-images, but, more often than not, they make the wrong moves when it comes to making changes. For instance, they choose crash diets to lose a few pounds rather than looking at the whole picture.

Think for a moment: How many people do you know who take real care of themselves, who make time for their physical and emotional wellbeing? Do *you* take adequate care of yourself?

Today, it seems that very few people are taking notice of their own – or anyone else's – needs. And that's where Holistix comes in.

Holistix is very different to any other health and fitness system you may have come across. In fact, we don't like to call ourselves a 'fitness system', or a 'health plan'. Holistix is about the individual making informed choices, so you will find that you are not dictated to. Most of all, it is about taking responsibility for yourself.

We are concerned with the whole spectrum of health and every aspect of a person's life – from their career to their personal relationships, from their emotional background and upbringing to their everyday ailments.

Holistix is not aimed at a certain type of person. We see a huge variety of people, ranging in age from seventeen to seventy: career men and women; company owners and directors; academics and professionals from the medical field; housewives and models; designers and quite a large number of celebrities, and many more.

The range of problems on which we are asked to advise is just as varied. Concerns about weight are, as you'd probably guess, very common. Stress, lack of energy, and recurring minor illnesses come up all the time. In addition, many clients come to us when they are suffering from – or have recovered from – serious illnesses or injuries.

It is not, however, just the physical symptoms of health, or ill health, that Holistix is concerned with. Dealing with the symptoms is no longer good enough. The only real answer is to get to the root cause of a predicament. By doing this, each individual is in a position to start making the changes that he or she wants to make.

We recognize that many men and women find it difficult (if not practically impossible!) to maintain a healthy lifestyle. Just because you are advised to 'Eat a balanced diet', 'Take more exercise', and so on, does not mean that you are going to find the discipline or desire to do so.

Holistix takes into account your individual strengths and weaknesses and recognizes that not everybody can do the same exercises to the same standard, that the same food does not suit each person, and that we all have differing physical and emotional needs. Therefore, you will find questions and charts throughout the book, especially designed to help you pinpoint your individual requirements.

For the last five years I've been running Holistix courses for all kinds of people from all different walks of life. What we all have in common is that often day-to-day problems and tensions stop us from taking proper care of ourselves. But we do share a desire to improve the way we feel and look, so that we can be more energetic and motivated.

I started Holistix out of a personal desire to be taught exercises properly, with consideration being shown to my own difficulties, in *all* areas of my life. At that time I was two stone overweight, covered with cellulite and very depressed! Also, I had a long-standing back injury which left me with one leg shorter than the other. I was stiff, lazy and incredibly uncomfortable with my body.

Utilizing the training I'd had from an early age in exercise, ballet, swimming and gymnastics, I formulated a series of exercises that helped me to correct my body. This not only resulted in my shape changing, but also enabled me to release an enormous amount of tension. Once I had taken this first step, I tackled nutrition, relaxation and skin. There is more to overall health than just exercise alone!

Each one of us is totally unique. Yet we are

all constantly sold the image of the perfectly toned and slim body, without any consideration of what is right for us as individuals, and what else we need to do besides exercise.

That's why in Holistix we take an interest in each person's nutrition, their day-to-day emotional wellbeing, and relaxation. Problems to do with lack of energy, recurring minor illnesses, insomnia, or bad skin, to name but a few, are all too common.

I know it's a tall order not only to try to persuade you to take exercise, but also to tackle these other areas. From my own experience, I know that if you do, you'll be amazed at how quickly both you and others notice the difference.

Because you have a history of habits to contend with, Holistix does not provide quick-fix, short-lived results. What this book *will* give you is a solid and thorough basis for taking care of yourself and for consistently achieving and maintaining the kind of results you want. What I would love to achieve through this book is that you make the improvements you want so that you feel better about the body you have.

My dream is for the Holistix physical and life skills education to be available for school children as a normal part of the curriculum. Then, perhaps, they won't have all the physical and emotional problems, and lack of knowledge, that we grew up with.

Before that happens, we've got to understand ourselves – examine the reasons for our health and fitness problems, probe into our pasts to discover why we act the way we do or don't, re-educate ourselves about our bodies and the way they work, *and focus on the excuses we offer to avoid taking action*. Think of your life as a puzzle: only when you have completely mastered and understood a part of your life, can you put that piece into the puzzle. When you fully realize all your capabilities, potential and strong and weak points, and are on the road to setting your life in order, you can complete the puzzle. This book will help you to organize those pieces of the puzzle by putting them within easy grasp, so that they fit together. And the finished puzzle could, if you wanted, be one of the most rewarding and satisfying results you ever thought possible.

Through teaching the Holistix courses over the last four years, I have realized how many people out there are capable of achieving real changes in their lives for the better. That's how the idea of the book came about – an attempt to reach many, many more people than we could ever deal with by ourselves. This book is just as thorough and helpful as participating in a course. But to start with we thought you might like to know how the Holistix course works in practice.

THE CONSULTATION

The course begins with a two-hour Consultation and a one-hour Pamper. Clear guidance on how to construct this course at home is given in the following chapters. The rationale behind the Consultation is to help you define for yourself what is and isn't satisfactory in your life, identifying the causes of when and where the dissatisfaction started.

We go into every area that affects the daily upkeep of the body; for example, medical history, nutrition, stress factors, mood swings, good and bad habits, the satisfaction factors in every area of life, ability to relax, tension, injuries, and much more.

This is where we begin to piece the puzzle together. From the information given to us, we are able to decipher the causes of problems. We then discuss, explain and agree what sort of action needs to be taken in order to eliminate problems, and improve physical condition.

There is a great sense of relief at the end of this session, for there is no longer any mystery surrounding daily wellbeing and ability to achieve the results we want. By answering the questions in this book and filling in the tables on pages 19 and 21, and taking in all the relevant information you will be able to do this for yourself.

THE PAMPER

Immediately after the Consultation, we take them through a complete face and body cleanse. This gives us a chance to show them how to relax properly at night, and to wake up feeling refreshed in the morning, rather than feeling the need to sleep for another two hours. We also

It is not the physical symptoms of health, or ill health, that we are involved with at Holistix. Dealing with the symptom is no longer good enough. The only answer is to get to the root cause of a predicament – be it nutritional, psychological, physical or emotional. By doing this, each individual is in a position to start making the changes he or she wants to make.

deal with any specific skin and muscle tension problems they may be suffering from.

From working with people in business, particularly women who run busy households, I realized just how much people neglect themselves. In the process of making sure that every part of a job and a household was attended to, they left no time for themselves, and would inevitably collapse in a heap at the end of the evening.

It became clear that both men and women needed to know how to look after themselves, particularly if their self-esteem was low, so that they could deal successfully with the strains of running a busy home and a career or business. Because many people's main consideration is time, I decided to design a routine that they could do at home. It also enabled me to recommend very specific treatments or remedial treatments that each individual could benefit from. Like nutrition and exercise, I felt that this part of taking care of themselves – pampering, hygiene, understanding how their bodies worked, organization and relaxation – had to be consistent. In Chapter Eight we will go into this

in great detail, showing you how to do this at home.

The Pamper is designed to deal with very intimate, everyday problems that arise – such as acne, psoriasis and body odour – and lends itself greatly to each person being more organized, and caring about their home environment and their bodies. All in all, the Pamper is practical, luxurious and fun – a simple reminder of how relaxing and rejuvenating the bathing routine can be for body, mind and spirit.

THE HOLISTIX EXERCISE PROGRAMME

There is usually a short gap between initial consultation and the start of the exercise programme; this gives us a chance to begin to work on the changes, and to note down any difficulties as they crop up.

We begin the eight-week course of classes with an introductory class, where we explain every exercise thoroughly. We go through posture and breathing, and take great care to correct every individual so that he or she can get as much benefit from the movements as possible. This kind of treatment goes on throughout the course, as we have two studios at our disposal and can take small groups of people, giving each person who needs it an even more private class.

Gradually, each person develops a personal knowledge of how their body works, what it needs and how to make the changes they want to make. Although the classes are demanding, they are a lot of fun, covering suppleness, stamina, posture, breathing, relaxation, reshaping, coordination and correcting injuries. We do this through a vast range of exercises that include floor- and barre-work. We firmly believe that increasing the heart beat by manically jumping up and down is *not* the only answer.

The participants never know quite what to expect from the classes, so they never become complacent. Even if they did the course consistently over a period of two years, they would never learn all the exercises and combinations. I am continuously creating new ones, being ever careful to change the classes daily and weekly to suit each person's needs.

There is always information and advice

Tracey-Joy

*W*hen Tracey first joined Holistix, she was one tough cookie. We found her unapproachable, hostile and sullen.

Physically, she was three stone overweight, and suffered from constipation and sallow and blemished skin. She was lazy and lethargic, and her posture was very poor, from slouching in an attempt to disguise her bust. In general, she was dissatisfied with herself and her life.

All this, despite a happy upbringing by adoptive parents, with caring brothers and sisters, good schooling and an active, intellectual and imaginative mind. At the time she was living with a long-standing, successful boyfriend in the height of luxury, with everything material at her fingertips.

There was obviously a problem, however, because Tracey, always a stone overweight, had gained a further two stone in recent months. She felt fat and unhappy, and at odds with the world. She was addicted to chocolate.

'I remember having things like a huge bowl of trifle for breakfast and I ate pounds of chocolates,' said Tracey. 'My real favourites were the expensive, handmade varieties, and I just thought: Why not? We can afford them.'

She was literally addicted to chocolate, and hardly a day would go by without one trip (or more) to the newsagents.

'I think it was when my generous size fourteens no longer fitted me, and when my bust reached 38FF and I was having to have bras specially made for me, that I realized something needed to be done. I'd tried all kinds of diets and what have you, but nothing had any real effect,' she remembered. 'It was all promise and no results. Then I saw an article about Holistix in Cosmopolitan's "Zest" supplement and I just knew that this was the one that could make a difference. I rang up and got straight through to Carole. She asked me loads of questions and we talked for ages. So much of what she said made sense. I immediately signed for the next course.'

One thing about Tracey, which we were to learn over the next few months, is that when she makes a decision to go for something, that's it. This made a potentially traumatic Consultation much less difficult. Consequently, although wary and defensive at first, she slowly opened up to us and we were able to establish a pattern.

During her childhood she had always felt big and clumsy – being the plumpest of the family – with her mother making much of her brains whilst attributing good looks to her sisters.

Her boyfriend, on the other hand, loved her looks and her figure, which she found impossible to deal with. The result? She gained weight, wore unflattering clothes, began scraping her hair back, and her perpetual slouch became worse, probably to hide an ever-increasing bust. It was as if she had set out to make herself big and ungainly, acting out her deep-rooted expectations around her looks.

Having got Tracey to the point of seeing this, we took her a step further, explaining how she felt out of place, and threatened by her boyfriend's business and social circles.

'I always felt one step behind him, as if I was running behind, trying to catch up,' she noted.

We talked her through all this, and she was able to see that she used the food, bingeing and overeating, as a defence mechanism.

The result of all this rooting around in Tracey's past and present lifestyles was that we enabled her to see that she needed to increase her self-esteem, that she wasn't out of control, and that it was entirely within her power to change.

Nutritionally she was all over the place, even without the bingeing. Her affluent lifestyle included late-night meals out, rich food in sauces, and three-course dinners every day, with no proper breakfast, other than the occasional full-blown hotel breakfast. She drank very little liquid to flush all this food through her system.

'I very rarely drank anything at all, and I could go for days without a drop of water passing my lips,' said Tracey.

---

offered at the classes, so that everyone can build on the knowledge they acquired at their Consultation. We will often pick up on low energy, bad moods, depression and other such idiosyncracies, and design the class with those prevalent feelings in mind. They're soon forgotten!

Throughout the course, we keep a constant eye on each person's results and wellbeing, and are available in class or at home twenty-four hours a day, seven days a week, to help with any anxieties or problems. We're also there to receive the good news! Chapter Seven concentrates solely on giving you a comprehensive understanding of how to exercise all areas of the body.

I hope that you have found this chapter useful. Perhaps, it has set you thinking about elements of your life that could be explored on the route to you becoming happier and more satisfied.

The next chapter will begin this process.

So we had to completely re-educate Tracey in terms of food and her eating patterns. We explained why she needed a balanced diet, and what exactly were the effects of the type of rich, spicy and creamy foods she was eating.

We suggested she come off all dairy products other than live, natural, low-fat yoghurt, eat muesli at least once a day to get her bowels working, restrict her food to wholesome, fresh ingredients, eliminate chocolate completely and start drinking two to three litres of water each day. She could hardly deny the logic of all this, and she decided to go for it.

Over the next few months, slowly but surely, a strong relationship developed between Carole and Tracey. Mostly, Tracey was able to stick to her new eating habits, but she would go through short bursts of rebellion and depression. Carole was always there to pick up on this, talk to Tracey, and get her back on the right track by repeatedly encouraging her to re-affirm her desire to change, and leaving her feeling excited and optimistic again.

Tracey steadily lost her weight. One of the main delights and immediate differences was that her bowels started working daily, and all the poisons and toxins in her body began to be flushed away. Drinking two to three litres of water each day also helped with this, and another bonus was that her skin, which had been problematic, began to improve. She was regularly following the skin-care and bathing routine, which contributed enormously to the improvement in her body and facial skin tone.

She began to make other changes – the way she dressed, her hairstyle – and, through the exercise classes, her posture changed dramatically.

'I remember seeing some friends who I hadn't seen for some time and, apart from being stunned by the change in my appearance, they were particularly amazed because I looked so much taller. And I realized that my slump had all but gone,' she recalled.

Later, and three stone lighter, Tracey was a different person: proud of her looks, stylish and elegant, tall with a certain grace. There were, however, certain areas of her life which she needed to work on and at this point she had a major crisis.

She decided to end the relationship with her boyfriend and change her career.

All her old fears and insecurities came flooding back and it wasn't until Carole took her aside and asked what was going on, that Tracey saw herself repeating old patterns. Somehow, she was trying to regain her 'safe' old self to compensate for the fairly hefty changes she was making.

The situation was hardly helped by a boyfriend who wouldn't let go, and 'played games', and in-depth and lengthy job interviews and assessments. In addition, at this time, her search for her natural parents began, adding further stress to an already tense situation. However, with support and encouragement from Carole and Holistix, she got back into the swing of good nutrition and she upped her attendance at classes. Once more her body started to function properly and her weight dropped.

Now, just a few months later, she has finally extricated herself from her boyfriend and has been working at her new job – which she loves! She also found the courage and confidence to meet her real parents, something which she wouldn't have dared do before. The BBC programme, 40 minutes, made a documentary about Tracey finding her parents.

'All in all it has been quite a year. I feel entirely different, as though I've grown up,' said Tracey, confidently. 'I'm now a woman confident in myself rather than just in my abilities. I've now established a life and lifestyle of my own, in which I am contented, optimistic, energetic and much more open to different people and ideas. Physically, I fit comfortably into size twelve clothes, and I'm now able to go to High-Street stores to buy bras. I'm much more daring in my choice of clothes, no longer trying to obscure my body. Whilst buying a swimsuit was always a major trauma, this year, I'm looking forward to having a bikini.'

Holistix works because you call the shots: you educate, question, consult with and pamper yourself. Then you choose from a variety of tips for healthy living, and set your own goals and guidelines, based on the kind of person you are, and the kind of person you want to be. It's been tried and tested: Only you can change you.

TWO

Becoming Aware

HOW OFTEN DO you feel that you are totally satisfied that you are doing everything in your power to attain all you wish for in your home life and your relationships, in your career and in your day-to-day wellbeing?

How much do you think the past events in your life have influenced your physical health today? Do you feel that your present outlook is affecting how motivated you are when it comes to looking after yourself?

I wonder how many of you have found someone who gives enough time and attention to help motivate you to get back in the driver's seat again – and to take control of your circumstances.

Today, the pursuit of health and fitness has concentrated for the most part on giving fast solutions to recurring problems. With Holistix we go much further. We believe that you cannot separate your physical wellbeing from your emotional and intellectual wellbeing.

From the ages of five to thirteen we are called upon to make decisions (both knowingly and unknowingly) which affect the rest of our lives. Personalities, ways of approaching problems and dealing with stress, eating habits, schooling, sleeping habits, choice of interests (for pleasure, education or work), attitudes, demeanour, posture, mannerisms and intonation are all developed through these years. And based on surroundings, encouragement, guidance, approval, criticism, parental and social relationships, we make choices and decisions that remain with us well into, and perhaps completely throughout, our adult years.

Take me, for example. One of the first things I can ever remember was that I did not want to be like anyone in my family – there was a messy divorce, and I was aware from a very early age of the games that were being played by the adults. Given the choice, I chose, at age ten, to go to boarding school. And there I got a further sense of what I did and did not want.

My decision not to be like my family created at first a rebellious, angry side to my character. I got myself into trouble any number of times and learned some pretty tough lessons before I made a conscious decision – at a very young age – to be different. I ended up despising deceit and mind games, and my personality developed from that.

I made decisions about education, and about the people I wished to have as my friends and mentors; I chose what food I liked to eat, and developed bad habits that took me years to change; I discovered that I liked socializing and sport more than I liked studying, something which led to the development of my inter-personal skills, and through that, my choice of career.

It's a frightening thought – our lives were in the hands of very inexperienced, young versions of ourselves. Would we make the same choices again?

It's impossible to stress enough how much effect our childhoods have on ourselves today.

So, in this chapter we will take you through your past and present life, asking you questions which will reveal the sources of your current difficulties. By becoming aware of certain personal issues you will then have very practical information which you can use to change your outlook.

Throughout the chapter we are going to concentrate on helping you to reach a degree of self-knowledge that will show you which direction is right for you. *We are not going to give you pat answers because no two people are the same.*

It is essential that we all become aware that no matter what life has thrown at us in the past, at the end of the day *everyone has a choice* in how we let those events affect us today. I would like you to realize that you have a great capacity to affect anything you choose, it's just a question of looking at the whole picture.

It's time for you to stop blaming events and other people for the things that make you unhappy. If you don't take it upon yourself to take full responsibility for your life, you will not achieve your goals. *Nobody else can do it for you.* However, there is a very exciting and positive side to this: the road to taking responsibility for yourself is challenging and rewarding. You will probably find that it is one of the most interesting journeys you will make. Please don't be put off by the 'New Age' sound of this! It really is very down-to-earth stuff.

WHAT BECOMING AWARE IS LIKE

When you are working through this chapter you will find it very much like having a complete clear-out of your cupboards at home, or your drawers and files at work. You know you have to do it sometime – you even know how good it feels when it's done.

However, for one reason or another, there never seems to be enough time, so you put it off until the nagging in your head becomes too loud to be ignored. First, you empty everything out and it's complete chaos, you don't know where to start. You feel really lethargic and can't imagine ever completing the task. Then, once you've begun, you come across bits and pieces of paraphernalia which distract you – you read scraps of paper, look at photographs or try on clothes you'd forgotten you had.

Then, the worst part comes, when you have to be tough with yourself and throw away things that you have hoarded, but that you know you won't use. When you're halfway through you want to stop. But you know that if you leave it, it will be harder to return to later. So you take a deep breath and plunge back in.

At some point, towards the end of the task, you feel your energy increase and, by the time you've completed the clear-out, you are wondering why you didn't do it much sooner. You may even feel inspired to handle lots of other menial jobs, like writing letters, speaking to the bank manager, or getting the car fixed.

In the process of clearing out, you will have found valuable items that you thought you had lost, and you will often re-organize your room or desk. And, as a result of all of this, you will feel immensely satisfied and optimistic.

Notice when you do a chore like this, the immense range of emotions and thoughts that you went through: lethargy, frustration, irritation, attachment, resentment, wanting to give up, being fully absorbed, increased energy, humour, satisfaction, excitement, feeling ready to tackle anything, and probably ending up by having the best night's sleep in ages. And, as a bonus, you'll probably wake up the next day feeling enthusiastic and refreshed. Some people even feel sexier and physically lighter.

This analogy is the best way that I can describe the range of responses you may encounter when working through this coming chapter.

*F*rom the ages of five to thirteen we are called upon to make decisions which will affect the rest of our lives. In order to understand yourself today – your habits, personality, ways of approaching problems and demeanour – you must become aware of the factors that influenced you and your early decisions. Only then will you have practical information which you can use to change your outlook.

THE COMMENTATOR

At this point, I would like to introduce you to someone who knows you intimately. He or she is sniffing disdainfully as you are reading this, with hands on hips and one eyebrow raised – waiting for the next line to appear. 'Who is it?' I can hear you asking. Let me introduce you to your 'commentator'.

Your commentator is the little voice in your head that passes comment on everything you do, passes judgement on your and other's actions, and screeches if you so much as dare to look risks and fear in the eye, or dare to express outwardly an emotion there and then.

Let me explain further. I am sure you can remember times when you've wanted to go for a salary rise, ask someone for a date or try something really different and haven't. It's at this point that the voice in your head has argued against you and has often won.

Well, that's your commentator. He particularly rears his little head when he feels out of his depth. He remembers the times that you tried things that didn't work out and, so, makes excuses for you not to try again. He wants you to stay 'safe'.

When you are looking at this chapter, listen with one ear to your commentator, but don't take him too seriously. If the questions here raise points that upset or irritate you, allow yourself to express the emotion. You don't have to feel a certain way or have a positive attitude to benefit from this chapter, or the rest of the book.

You will find that your commentator will acquaint him or herself with you at every opportunity. If push comes to shove and your commentator stops you opening the door, you can always buy some darts, put the front cover of this book on a board and throw them at me!

WHAT'S THE RIGHT ATTITUDE?

I would like to get rid of the popular belief that in order to get value from doing this kind of work on yourself you have to 'Think Positive'. We see many men and women who are experiencing feelings of guilt and poor self-esteem, *because of* the Think-Positive approach that was very much a part of the 1980s.

Assuming that you are a normal human being, it almost goes without saying that your emotions swing from one extreme to the other. There are days in your life when everything is going to plan, you wake up with energy and look forward to whatever life has in store for you.

Patricia

Patricia is a young woman of twenty-three who had some fairly severe physical symptoms. These included recurring cystitis, discharge, constipation and painful flatulence. On the emotional side, she was prone to depression, boredom, restlessness together with drug and alcohol abuse at various points in her life.

Her childhood was miserable: rowing parents who eventually divorced. She was then brought up by her grandmother who neglected her. She was often bullied at school and subsequently couldn't relate to normal care and attention.

Throughout her Consultation she was quite hostile and found it almost impossible to open up. She eventually revealed that she had a history of sexual abuse, but was highly offended by the idea that in some way she had contributed to the situations because they fed her overriding need for attention and love.

Her nutrition was appalling – she sometimes went without food for days and, at other times, overate. It was explained to her that her eating habits would need to change but for every suggestion offered, she found a valid reason not to change anything. 'I don't like healthy food', 'I don't have time to cook', 'I share a kitchen', 'I'm abroad a lot'.

It became obvious that she wasn't prepared to make any attempt to help herself. She wanted us to do it for her and present her with a miracle cure. We tried to point out and get her to see that she was living her life as a victim, holding on to emotions and feelings from her upbringing and childhood, and we tried to encourage her to see the patterns, let go of them and start living life afresh as an adult. She refused to acknowledge this possibility. When it was suggested, however, that her attitude to the Consultation simply perpetuated the patterns of behaviour, which were to be very pious and attention-seeking, be it in the form of depression or physical illness, and that she seemed to want to hand over responsibility for her life to other people – doctors, boyfriends, us – she became very hostile and left.

Why waste time trying to improve yourself? It's hopeless. Relax and have another chocolate..

There are also just as many times – if not more – in your life when you wake up feeling depressed, scared, cynical or just plain numb. 'Thinking Positive' at these times is just impossible. *It's normal to have ups and downs.* Whether or not you recognize how those ups and downs affect your physical wellbeing is another question entirely.

Let me give you an example. Often we see people who want to lose or to put on weight. Most of these people have a list of doctors they have seen, diets they have tried, and books they have read. None of these have sufficiently maintained their interest or their will power for them to stick to a regime long enough to reach their desired weight. Others may have reached their targets and then have shot back up, or down, again within months.

It is easy for us to impart all the relevant information and advice about nutrition, digestion and where to shop for good foods in a particular part of town. However, this is usually not enough to produce the result. What really governs their improvement, or lack of it, are the upsets and traumas they have been through in the past, and the ups and downs they are going through in their daily lives. It is the extent to which they are affected emotionally by those problems and ups and downs that determines their commitment to following the advice given. Most of us are unaware that this is what is getting in the way of achieving, say, our desired weight. Hopefully, this has illustrated that there is no 'right attitude'!

WAITING FOR THE RIGHT TIME

When problems crop up, how often do you use the excuse: 'Now is not the right time' or 'I've got too many other problems to deal with'? Waiting for the 'right time' to deal with a problem, or waiting to feel enthusiastic, is probably the worst thing you can do. There is no right time, and you could wait forever to feel more enthusiastic.

The most useful skill of all is to learn to get on with tackling your fears and problems, no matter how you feel. At times, you are going to feel lethargic or depressed, but it is important

not to let those states take their toll on your physical wellbeing by not looking after yourself properly. In fact, it is vitally important that you pay special attention to your body at these times.

Consider your answers to the following questions carefully, and illustrate your answers with examples of the most common situations in which you do this.

1. *In the last three months, how many times do you recall having used the excuse 'Now is not the right time', when tackling a problem concerning:*
   ○ *a) Your weight and your eating habits;*
   ○ *b) Your personal finances;*
   ○ *c) Your relationship; or*
   ○ *d) Your career.*
2. *What is the longest period of time you have waited between knowing you should do something about a problem, and actually starting on a course of action?*
3. *Are you someone who starts a course of action immediately and then, halfway into it, gives up?*
   If the answer is Yes, then think back to the last time this happened and explain your circumstances and reasons for giving it up.

The information your answers have provided will indicate whether you procrastinate or not. *If you are one of those people who does, this has to be addressed before any physical results can be attained.*

TAKING STOCK

Consider for a moment when you last sat down and *really* took stock of all the elements of your life. Do you feel that you are doing everything you can to attain all that you wish for in your relationships, your home and social life, your career, and your mental and physical wellbeing?

In answering this question, do you find it easy to see the role you are playing in all these areas? Or, do you feel that the situations in your life are largely controlled by other people, who constantly get in the way of you being totally

Elaine

Elaine had cancer of the womb. She had been to see psychiatrists who treated her badly, specialists who terrified her and hospitals where she was ignored.

Her history included depression, suppression of desires and emotions, a childhood deprived of love and affection, and a father prone to violent rages. Since then she had repeatedly had disastrous relationships with men of a similar nature.

Her Consultation was pretty tough going – she had expected tea and sympathy and, instead, we explained that her life was just one recurring pattern. She always 'expected' to be treated badly, to be abused and to be a victim of circumstance and, consequently, she set herself up for that to be the case.

For the first time she was suddenly able to see the various dramas and crises in her life from a completely different perspective and see that perhaps blaming everything and everyone for each of her predicaments did nothing to help the situations.

The truth was that she was a victim of cancer – but she had complete control as to how to deal with it and move forwards, and live her life positively.

To Elaine, with a life-long history of being the victim, underdog or loser, this whole concept came as something of a mind-blowing eye-opener. She immediately made a decision to create a different life for herself. We suggested that her first step was to begin looking after herself physically, on a consistent basis, in terms of nutrition, relaxation and generally pampering herself to give her body a real chance. We were also able to suggest some alternative treatments and doctors to help her, and that she needed to take some of her attention away from herself and on to other things.

Although she is still fighting cancer, she now works from a position of strength, rather than weakness. Physically, she looks and feels 'healthy'; her energy is much improved; she grabs opportunities with both hands (she is off to Africa travelling, shortly); she has become actively involved in the social side of the Church, and although, as with anyone else, life doesn't always go her way, she can now shrug her shoulders and say: 'That's life' and go forward from there with enthusiasm. When it all does get too much for her, as it sometimes does, she immediately gets on the phone to us, for support and a reminder of her decision to have the rest of her life work for her.

Elaine's story

My first visit to Holistix was a very important step towards recovery from six months of operations and radiotherapy treatment for cancer of the uterus. I had been pronounced clear of the cancer but I was completely exhausted and horrified at the prospect of now having to have a hysterectomy. I needed to talk to someone who was both practical and caring. The hospital, unsure of exactly what I needed, sent me to the psychiatric unit. A little perturbed at this, I sat down to talk to the doctor who immediately ran out of the room to answer an emergency call. In my rather sensitive state, I took it personally and as another indication that people were avoiding discussing this with me.

At Holistix, they listened carefully to my tale of woe and asked many probing questions about all aspects of my life. The very next day they went to meet an eminent gynaecologist, Mr Edmunds, to ask him questions on my behalf. On their insistence, I went to see Mr Edmunds and found him a very caring man. We decided on an appropriate date for my hysterectomy. What a relief to have come to a decision that allowed me time to prepare myself.

I was now regularly attending the exercise classes and could feel my vitality and body tone returning. Physically, I was improving tremendously, but mentally it was a different story. Looking back, I can see that the depression I was suffering from was due to the fact that I was grieving for the children I would never have. On top of this, I wasn't even in a meaningful relationship. My job became unfulfilling, I squandered my salary, my flat depressed me but I didn't have the energy or inclination to find another. Unsurprisingly, I became ill again with cancer and had to have an emergency hysterectomy followed by chemotherapy treatment. After the treatment, I was told by doctors that there was still a little of the cancer left but there was no other treatment available.

I suppose I should have been depressed. My life had been completely turned upside down. I had lost my job through being ill and had to move flats two weeks after my operation. Far from being despondent, I found the challenge exciting. The operation I had long feared was finally over and I'd recovered very quickly. I had time to renew many friendships and came to realize how loved I was. Very importantly, I came to love myself after years of self-hate.

At one time, I asked all my friends: 'I am going to be all right, aren't I?' but I now know I am the ultimate authority regarding myself and I'm beginning to trust in that. I know that what is right for someone else is not necessarily right for me. What a relief to feel that inner strength emerging at last. I may be nearly forty but I feel quite new. My sabbatical from a working life has done me a power of good. I travel a lot now and am never bored. I can remember at one time never enjoying anything very much because I was always in such a hurry; but now I take pleasure in so many of the little things in life. There is still a long way to go but now I look forward to the journey.

satisfied? You may find that, for you, it is a mix of the two.

On the other side of the fence, when situations, events and problems work out miraculously well, are you able to define the personal strengths which contributed to those positive outcomes, or do you just sigh with relief and put it down to good luck?

The key to achieving a balance in all this is to develop your ability to give yourself objective, truthful feedback. By doing this you will recognize your strengths and weaknesses, and be able to put aside the part of you that is coy or self-effacing. A weakness is simply a weakness. It is not good or bad, just something to note and address to the best of your ability. A strength is not something to shy away from or put down or write home about. It's simply a strength that should be acknowledged and built upon.

GIVING YOURSELF FEEDBACK

Receiving praise and criticism from outside sources is not always easy to swallow. Often when we receive criticism we take offence, feel guilty, or become defensive. When receiving praise we may feel embarrassed, try to joke about it, or try to minimize the effect we've had.

In giving yourself feedback throughout this chapter, you must be careful not to justify your weak points. Instead you must articulate, truthfully, what they are. One of the hardest tasks is to get you to own up to your good points and your strengths. But this is extremely important, and that is why there are two tables coming up to complete – one which will show the weaknesses, and one the strengths.

Unless we are very schooled and disciplined in being objective and fair-minded with ourselves, which is hard at the best of times, we often swing from being over-sensitive about certain situations, to mentally beating ourselves over the head about how bad we are. These are very unconscious, subtle excuses for not nipping the problems swiftly in the bud.

When you become accurate and comfortable in pinpointing your strengths, you will find it a lot easier to clarify your weakness; the emotions,

embarrassment and anger that surround owning up to your strengths and weaknesses will practically cease to exist.

This is one lesson, like many others, that takes time and patience and consistent practice. Once mastered, you will feel more in charge of the outcome of your life. This skill will also make the job – for instance, of managing people at work, or bringing up children – much easier, and they will benefit enormously from this skill being passed on by you in a relevant and appropriate way.

The following tables clarify the points raised on the previous pages. The first table is for situations which you are not happy with, and that are unresolved. The second table is for situations that you are happy with, or that have been resolved satisfactorily.

HOW TO USE THE FOLLOWING TABLES

Table One is divided into four columns, Table Two into five.

TABLE ONE

With every predicament, no matter what the circumstances, there are always two sides to the story – yours and theirs. 'Their side' is usually easy to define and explain. We are not taught, however, to objectively explore with no fuss or guilt what our side has contributed to the creation or development of a problem or predicament. The more depth of understanding that we can develop around this skill, the more we can learn from and affect the outcomes in our life. To give you an idea of what I mean, here is an example:

1. *My current situation:* A reply in the 'Work' category might be 'I'm never considered for promotion'.

2. *The outside factors responsible:* You might reply 'My bosses don't take me seriously'; 'There are people who have been there longer than me who haven't been promoted yet'; 'I don't think they believe I'm capable enough'; 'There's too much competition'; 'There are some people who don't want me to get ahead'; and so on.

TABLE ONE

WHY ARE THINGS NOT WORKING OUT?

Category	My current situation	The outside factors responsible	My part in all this	How I can change matters
Partner (as in personal relationship)				
Parents				
Children				
Flatmates				
Friends				
Social life				
Work				
Boss				
Colleagues				
Money				
General personal organization				
Health				
Weight				
Sex				
Relaxation				
Level of confidence				
Boredom				

Now, for the most difficult category:

3. ***My part in all this:*** You might say here 'I have never stated to my manager that I want promotion'; 'I make out that I'm really happy and that I don't care anyway'; 'I am afraid of going for promotion because of the competition and because I might fail'; 'I'm waiting for it to be offered to me rather than letting people know that I want to get more involved with the company and therefore move on'.

4. ***How I can change matters:*** You might include the following:

   a) 'I must decide if staying in my current position for a while longer would give me the confidence I need to go for promotion';

   b) 'Rather than be swamped by my fear of failure, I am always going to bear in mind that it is quite normal to have self-doubts, and am going to research what the promotion will entail so that I can make a decision whether or not to go for it';

   c) 'I will make a list of people who can advise me, and contact them regarding my becoming a serious contender for promotion';

   d) 'I will consider carefully whether the image I am presenting – both in terms of my appearance and in the way I verbally express my points of view – is in line with the promotion I want'; or

   e) 'I must not make guesses about how people view me, and why they may not think I am capable enough. I must develop the courage to ask them how they see me'.

BEFORE YOU BEGIN

OK, it's your turn now. Be as specific and descriptive as you can be, when filling out these tables. Don't worry if you go blank. Just relax and the thoughts will come fast and furious as you begin writing.

You need to get a large notebook and a pen, so that you can keep a record of your thoughts and responses. It's a good idea to sit or lie in your favourite spot, and to be sure that you have

got some peace and quiet to relax and spend this time uninterrupted.

TABLE TWO

1. ***A current or past situation:*** A situation in the 'Money' category could be that you had difficulties meeting your mortgage payments, along with the day-to-day cost of living. In addition, there were a number of credit-card bills outstanding, and requests from the bank manager that you better maintain your account. Everything is or was in complete disarray.

2. ***What I can do (or did) to address the problem:*** Bought a ledger book and made a list of everything you had to pay out weekly and monthly, to get a grand total. You balanced this against your income, then made a plan of action to find the quickest way to eliminate the debts.

3. ***Making use of outside resources:*** Made appointment with bank manager; worked out a position where one loan would simplify existing debts; sat down with a bookkeeper and learned how to tally your accounts properly.

4. ***Risks taken, if any:*** You decided to own up to your parents about your financial situation and were then able to ask their advice.

5. ***The long-term outcome:*** Completely out of the blue your parents offered financial help and you cleared up the debt in half the time you thought it would take you. You cleared up the loan and set aside time each week to ensure that you never got into that position again.

PERSONAL HISTORY

Every problem has a beginning and a history. Before looking at your physical background, it is important to be able to trace back to events in your life that may be at the root of the problems, and to look at your upbringing.

The range of problems that are related to past events is very wide and includes the following:

TABLE TWO

STEPS I TOOK TO GET THE OUTCOME I WANTED

Category	A current or past situation	What I can do (or did) to address the problem	Making use of outside resources	Risks taken if any	The long-term outcome
Partner (as in personal relationship)					
Parents					
Children					
Flatmates					
Friends					
Social life					
Work					
Boss					
Colleagues					
Money					
General personal organization					
Health					
Weight					
Sex					
Relaxation					
Level of confidence					
Boredom					

Sylvia

Sylvia danced in her first ballet class at two and a half years of age, and danced in her first movie at four and a half. At six, she was sent to school and the school dance teacher advised her parents that she was so talented, she should receive proper training. She was then sent to the Arts Educational School in Tring, Herts., where she was fully trained in ballet – Cecchetti, the Russian method, and R.A.D. Along with this she learned, to professional level, all forms of Dance, Stage, Speech and Drama. At twelve and a half, she was asked to take the leading role in the film A Little Ballerina, but parental opinion opted for 'education'. By fourteen, however, having already danced in a musical as a soloist with Audrey Hepburn, she became the youngest member of The Festival Ballet Company, dancing her way through the repertory, highlighted by Massine's 'Beau Danube' which he directed himself. She then left, in order to express dance in a wider context, and performed in film, TV and musicals.

At the age of nineteen she married. Ten brief days after her wedding she was invalided in a near-fatal car accident and suffered multiple injuries which resulted in two years of operations and she sustained a back injury which was to return later in her life and which, in part, led her into teaching, giving her a painfully vivid insight in dealing with injury, illness, and depression. Ten years later, with two small daughters dependent on her and in poor mental and physical health, she struggled on all fronts for quite some time. Then a friend introduced her to the couple, Pat and Gary, who ran the dance centre in Floral Street, Covent Garden. She was persuaded to starting teaching classes there. These classes took off in an amazing way, with long queues each evening of people waiting to learn her unique method of teaching.

During this period she taught Mia Farrow, John Hurt, Jane Fonda 'Pre-Aerobics', choreographed The Naked Civil Servant with John Hurt for Jack Gold and Julia with Fonda and Redgrave for Fred Zimmerman. Then her back injury recurred and only with the help of her sixteen-year-old daughter Carole, she carried on teaching, while lying on the floor, for eighteen months. She was told she would never be able to walk, teach, drive, or be mobile again and would be in a wheelchair for the rest of her life. With Carole's consistent and constant encouragement she went to alternative practitioners for help, and formulated a course of exercises to alleviate pain, strengthen the muscles, and limber up the injured area, and slowly but surely Sylvia's back was completely cured.

By this time Sylvia had studied and learned a fascinating amount from the famous homeopath Ashwin Barot and as a result of her knowledge her advice was sought by more and more pupils. Ashwin Barot asked her to consider becoming a consultant, as, to quote Barot, 'She was able to address more than he on the psychological/emotional side of holistic health'. And so the consulting started, steadily gaining a large following of satisfied patients whose own doctors approved the advice, and their friends spread the word about this woman whose logical knowledge was proving to be unusually helpful in an extremely wide area. By this time the list of famous names included Roger Rees, Daley Thompson (who wrote a chapter in his first book about Sylvia), Janet Street-Porter, and her long-time friend and pupil Felicity Kendal, whose record Sylvia choreographed ('Shape Up And Dance', which soared into the charts and went gold). Selina Scott and many more, such as Gemma Craven and her husband David, are now on a long list of her grateful patients.

Sylvia continues her research into both sides of medicine and her interest now lies in drawing on the spritual side of healing in her work. She would like to acknowledge that the many patients she has helped have, in return taught her so much.

○ Recurring illness;
○ Depression;
○ Weight problems;
○ Skin problems;
○ Lack of energy;
○ Shyness;
○ Lack of confidence;
○ Disastrous relationships;
○ Injuries;

○ Headaches;
○ Boredom;
○ Sexual fears or revulsion; or
○ Feelings of inferiority.

The events themselves won't necessarily be obvious, so I have listed some common causes and their possible results in order to trigger your memory. The events usually occur from a very early age, as young as three. It is important to note here that many people don't have any memory before the age of ten. If that is the case for you, don't worry, just go back to whenever your earliest memories are.

1. BEING TEASED AND BULLIED

This is a threatening situation, and memory of waking up with fear in the pit of your stomach can cause equal stress, panic and tension now. This kind of treatment has enormous emotional repercussions in later life. A feeling of self-worthlessness, panic attacks, and general lack of self-confidence will naturally build. Until you can relax and confide in someone who appreciates you for yourself, it's sometimes difficult to accept that *you are accepted.*

Certain fears of social situations, attention, friendship and high-profile work develop from early taunting.

It's important to remember that the only person's opinion of you that *really* matters is yours. When you accept that, and allow yourself to relax and *be* yourself, you'll certainly find that other people like that person as well.

Counselling, talking it through with a close friend, taking steps to look after yourself, and gently seeking attention from other sources may help.

There are plenty of ways that childhood teasing and bullying manifests itself. For instance, anorexia and bulimia are cries for help; while obesity is a way of saying you don't really care. Other ways that this can turn up in later life include:

○ Shyness;
○ Lack of confidence;
○ Depression;
○ Difficulty in relationships;
○ Feeling inferior – or being bossy;
○ A nervous disposition;
○ Headaches;
○ Being overweight;
○ Anorexia and/or bulimia; or
○ Digestive problems.

2. LITTLE OR NO ATTENTION FROM PARENTS, CONSTANTLY MOVING THROUGHOUT CHILDHOOD, ARGUMENTATIVE PARENTS, AND/OR PARENTS' DIVORCE AT AN EARLY AGE

Parental attention, lack of attention, and actions have a great influence on a child's personality and demeanour. When one or both parents fail to focus enough attention on a child, he or she will seek it elsewhere – outside the family unit, usually. Anyone who has suffered this type of rejection as a child has a propensity to look for rejection later in life, almost to prove the point that they are worthless.

Remember, your parents' actions are no reflection of your worth as a human being. If there was no one to hold you, it was not because you were not worthy of being held. There are a number of ways that rejection, or an unsettled childhood can affect an adult in later life. You might constantly seek attention and become overdependent, for fear of being hurt again. Alternatively, you may find relationships frightening, and push people away, or close up altogether.

Certainly, if you feel that you have suffered any of the above, talk it out with a partner, friend or, if necessary, a trained counsellor. There are always reasons for our adult actions, and physical and mental state.

The most common threads here have been seen in people suffering:

○ Recurring illnesses;
○ Overdependency on friends and partners;
○ Pushing people away;
○ Dramatic mood swings;
○ Insecurity and fear – or the complete opposite, being tough and uncommunicative;
○ Total absorption in career, to the exclusion of everything else;
○ Insomnia;
○ Digestive problems; or
○ Inability to make and keep commitments.

3. BEING DISCIPLINED UNFAIRLY FOR EXPRESSING EMOTIONS AS A CHILD

Unfair discipline always has an affect on a person's level of confidence, no matter what age it takes place. Later in life, this can result in both the suppression of negative emotions, such as anger and emotional upset, and in the suppression of desires and needs. Always remember that freedom of speech, emotion and affection are essential to well-developed and stable psyches. If you have ever suffered unfair suppression, think about why. Were you too zealous with your emotions for quiet or refined parents and teachers? Were you overemotional in expressing views or opinions? Were you warm and loving in a cooler home environment? No emotion is wrong; it's simply a clash of personalities or expectations. Feel proud of your emotional make-up; don't ever hesitate to let it all out. Suppression can be dangerous; it is one of the most common causes of:

- ○ Weight problems;
- ○ Digestive problems;
- ○ Asthma and shallow breathing;
- ○ Depression;
- ○ Problematic relationships; or
- ○ Meanness.

4. BEING LEFT OUT AT SCHOOL/NOT BEING ONE OF THE GANG

Childhood relationships are enormously important for developing communication skills, personality, confidence and a good self-image. If you felt left out at school, you might have been led to believe that there was something wrong with you. It's the 'Why me?' syndrome – What's wrong with me? Why does nobody like me? Why can't I fit in? A child's mind is often at a loss to discover the answers to these questions, and the natural reaction is to hide, or to *make* yourself dislikeable, to create a reason for lack of popularity. Later in life, these feelings can manifest themselves in any number of ways, including:

- ○ Shyness;
- ○ Lack of confidence (that as an adult can come across to other people as being

eccentric or standoffish);
- ○ Awkwardness;
- ○ Poor posture;
- ○ A greyish tinge to the skin;
- ○ Drabness; or the opposite extreme,
- ○ A purposefully outlandish and gaudy appearance.

5. BEING ADOPTED

The effects of being adopted depend on how and when you've been told. Adoption is one area that must be dealt with more sensitively. Whatever your personality and character, you may always wonder *why* you weren't wanted. If you have ever been teased about it, or made to feel that you are incomplete in some way, that feeling will be compounded. Adoptive parents often try to make adopted children feel 'special' and 'chosen'. This is an excellent way to deal with the possibility of children feeling unwanted, but alternatively, it might make them 'different', which children may not want to feel.

If you have been adopted, and depending on how satisfied you feel now, you may suffer from:

- ○ Bitterness;
- ○ Confused emotions;
- ○ Clinging and coddling in relationships;
- ○ Poor posture;
- ○ Digestive problems; or
- ○ Lack of confidence.

6. BEING REJECTED AND IGNORED FROM AN EARLY AGE OR LATER IN LIFE BY SOMEONE VERY IMPORTANT TO YOU

Rejection often produces the gloomy view that it is our lot in life, that we are doomed to be rejected again and again. Very little self-worth is able to develop in later life, and attention-seeking mechanisms become a daily ritual. You may not feel inspired to look after yourself – after all, what's the use? Does that sound familiar? Rejection of your ideas, emotions and character will preclude confidence developing. Your decisions, which will affect the rest of your life, are half-hearted and thoughtless. You may not want to make commitments, which will inevitably cause strain, tension and ill health in adult life. In

Judy

Judy was a depressed, overweight, self-abusive woman who drank too much, became upset and over-wrought over trivialities, moaned about her life, and had very little energy or drive. As a result, she was overweight, her face was puffy and marked by red veins, her eyes were dull and glazed, and her features generally listless.

All this, in spite of her boyfriend leaving his wife to be with her, and her enormous material and business success.

We pointed out during her Consultation that she had two options – either to remain as she was, or make some changes, and that the bottom line really was that simple. She opted to make the changes.

As the Consultation progressed, it became obvious that she felt the relationship between herself and her boyfriend was breaking down. But we pointed out that this seemed largely to be due to numerous assumptions that she had made around him: 'He prefers his son to me', 'He doesn't desire me anymore' and 'He won't support me or like it if I decide to get my act together'.

It was suggested that until she sat down with him and checked all these assumptions out, that she was in danger of losing what was once her most valued relationship, and that she'd never really know why. With most suggestions of this kind, she had tons of excuses. So we came up with answers to each and every consideration until there were no more left.

So she decided to talk to her boyfriend, no matter how scared she was, and when she did, she was amazed. He'd made his own assumptions and as a result had started withdrawing from her and the relationship. So, as we had suggested, they literally went through every single thing that they were either assuming, uncertain of or irritated by, and talked long into the night.

After their discussion, they made a conscious decision to work things out together and have their relationship become different and more satisfying.

In order to help achieve this, Judy wanted to get both herself and her boyfriend into shape physically. So we went into nutrition, weight, drinking, presentation and exercise with her, regularly checking upon how she was doing and making suggestions whenever we could. Just a few short months later, she is a happy, bright, elegant and slim young woman. Her face has an even tone and texture to it now, and her body is firm and supple. She lost sixteen pounds, started communicating at work, got her man to knock the booze on the head, their sex life soared and she felt fresh and young and optimistic about life again. Physically, she actually looks as though she is looking forward to her life.

Oh, and she has just told me that she is going to have a baby!

---

later life, this may manifest itself as:
- ○ Being standoffish;
- ○ A highly strung character;
- ○ A 'don't-care' appearance;
- ○ Sallow skin;
- ○ Dull eyes;
- ○ A pessimistic outlook;
- ○ Indecisiveness;
- ○ Self-righteousness;
- ○ Defensiveness; or
- ○ Being a victim of circumstance.

7. BEING THE BLACK SHEEP OF THE FAMILY

From your earliest experiences, you may not have felt you were good enough. And when you are constantly rejected or made to feel unusual or inadequate, your defence system is sparked into action. 'Screw them', you may think. And from there you may go on to develop a purposefully annoying and attention-seeking series of personality traits. That attitude inevitably causes enormous problems in later life, compounding the rejection or lack of understanding suffered as a child. If any of this sounds familiar, take steps to avoid self-destructive action. At the end of the day people are important to us and, as a result, what they think is also important to us. Creating constant battles out of everything is in the end self-defeating. Calm down, take stock of your good points and focus on decisions that can change your defensiveness, if you suffer from any of the following:
- ○ Rebelliousness;
- ○ Punishing in relationships;
- ○ Extreme pride;
- ○ Revengeful nature;
- ○ Defensiveness;
- ○ Toughness; or

○ Behaviour that is deliberately hurtful to others.

8. FEELING GUILTY FOR NOT HAVING DONE WELL AT SCHOOL, COLLEGE OR UNIVERSITY

If you have not done well at school simply because you didn't try, take heart, academia is not for everyone. Now is your chance to find your niche in the world. Never feel guilty for lack of achievement; there are always extenuating circumstances which preclude all of us excelling in academic life. Maybe you were bored or too bright. Or maybe you need to learn some self-motivation skills, and focus. Whatever the results, it's never too late to begin succeeding at something else, in another part of your life. Don't allow yourself to suffer from the common manifestations of this guilt, which include:

○ Lack of confidence;
○ Lack of concentration;
○ Defensiveness;
○ Being a loner or unnaturally popular;
○ Being either very flashy in appearance, or very drab; or
○ Feeling the underdog.

9. BEING ABUSED AS A CHILD

Most people will not have admitted this to themselves or anyone else. The most important thing to remember is that you are not bad or guilty in any way. When physical and psychological problems stem from child abuse, it is simply your mind's attempt to deal with any psychological damage in the only way it knows how.

For you to heal yourself properly, and resolve it, you may need specialist counselling. Working with professional help in this area can change the whole of your life. What *is* important is that you look at how this is affecting your wellbeing today. For instance, one of the best self-protective measures that the mind will adopt is to not care for your body. There can be great hatred, in fact, for things like the genital area, or other private areas of the body, which would make love-making unthinkable or traumatic. If you're at the point where you want to make love to someone,

Waiting for the right time to deal with a problem, or waiting to feel enthusiastic, is probably the worst thing you can do. There is no right time, and you could wait forever to feel more enthusiastic.

and haven't let this out of the bag, your partner may think something is wrong with *them*. You'll feel rejected and withdraw, adding insult to injury.

Remember: you are not inadequate, and deserve no punishment.

Take a look at your life and see if child abuse has affected you in any way. This includes being hit, sexual or mental abuse, and/or harrassment. In addition to the predicaments above, there are other problems which can stem from abuse including:

○ Insomnia;
○ Irritable bowel syndrome;
○ Nightmares;
○ Recurring back problems;
○ Concaved chest and bad posture; or
○ Physical abuse to oneself and others.

10. LOSING SOMEONE CLOSE TO YOU THROUGH DEATH OR SUICIDE

Many people who do lose someone retain a great deal of anger and guilt about it. Grief has a lot to do with our own fear of death, and our brain goes into overdrive when it registers complete panic at not being able to feel, see or touch that person again. There is a fundamental loneliness, no matter what. Although others may have shared your loss, every person is something different to someone else. You may try to avoid becoming close to people, for fear of suffering another loss. Other symptoms may include:

○ Bitterness or deep depression;
○ Irrational impatience;

○ A hard attitude in future relationships;
○ Poor posture;
○ Self-neglect;
○ Suppression of emotions;
○ Nightmares;
○ The inability to sustain relationships; or
○ Loss of purpose, giving up, feeling numb inside.

11. THE BREAK-UP OF A LONG-TERM RELATIONSHIP OR DIVORCE

The divorce or break-up of a family or a relationship is much like losing someone through death. You may feel ill, depressed or unworthy, and rejection of this nature can drive you crazy with worry, self-doubt and anger, causing a number of physical problems, and often, a manipulative character. You may feel driven to control your relationships from thereon in, and take steps to do so by being bossy and constantly in control. Physical symptoms are also a way to attract attention that will fill the gap in your life, and make you feel worthy again. Common symptoms may include:

○ Bitterness;
○ Anorexia, bulimia or obesity;
○ Constantly feeling rundown;
○ Suppression of emotions;
○ A hard attitude in future relationships;
○ Nightmares;
○ Irritable bowel syndrome;
○ Extraordinary tiredness; or
○ Recurrent, minor illnesses.

12. FEELING GUILTY ABOUT A CLOSE ONE'S DEATH

The feelings that accompany guilt are never productive. As we noted earlier, guilt is our attempt to rationalize death. The 'what if' syndrome is strongest when we are faced with the death of a loved one. What if I'd called him? If only I had a chance to say goodbye. If only I'd noticed she was unwell. What if I'd treated him better, would this have changed things? Stop now. Thoughts like these, and self-castigation, are totally unproductive. Rationalizing a death in your own mind will never change the fact that it has occurred.

Give yourself a chance to heal – mourn, cry, yell, scream and be angry at death for robbing you. Don't be angry with yourself, you really are unlikely to have been able to change things. Remember this if you are suffering from:

○ Periods of deep depression;
○ Introspection;
○ Low self-esteem;
○ Slumped posture; or
○ Nightmares.

13. FEELING GUILTY IN SOME WAY ABOUT HAVING BEEN RAPED

If you have been raped, you must work through your plethora of emotions with a professional, for they won't try to smother your experiences.

Talking to friends before you have healed emotionally can sometimes result in your feeling misunderstood. They also have their fears and upsets to deal with personally, and in relation to caring for you. Speaking to a professional first and working with them to understand and come to terms with this predicament is vital. They will also help you to define the kind of reactions that can occur when telling others about it and how to deal with these

Unless we are are schooled and disciplined in being objective and fair-minded with ourselves, which is hard at the best of times, we often swing from being over-sensitive about certain situations, to mentally beating ourselves over the head about how bad we are.

These are very unconscious subtle excuses for not nipping the problems in the bud.

reactions so they don't push you in a corner. When that is done it's important for you to talk to your trusted friends and relatives so that the incident becomes less traumatic and you can see that they think more and not less of you.

Talk, talk, talk. Let all your feelings out. Kill that guilt stone-dead. Transfer that feeling to anger and express it – it's a lot more short-lived. You may find that guilt is the reason that you are:
- Not taking care of hygiene, or being obsessive about it;
- Being very needy;
- Purposefully making yourself unattractive;
- Suffering a dislike or fear of sex;
- Constantly putting yourself down; or
- Suffering sleep problems.

14. FEELING INADEQUATE BECAUSE OF FAILURE TO KEEP AN IMPORTANT RELATIONSHIP OR MARRIAGE TOGETHER, OR BECAUSE OF FAILURE AT WORK

Failure is cleansing. It teaches you what does and doesn't work, to experience your own strong and weak points, and to experience what you really do want out of life. Failure also calls for self-appraisal, which can only be good. Don't brood or become overly introspective. This is your chance to start fresh, all over again. The possibilities are endless. Learn how to talk to yourself, parcel up your experience and use it to avoid future mistakes, but give yourself the freedom to try again. Be imaginative and help yourself get over the initial pain and embarrassment by making lists of what to do, who can help and what to change. Getting to the point of being able to undertake any of these suggestions requires one thing – energy – especially when you are feeling numb and lethargic as a result of failing at something. Everyone fails at something at some time in their lives. Remember that and call on your friends for support. Otherwise, this feeling of inadequacy can or may have led to:
- Letting everything collapse physically, emotionally and careerwise.

All these situations and many more that I haven't mentioned affect both how you feel and look physically, and your emotional wellbeing. Your enthusiasm, self-esteem and motivation may be very low, making it difficult for you to tackle your physical health, no matter what 'good advice' you have been given.

WHY WE MAY FEEL INADEQUATE

It is clear that almost all childhood events affect the way we feel now. In addition, you probably had lots of rules imposed on you in childhood that you have brought into your adult life.

The remarks frequently made to us as children affect us in different ways. When they were given as simple disciplinary measures, but were made in a derogatory fashion, we may have been too young to differentiate between the two. As a result, they can deeply affect how we think about ourselves, and how we put ourselves across. Because we are made to feel inadequate by most of these remarks, those inadequacies then become 'real' to us.

Here are examples of remarks you'll probably recognize:
- Don't show off;
- Do as you're told and don't question it;
- Be quiet when adults are around;
- Don't speak unless you are spoken to;
- Don't interfere;
- Don't keep asking so many questions;
- Don't be so stupid;
- Keep your thoughts to yourself;
- Stop being a cry-baby;
- Slow down;
- Get on with it;
- Don't answer back;
- Your elders know better;
- If you don't do as I say you'll be punished;
- You can't have any dessert or leave the table until you've eaten all your food;
- If you're good you can have some sweets;
- You'll never get anywhere if you carry on like this;
- Your Daddy/Mummy won't love you if you do that;
- Run along and stop wasting my time;
- Don't bother other people, they've got better things to think about;

Jenny

Jennifer was a hyperactive, twenty-eight-year-old fashion designer, with a successful business and a fascinating love life. She was obviously anorexic and, on the surface, a flirtatious socialite.

All she wanted was a 'bit of exercise', and she couldn't understand the need for a Consultation. She was quite offended by the nature of the questions.

The first stumbling block was getting Jenny to admit that anorexia was not a normal state of being. We explained in detail the damaging effect it had on the internal body and nervous system, detailing the kind of symptoms she could expect. And she admitted to not having had periods for eighteen months, and that anorexia had directly caused this. Although this suited her promiscuity, it simply wasn't 'right', she felt.

We discussed her childhood, and she found this very upsetting. Her parents had had an acrimonious divorce when she was three, and until the age of eighteen, she lived with her mother and her series of boyfriends. Schooling was difficult, as her mother had quite a reputation with the local wives, who discouraged their children from mixing with her. She became very isolated and felt the only way to win affection and attention was to be flirtatious and promiscuous. This led to two failed marriages, and a series of short-term lovers (she currently had three in tow), but no emotional stability.

She realized what a dangerous game she was playing, and asked to come back to do further work to sort out her life and emotions.

We're still working with Jenny, who is beginning to show some progress. The biggest step forward has been Jenny recognizing how shallow and pointless the sex life and relationships she has had to date really are.

○ Stop letting your imagination run away with you;
○ You look a mess;
○ I can't take you anywhere;
○ You've never had it so easy;
○ You should be grateful for everything you've got; and
○ Look how much I've/we've done for you (i.e. emotional blackmail).

These rules, in addition to encouraging feelings of inadequacy and resentment, also have an impact on us in the long term.

· It is very useful if you make your own list, noting particularly the key comments that you feel affect you today.

LET YOURSELF OFF THE HOOK

In exploring the ideas and questions in this chapter, you may have begun to locate the core issues that are governing your emotional and physical dissatisfaction. You can't change the past, but you can become aware of how your outlook on life and your physical and emotional wellbeing is affected, by not letting yourself, and perhaps others, off the hook.

Just a note here about 'letting people off the hook'. This means that you take on board the idea of forgiving, or letting go sufficiently of the upset and anger caused by people or events in the past. You must stop blaming yourself and give yourself the chance to heal in order to allow the rest of your life to provide you with the things you want.

In this chapter, I have mostly mentioned the downside of the effects of early experiences. As with everything else in life, there is also an upside. There are those of you who have had similar or other traumatic events in your lives, and you have worked hard to attain happiness and satisfaction in your present lives. You have made a conscious decision to ensure the rest of your life is not coloured by these past events.

For those of you in the second category, this chapter will have alerted you to some of the ways you came to your decision. By connecting your past to your present, and by letting yourself off the hook, you are giving yourself the chance to heal and to start fresh. Long-standing problems can now be tackled in a completely new way.

Once you become aware, you can get back in to the driver's seat, and start on a new journey. To begin with, all you have to do is understand that fear of change and any other negative emotions you may feel are normal and healthy. Then you can take on board the lessons that life has provided you with so far, as well as the ones it will offer you in the future.

THREE

The Nuts and Bolts of Problems

IN THE PREVIOUS chapter we worked on becoming aware of how past and present events may have prevented you from achieving your physical goals up to now. Before tackling specific problems, it is important to explore those parts of us that have prevented us from dealing with these problems. In this chapter you will wrestle with the reasons and excuses that have led you to say 'I can't' or, 'I won't deal with this problem'.

Bearing in mind that everyone has different opinions, some of you will be nodding your head in agreement when reading this chapter, while others may be confused or cynical. Perhaps at this point, it would be a good idea for me to remind you about your commentator. He'll either love this stuff or he'll hate it. If you find that your commentator baulks at the material here, this usually means that the information has struck a chord.

This chapter will get your butt into gear to do something about these problems. And in doing this, you will be able to detect just how much choice is available, when it comes to making the changes you say you want to make. Before going into the whys and wherefores of problems, it is useful to note that we all have the following in common:

1. If a friend of ours has a problem, we can usually see clearly what they should do to rectify it. If you regard yourself as a loner, or so shy that you are never in a position to give advice to others, you can detect this ability when you are watching a film, or reading a book that involves a mystery being solved, or a love story unfolding. There may be a scene in a book or movie that shows a man and a woman in a private state of wanting each other, but neither has any idea that the other feels the same. They create scenarios of chaos and drama that have you silently commenting about what they should do or say to produce the eternal happy ending.

2. It can be the case that when it comes to solving problems in different areas of your life, you may be lousy at dealing with relationship problems but great at dealing with career-orientated problems (or vice versa).

3. Even if you're the kind of person who thinks you are not good at solving problems, you will probably be able to come up with at least one example of a difficult problem that you have successfully dealt with.

4. Whatever your circumstances, you will often find that you have a vast reservoir of ideas and energy when it comes to solving problems that you find easy.

WHY IS DEALING WITH PROBLEMS SUCH A PROBLEM?

Generally, when we think of the word 'problem', many of us view it as a negative element. This is because when we face a problem we often feel uneasy and uncomfortable. We have memories of past problems that were difficult or painful either

Timothy

Physically, Tim was a disaster area. Grossly overweight and suffering from psoriasis, he was lethargic and very prone to bouts of depression. He was also constipated and suffered to a fairly severe extent from flatulence.

At first, he was rather uncommunicative in his Consultation, skirting around all the questions, particularly nutrition.

At that point, we had to make a decision as to whether we should curtail the discussion. We asked him if he wanted to continue the rest of his life feeling as he did then. And he said no. We then suggested that for any change to occur, we couldn't achieve it for him. He would have to, at the very minimum, meet us halfway. He eventually agreed that the only person who would lose out if he walked away would be himself, so he decided to go for it.

He then revealed a background of upset, insecurity and unhappiness, and a pattern, since childhood, of eating for comfort. Tim could not actually remember not being overweight.

In his life at this time, he was happily married and a fairly successful painter, with no longer any need for food as a comfort. The only real down-sides to his life were all the physical effects of being so overweight. We took him off all dairy produce, red meat, and most fats, recommending muesli for breakfast, salads for lunch and chicken or fish with vegetables for dinner. We had to wean him off fried, fatty and stodgy foods, replacing mashed potato with organic brown rice and parsnips, pork chops with chicken fillets, bacon and eggs with fruit, porridge and muesli, and so on.

We also made the exercise classes a priority for him, so that he not only lost weight (he lost twenty pounds) but he also toned and firmed his muscles. Over the next few weeks he was consistent and thorough in his attitude to the nutrition and classes, constantly asking us questions and letting us know his progress and problems. It really paid off. He regained a natural, healthy complexion, was no longer constipated or bloated, and due to the information he'd received in his Pamper, even the psoriasis began to disappear.

Most importantly, he now had masses of energy and a totally different look on his face and in his eyes. We'd see it each week when he would get on the scales, smile and then wink.

---

in direct relationship to ourselves or others close to us.

We can experience a host of different emotions and feelings, depending on the kind of problem we have. For example:

○ Frustration;
○ Anger;
○ Fear;
○ Sadness;
○ Loneliness;
○ Guilt;
○ Regret;
○ Anguish; and/or
○ Despair

These feelings are often so uncomfortable that the pain is as bad as the worst physical pain you have ever endured. That is why we often avoid facing up to, or dealing with, problems.

In order to avoid having these feelings, we may make any number of excuses:

○ We procrastinate, hoping that the problem can be dealt with at a later date or that it will go away;

○ We turn a blind eye and pretend it doesn't exist;

○ We will moan and groan: 'Why me?' and 'It's somebody else's fault' and get as many people as we can to agree with us;

○ We believe that our problems are unique to us, and therefore impossible to solve;

○ We complain that we are so weak-willed we are just not able to deal with the problem at all;

○ We put the responsibility on to somebody else;

○ We can sometimes talk ourselves out of having the problem, denying it exists, which lulls us into a false sense of security – but the problem is really there, lurking in the background; or

○ Some people turn to drink, take drugs, become anorexic, bulimic or obese, become very ill, or attempt to commit suicide as a way of not facing up to a problem

We can see from the above that if we want to

attain a physical change – we may wish to lose weight, for example – simply dealing with the problem on a nutritional or medical basis is not enough to get the result.

Take risks, make yourself do things that were previously out of character. Override any apathy, lethargy or negative feelings by simply putting out a vast amount of energy, physically or otherwise. Congratulate yourself on every little victory along the way. If you've taken steps to overcome shyness, your own particular problem, and you've met three new people through your perseverance, take pride! That's more than one step on the road to recovery and total wellbeing.

PROBLEMS THAT DON'T GET DEALT WITH – AND THE REASONS WE GIVE

There are many problems which we avoid solving. Here are the most common and the chief reasons we use for not dealing with them:

○ Relationships – being unhappy in a relationship and not wanting to rock the boat;

○ Marriage – the marriage is no longer working out but you can't split up because it would affect the children and, besides, you can't afford to;

○ Job – knowing you hate your job but you are too scared to do anything about it because you need the money and, these days, times are trying;

○ Parents – your parents just won't see your side of the matter so communication is kept to the bare minimum, with you getting more and more frustrated;

○ Children – one of your children is going through a difficult stage and you think nothing you do or say will make a difference;

○ Weight – I can't stick to a reasonable way of eating because I have to socialize a lot; and

○ Boss – you are dissatisfied with your relationship with your boss, but you don't feel it's your place to speak your mind.

Problems can be as big an addiction as any other type of addiction and just as difficult to

knock on the head. For many people, not having a problem to occupy their thoughts is more frightening than having one. If you are in this state, you may be the last person to know it, as the clues are very subtle. The following are some key points to recognize those clues:

Loneliness: Consistently having other problems takes us away from dealing with the most important problem of all – loneliness itself.

The past: We often suppress our feelings about situations or about people we have had to deal with in the past. We may have withdrawn from particular people, blaming them for this, that or the other. This anger or emotional upset is very deep-rooted so we often won't know we are doing this. We will often complain constantly that we get the rough end of the deal.

On-off relationships: When we are in a relationship that keeps breaking or making up, we can't talk enough about the situation to our friends. We cry one minute and get angry the next, and sometimes we feel completely indifferent. Our friends give us good advice and sympathy, time and again, but that isn't enough for us to deal with the whole problem. It's easier, we believe, to have this problem rather than the one we imagine we would experience if we finished the relationship completely.

P roblems are an intrinsic part of life, and they will always be there. Instead of spending a lot of energy worrying or procrastinating, you must learn to tackle your problems and put aside your fears that the outcome may not be exactly as you'd planned.

All these examples illustrate to different degrees the misapprehension 'Better the devil you know than the devil you don't'. People often find that deciding to deal with that one big problem opens a whole can of others that will have to be dealt with.

This is where our imaginations run away with themselves, coming up with hypothetical problems or jumping to disastrous conclusions. This can, however, be a positive thing. Once we have figured out why we fail to do things, why our life is the way it is, and what has caused it, we can do battle.

HIDDEN FEARS

Here are a few examples of the underlying fears you may come up against:
- ○ Fear of failure;
- ○ Fear of making the situation worse;
- ○ Fear of losing someone's respect or friendship;
- ○ Fear of looking stupid and inadequate;
- ○ Fear of losing a job or a personal relationship;
- ○ Fear of hurting somebody; and
- ○ Fear of the changes we have to make within ourselves in order to address and rectify the problem at hand.

These fears are very real. However, you have to decide whether they are good enough reasons for not tackling the problems at hand. If your decision is that your fears are more important, the chances are that the problem will escalate and your fears will increase until they get blown out of proportion.

For example, the fear of hurting someone. Ask yourself the question: 'Could it hurt the person more if I don't tell them what's on my mind?' You will usually find that the answer would be 'Yes'. Just imagine that the roles are reversed, and there is an issue that someone has with you. Wouldn't you rather know what it is so that the air is clear between you? As long as you make clear to them that you are anxious not to hurt their feelings, you will probably both feel a huge sense of relief and bring your relationship a lot closer as a result.

Furthermore, when a problem that is not voiced arises between two people, the person concerned usually has an idea that something is up. I mentioned earlier in this chapter that the problem with problems is that they are viewed as negative elements. Partially, the reason for this is that an explanation of the true meaning of the word 'problem' does not exist in our everyday vocabulary. *The New Dictionary* definition of the word 'problem' is: 'A proposition requiring something to be done'. It doesn't sound as frightening in those terms, does it?

Problems are an intrinsic part of life, and they will always be there. Instead of spending a lot of energy worrying or procrastinating, you must learn to tackle your problems and put aside your fear that the outcome may not be exactly as you'd planned.

Too often, we think we should be able to handle our problems on our own. Don't let pride prevent you from asking for help from a person close to you, or from a professional. We can be so close to our problems that we don't see a solution ourselves. Without having problems or making mistakes we wouldn't learn or know how to do things better.

BEHAVIOUR: APPROVAL AND CONTROL

In addition to the hidden fears we have looked at, there are a number of other influences on our behaviour.

Firstly, we often strive for approval. This is probably one of the first things that we learn, and it makes us feel more accepted, safe and secure. Approval-seeking behaviour includes smiling a lot, being nice and, most of all, doing what you think others expect of you.

Approval-seeking has its time and place. For example, being nice may win you a personality contest; however, if you're feigning being nice to your best friend when you are angry, the relationship is built on a lie. Ultimately, seeking approval is done because we fear the loss of love, friendship or respect.

We also turn our approval-seeking behaviour on to ourselves. We pretend that something that went wrong was 'all right, really'. For instance,

Mark and Sarah

When Mark first contacted us, he was extremely effusive, said he was slightly overweight and had a niggling back problem. He arranged for his wife to come, too. Their physical symptoms differed quite dramatically, but there was an underlying tension and nervousness in their health. She was overweight, untidy and unappetizing: she looked like she needed a good scrub and shampoo, having let herself go to pot.

He, on the other hand, was well presented, hyper and extremely uptight, which was apparent in his face and twitchy hands. Quickly it became obvious that he had seen numerous medical people regarding his chronic back problems; he chose to ignore all their advice which included giving up squash, cutting down on drink and calorie intake. As soon as he sensed that we were not about to sympathize mindlessly with him, and that we would, in no uncertain terms, address these problems, he became extremely annoyed and upset and stormed out, leaving his wife sobbing. She told us the behaviour was not unusual, and that she was desperate for him to see what he was doing to himself and their marriage.

Mark consciously chose to ignore what he knew to be the only course of action that would correct his physical and behavioural problems. He was jeopardizing his marriage, his health and his life. He thought he was more in control and comfortable, repeating these life-long patterns of behaviour, rather than addressing and coming to terms with his problem.

Some time later, they separated because Sarah felt she needed to create a life without drama for herself. She is now very happy in another more fulfilling and equal relationship. Her weight is correct and she looks elegant, happy and satisfied.

---

when we haven't replied to a friend's letter, we may tell ourselves 'It's OK, I'm too busy. She'll understand' when really we know that it's far from OK, and every time the phone rings we have a sinking feeling in case it's her calling.

Then there is control. Controlling behaviour is the 'lion's face' of approval. Fearing loss of love so badly, the control merchant must get in there first to circumvent any possible breakdown of respect before it happens.

When using controlling behaviour with others, we may be loud or aggressive, talk over the other person, or be extroverted. Being ill is also used as a form of control. One of the most common control merchants is the shy, introverted character, and the insecure person – another is a boss who is never satisfied, and is constantly panicking and blaming others.

You know those shy people with whom you are constantly on guard – those people whom you go out of your way to make feel comfortable. You have to draw a conversation out of them. Think back to how you felt afterwards – probably drained and lethargic.

The insecure characters are the people with whom you can't be yourself; you have to put on an act in order to cope with their dramatic personalities. They are the ones who criticize anything and everything.

There is an up-side of control. Being 'in control' can get the job done, and help you to cope; however, it can mean that you do not, ultimately, create any real, close ties with people. Sooner or later, they bow out and the controller simply searches around for others they can control.

As well as controlling others, you may also enact controlling behaviour with yourself. This can include the 'I must, I should' type of internal dialogue. Afraid to make mistakes, the controller assumes a self-righteous attitude, to try to avoid any loss of face.

So what can you do to change either of these?

By catching yourself going for approval or control, you are then in a position to change your actions. You can go some way towards releasing the traps and can go for satisfaction instead. Ask yourself what there is to be afraid of: Fearing that people won't love you? Or that they'll kick you down? Guess what, thinking this will produce just that. OK, there is a little bit of risk involved – it's a little like holding your nose and jumping in at the deep end.

THE VICTIM SYNDROME

Making yourself the victim is a way of punishing

yourself, and of avoiding responsibility. Visualize it like this: You take yourself out of the driving seat and lock yourself in the boot of the car as it hurtles at 100 miles per hour down the wrong side of the motorway! You are entirely at the mercy of other people's actions, but were the cause of the disaster.

'Victims' include: the 'unhappy' wife/girl-friend; the 'misunderstood' husband/boyfriend; the person who is continually below par; the person who is always getting 'hurt'; the women who choose relationships with men who physically abuse them; men who go out with women that use them; and the person who lives his or her life in a state of disorganization.

It is essential that you recognize you are the cause, no matter how persuasive the evidence is that you had nothing to do with the situation. You must get back in the driver's seat.

Suppose you are going to a party. You expect lots of your friends to be there, and you feel happy, confident. You go along and find there's only one person who you know. However, feeling happy and confident as you do, you have a great time, entertain your friend, and meet a few new people along the way.

Now suppose, on the other hand, you expect not to know anyone there. You feel anxious and depressed. You go along to the party and find there is a person there that you know. Thank goodness! You cling to that person all night, bore them and yourself, and no one else attempts to speak to you.

The party hadn't changed. It was you who determined the experience.

BELIEFS

As well as being governed by our fears and the desire for approval or control, our decisions are also affected by our beliefs. Beliefs are preconceptions, often instilled in us through our upbringing.

While it is difficult for us to change our beliefs, it is important to realize that our beliefs affect how we view reality. There are many positive beliefs that enhance our lives, but we must also watch out for the unproductive, negative beliefs. For instance:

1. Believing that nothing really makes a difference;
2. Believing that the more money something costs the better the product;
3. Believing that it is not right to spend time relaxing and looking after yourself;
4. Believing that it is wrong to speak out and express dissatisfaction;
5. Believing you are not good enough;
6. Believing that you can't change anything.

Ascertain whether you run your life around particular beliefs, and whether you have any negative beliefs about your body. Making a list of your beliefs will help you to see that they are not necessarily part of the real picture. Remember, they may be standing in the way of you achieving your goals.

INTEGRITY

When making a decision to change any part of your life, integrity is the key to your success. Integrity means doing what you *say* you are going to do. It takes hard work to have integrity, and it means making a commitment. That commitment has to be re-affirmed every day.

Our integrity often battles with our addictions to our problems, and may break down when we are trying to change our habits. We have to fuel our motivation, and this is something we have

*U*ltimately, seeking approval is done because we fear the loss of love, friendship or respect. By catching yourself going for approval or control, you are then in a position to change your actions. You can go some way towards releasing the traps, and can go for satisfaction instead.

Tania

A young girl called Tania was going out with a man who lived abroad. He asked her to marry him and to emigrate to his country. She accepted and was very excited. After her initial high she became worried, as it meant uprooting her life, selling her share of the business to her partners, and finding a buyer for her home.

She didn't want to talk about it to her boyfriend because she didn't want to show the side of her that was uncertain and doubtful about maybe not being happy once she joined him. She imagined her partners would be furious and that, given the difficulties in the property market, she wouldn't be able to sell her flat.

She got so worked up that she started to lose weight rapidly, and her results at work were greatly affected. Rather than deal with the problems directly she started to consider calling the whole thing off.

After having a long discussion with her, we helped her realize that staying silent was responsible for her worry, and that all of her reasons for not tackling the problems were unsubstantiated at this point.

Tania made a decision to talk to her partners about her predicament and got one of the biggest surprises of her life. They were delighted for her and told her that, of course, she must go and do what she wanted to do. They asked her how much money she needed for her share of the business. She then mentioned the problem of her house and they said they could rent it out to one of their executive managers until she found a buyer. She was so relieved that she burst into tears.

The hardest part was yet to come – talking to her boyfriend about her doubts and fears of living abroad. He visited her the following weekend and she told him what had been going on in her mind about the house and job. He was really pleased for her, but said he felt there were other things on her mind that she wasn't telling him. Because she was so scared she became defensive; they had an argument and went to bed in silence.

The next day she apologized and told him all her fears about leaving her friends and family. He understood completely, and told her off for not telling him these thoughts sooner. He said that he wanted her to consider carefully the commitment that she was making, as he wanted a marriage where there were no secrets between them. It was tough-going, but at the end of the weekend they had talked about things they had never discussed before – and their relationship took a giant leap forward.

Tania said she felt more committed, secure and in love as a result of coming clean. Needless to say, everything worked out in the end. Without facing her problems, especially with her boyfriend, she later could have created all sorts of difficulties that may have set up an underlying tension in the marriage. His questioning of her commitment was scary, but he was helping her and himself to ensure a clean start to their life together.

---

never been taught at a practical or theoretical level. To motivate yourself, you have to continually remind yourself of your intentions.

GOOD INTENTIONS

We often say that we intend to do something, but we do not see it through to a conclusion. The fact is that intention on its own is not enough to get the job done. We need to do all the things in between in order to move from A to Z. For example, how many people say that they want to switch to healthier eating habits? And how many really do it? I would say that only one in two hundred people do what is necessary to get the results they say they want.

The failure to achieve intentions occurs because we don't look at what has got to be done in order to reach our target; therefore, we have little or no hope of getting there. Yet, this process in itself can be immensely rewarding. By tackling all the things that need to be addressed, we can reap many benefits.

Get used to tackling problems as soon as possible, not in a desperate way but in as thorough and methodical a way as possible. Go towards your greatest fears first, whether that be confronting an individual straight on or asking for what you want. The more you do this, the less scary it will be. Remember, your problems won't just disappear – and nor should they. They are useful and have presented themselves for you to learn something.

Throughout your life you will find that certain problems recur. Hopefully, having worked through this chapter, you are now equipped to see that the ball is in your court, even when you think it isn't.

The next chapter offers practical steps you can take to do just that.

FOUR

Making your life easier

MOST OF US tend to think that in a perfect world we would have everything that we want and, above all, we'd be happy – happy in love, happy at work and in play, and have enough money to do the things we'd like to do.

We often think that the people we see as having achieved this are just plain lucky. In actual fact, if you sit down and talk to these people, they'll probably tell you some fascinating stories of the ups and downs, and the taxing lessons they had to go through in order to get to where they are today. They'll also tell you that maintaining this is not a foregone conclusion, but that it takes just as much hard work as getting there. When they're telling you the story, you'll notice there will be very little drama in the way they disclose this information. They'll also probably have a great sense of humour, and they'll tell you they wouldn't change a jot of it for anything in the world.

Most of us are still in search of the eternal happy ending – wherever that may be, and whatever that may look like. Well, for one thing, we've never really been given the guidance needed to steer ourselves in the right direction. First think of yourself now – how you look, what your body feels like, what your moods are like and especially what your image is. Is it:

Powerful	Shy	Downtrodden
Hard done by	Know it all	Introverted

Innocent	Unlucky	Over-confident
Tough	Suicidal	Understanding
Frightened	Cool	Careless
Cocky	Depressed	Goody Two Shoes

or, do you simply say: 'I'm not any of these things, I'm just me'?

Once you've really considered all of this, try to find an early photograph of yourself, and see what the person in that picture has in common with you today.

You'll probably find that the answer is not a lot.

Let's take children, for instance. They can have a day when they've been grouchy one minute, laughing the next, bursting into tears another, only to end up saying they had a great day. Their questions are blunt and to the point, and they seem strangely adult in their acceptance of your answers, provided they are truthful and logical. If they are in any doubt, they'll keep questioning you until they are satisfied. Whatever their negative emotions, no matter how big the trauma in their little lives, they're quickly aired and they don't dredge it up several weeks later. For children, everything is black and white. They know what they like and what they don't like. They have loads of energy and have a curiosity that is second to none. Sadly, none of this lasts long, and children find themselves slowly but surely becoming less and less free with their thoughts and expressions.

The obstacle course begins when the influences of the adult world come into play, making the child aware of sometimes being self-conscious, inadequate, embarrassed or wrong. Children are restrained, disciplined, over-powered and often suppressed. That's where natural honesty, and freedom of action, emotion and speech become stifled and altered.

At school, we mainly learn to remember academic information. It is in these formative years that we are conditioned not to say or do things 'out of place'. And whilst all this is going on we are going through fairly major first-time experiences emotionally and physically.

So while we are being programmed to take in academic information, we are not necessarily encouraged to understand and explore the personal areas of our lives. If priorities had been different, our lives today would be freer of the constraints and limitations we put on ourselves and others, which hold us back from doing what is necessary to get what we want.

When you were a child, the reason you were so spontaneous was because you didn't analyse or ponder over what or what not to do, or what not to be. Your body was your main barometer, and you would feel sensations such as butterflies in the tummy, sweaty palms, dry throat, etc, and act accordingly.

Because you didn't ponder, you more often than not announced the way you felt in your own style. You did this until you were told to shut up or behave yourself. When that happened, your body would have freeze-framed, and you would have felt any of the five negative emotions:

Pride
Anger
Grief
Fear
Apathy

It is that kind of incident that sets the precedent for how we do and don't express ourselves as we get older. We then start to think

Cathy

*B*asically, since being a young child, Cathy had always been a victim of her circumstances. Every time anything went wrong in her life, she allowed herself to be completely affected by it.

She'd had an unhappy childhood, with a violent father and a bitter, jealous mother. She was plagued by a catalogue of illness and injury, sexually abused by a neighbour, harrassed by men at work and, by the time we saw her, had convinced herself that that was how life should be – one long, difficult struggle. She dealt with these blows by overeating, and now weighed fourteen stone.

Our first job was to make her aware that she had complete power over her life, and that the only way things would change, would be if she took total responsibility for her life.

While we couldn't promise a trouble-free life, what we could do was help her deal with life's disasters more effectively, without always letting them get the better of her.

So there were some obvious things to address.

The day after her Consultation, she walked out of her job, leaving the two guys who had been harrassing her feeling guilty and embarrassed. She felt amazing; for the first time she was in control. When she went to see her boss he amazed her by not sacking her, but offering her any support and help she needed.

As a result of this, she was less stressed generally, her marriage improved, and she was able to commit herself to classes and getting herself back into shape.

Over the next few weeks, Cathy came back to see us a couple of times and spent many a long hour talking to Carole, who encouraged and supported her. Gradually, she took control in other areas. She dealt with her nutrition and was consistent at class. The changes in her body, skin and her demeanour were really exciting, and spurred her on until she had lost three stone, changed her appearance, and gained a confidence she had never felt before. Through this, she was able to talk to her mother and father, and improve her relationships with them; she applied for and got a job, for which she had never dreamed of going before; and, her marriage went from strength to strength.

For Cathy, the biggest lesson was that while there would always be problems and pitfalls in life, she had a choice about how she either dealt with them, or let them affect her. She could choose not to overeat when she got upset, or not to be depressed and miserable about a problem at work, and so on. Once she had grasped this principle, life took on a whole new meaning.

too much about what's right and what's wrong, and not enough about what works for our own satisfaction and the satisfaction of those around us. We censor much of what we want to say to each other, therefore not catering for our own and other's needs.

The main way to simplify life is to revert to the instincts we had as a child. Be *completely* honest at all times, in all your communication with people, in all areas of your life – including with yourself. An honest person does not necessarily mean a tactless or unthinking person – that's where phraseology and consideration come in. Honesty inspires trust, and although your honest dealings may sometimes shatter other people's expectations, they'll learn to trust you, and to regard your integrity with respect.

We all surround ourselves with people who tell us what we want to hear; it's the most common form of dishonesty. Change that. If you tell others what you honestly believe, they'll more often than not return the favour. Honest dealings are in the end more comforting – they inspire confidence because you truly know where you stand.

Before you can develop your honesty skills, you must acquire a certain amount of confidence to begin with. And that is what self-knowledge is all about. Dress comfortably, improve your physical appearance, take pride in your decisions and your ability to achieve your goals. Being honest with yourself makes being honest with others that much easier.

Stifled, repressed or suppressed emotions, thoughts, ideology, opinions and intelligence cause extraordinary stress, which leads to minor and serious health problems, out-of-character actions, undeveloped personalities and depression.

The following are some of the key areas where honest dealings and forthright behaviour will change parts of life that cause stress and unhappiness.

STRESS IN THE WORKPLACE

It is at work that we most often censor our true feelings and personalities. Because work takes up a large part of our lives we have to start

> *T*he main way to simplify life is to revert to the instincts we had as a child. Honest expression and emotion will be complemented by our years of experience and knowledge. Finding the child in you is like finding a long-lost friend.

seeing the urgency with which we need to address anything or anyone that is causing us major worry.

1. If you are in a job you want to do but are unhappy with a boss or colleague, you won't want to speak out in case you lose your job or make the relationship worse.

2. If you want a pay rise, you may not ask for fear of rejection, of losing face or, worst of all, of being told you're not worth it.

3. When you are working long hours, day after day, you start to resent this but find yourself caught in the competition or survival trap. More people lose their perspective here than in any other work situation and this ends up adversely affecting every area of their lives.

Workaholics lose touch with friends, eat atrociously and increase their reliance on addictive substances such as coffee or chocolate to keep them going, or alcohol and social drugs to calm them down. They inflict the pressure on their partners and/or families, become ill, temperamental and tunnel-visioned. Their bodies go to pot, tension builds up, no time is left for exercise and, instead, they sit all day long with bad posture.

4. Where there is a threat of redundancy over a long period of time, you may be too scared to try to clarify your position within the scheme of things, for fear of the

spotlight falling on you. This leads to great anxiety and stress.

5. If you believe your immediate boss is showing poor judgement, to the detriment of the company and with the possibility that it may reflect badly on you, you may need to go over your boss's head to address the situation. But you hesitate because of the possible repercussions and the conflict of loyalties.

6. Another stress situation can arise when you're in partnership with someone you once trusted implicitly. Yet now you feel that you're putting more than your fair share of time and dedication into the business, whilst they seem to be having all the business perks: lunches, trips abroad and time off. However, you let the anger and resentment build up, refusing to confront your partner for fear of risking everything you've worked for and put into the partnership thus far.

The first thing to remember is that *you* are the most important consideration – not the job. Sit down and think about what you expect from your job, and what you are actually getting. Satisfaction is vital to wellbeing. Make a decision to deal with any unhappiness in your career, with contingency plans to back you up if necessary.

There is no right time to deal with this. Obviously some times will be inconvenient to discuss problems with colleagues or your boss. But make a concerted effort to deal with anything you come up against within twenty-four hours. Make that crucial telephone call now. Try saying, 'I know this is not the right time now, but can we make a date to discuss this?' That throws the ball in your colleague's court; he or she will have to choose a date. Unless that person is critically ill or out of the country, insist on a meeting within your twenty-four-hour limit.

Get very clear in your own mind what specifically it is that you want. Present a document or report on your achievements and what you intend to improve on. Be prepared with facts, figures and a clear idea of the purpose of your meeting. Make it clear that you will not compromise. If you're honest and forthright – and unemotional – respect and sincere interest will come your way.

Never stay in a job for safety; being unhappy in your job makes life hell for those around you, not to mention you! If you cannot reach an agreement about the points of your job or work life that are causing you some stress or unhappiness, then perhaps it's not the job for you. Honestly assess the pros and cons of your job and take action.

Then breathe a sigh of relief.

STRESS IN A MARRIAGE OR LONG-TERM RELATIONSHIP

These situations can lead to an overload of stress, as they tend to affect every day of our lives.

1. You've been with your partner for some time, and although you love them dearly, you are basically bored. You start blaming the other person for anything and everything – from not putting the top on the toothpaste, to flirting with a friend at a party. You're touchy and irritable, create constant dramas to try to inject some energy into the relationship. Because we haven't been taught how to catch ourselves doing this kind of thing we are unaware of the fact that it is because we are bored

Never remain in a job for safety reasons. Being unhappy makes you unproductive and tense; it also makes life hell for those around you. If you cannot come to a compromise about the parts of your job or worklife that cause you strain, then perhaps it's not the job for you.

that we create these dramas. What you avoid doing is sitting down with your partner and saying how you feel – you may not want to hear that you, too, perhaps, are boring, and that you no longer stimulate your partner. Instead, the two of you can go on for months or years until there really is nothing left of the relationship to salvage.

2. After a very steady courtship you and your partner decide to set up home together, but you soon realize that there are some real basics in which you differ on a day-to-day level. It may be that you are obsessively tidy whereas he or she throws things all over the place, or you like to stay in when he or she wants to go out. Either way, you avoid discussing these issues frankly, because you are scared of facing the possibility that after all this time you may be incompatible and that the entire relationship could be jeopardy. This will be especially daunting if you've just married, or bought a home together, because you would have the added humiliation of facing your friends and family, on top of a failed relationship.

3. Despite your best efforts, your partner is extravagant with money to the detriment of your joint bank account. He or she seems to value a meal out above paying the gas bill. Rather than sit down and confront your partner with the anger and resentment you feel, not to mention the worry and anxiety, you constantly make little digs at them, with sarcasm and malice thrown in for good measure. You refuse to state your case clearly and directly because it makes you appear mean and tight-fisted.

4. On the other side of the fence, you could be living with someone who keeps a tight rein on the finances. You may be dependent on that person for money and may face an angry response when you ask for money for anything other than the bare necessities. You feel completely unable to tell your partner how you feel about this,

for fear of risking rejection.

5. Despite the fact that your partner tells you he or she really does care for you, they constantly undermine your confidence. They badger you about your weight, appearance, taste in clothes, your abilities at work, your friends, your parents, and so on. You end up feeling worthless and humiliated.

Somewhere in the back of your mind you wonder why they love and stay with you, but because this relationship seems preferable to none at all, you refuse to let them know how they make you feel, or question their motives. Consequently your self-esteem falls, and you become introverted and indecisive. There are varying scenarios of this type of relationship.

This is the most common problem in relationships and also the most addictive, as, for some reason, the interest of the victim is stimulated by the want to 'win that person over'.

6. You always seem to end up arguing with your partner when it's time to visit parents or family. Instead of explaining that you always feel uncomfortable, on show, inadequate, humiliated or not good enough, you become sullen and moody, withdrawing from the entire proceedings. It almost seems to come down to a choice between you and the family, and letting your partner in on your feelings is tantamount to asking them to choose sides. You cannot face the fact that they may choose the family's side, so you stay quiet, keeping your feelings to yourself. Again, this is one of many scenarios. The key point is that survival and safety wins at the cost of everything else.

7. One of you wants children, the other does not. At the end of the day, in this scenario, there is little room for compromise. Either you postpone the decision, one of you gets their own way or you split up in order to find someone with similar ideas. In the meantime, however, you do everything to

It's important to decide why you are in a relationship. Loving and fancying are important, but there have to be other reasons. A good relationship should be equally beneficial and rewarding for both partners. It should be the stable base upon which you are able to do anything in the outside world.

what you appreciate about each other, what makes you angry, what turns you on and off – and most important, you must invite the other person to do the same back.

More often than not we will find ourselves in relationships where we remain for the comfort, or the safety. Like staying in a job we dislike, we may have a fear of starting again.

Often, there is a constant battle going on. Neither person has the courage to finish a relationship or to address the problems within it. Very often we perpetuate the scenario by becoming addicted to the drama.

What all of the above relationships have in common is a lack of honest communication. More times than not, any communication is hidden behind repressed fear, anger and other emotions.

To properly communicate you have to set the stage for opening yourself up. Get the place really clean; set up a candlelit dinner and take the phone off the hook. Try to rationalize anything external from the relationship that is bothering you.

Calm down and chat with yourself – think out a conclusion that would be satisfying for you both before you even broach the subject. Listen to your partner; invite them to say how they feel about your fears. Give them an opening, 'I don't know how you feel about this, but. . . .'

If you are giving them a hard time, or telling them off, make sure you say at the beginning, 'I love you; I think you're great'. When communicating, they must be able to disclose what they think it is about them and you that is provoking this behaviour.

If your relationship just won't work and you know this, don't panic too much. Concentrate on preparing to end this stress-filled part of your life. If you can bring yourself to communicate and invite communication back, both good and bad, you can allow yourself to consider the idea of healing your heart and eventually being friends with your partner. Never feel inadequate or blame yourself. Acknowledge what you gained from the relationship and also what you gave to it. Don't allow yourself to take your hurt into another relationship, where a similar pattern could develop. Instead, focus on being honest

avoid the confrontation and discussion. You maintain the status quo by keeping quiet about the subject, but unfortunately the silence becomes tense and uncomfortable, leading to scenes and arguments on any subject other than the relevant issue.

8. You're both career-minded and feel that the other puts their career before the relationship. Maybe that is the case, but you will not risk bringing it into the open for fear that you may lose your career to your partner or vice versa. Either way it seems to you that frank discussion will inevitably lead to you losing one or the other.

It's important to decide why you are in a relationship. Loving and fancying a person are important, but there have to be other reasons. A good relationship should be equally beneficial and rewarding for both partners. You should thrive in a relationship, it should be the stable base upon which you are able to do anything else in the outside world.

To keep a relationship fresh and alive, you have to constantly re-establish your desire and purposes within the relationship. Don't bother waiting for your partner to wave a magic wand – if you're unhappy the initiative must come from you. You have to invite communication – disclose and up-front in future relationships. Do lament or grieve the end – that's natural. But then, take your life back in your hands. You've taken a positive step, and that's a victory.

Every relationship loss should, in theory, teach you more of what you want in future relationships. Loss can also give you more strength to go for your satisfaction as opposed to safety and survival of a relationship.

Even in the most painful situations, you have to see that for whatever reason you chose to stick around for as long as you did. Reaching the depths of despair, coupled with the inability to end a relationship that you know is no good for you, can eventually change enormously the way you are in future relationships for the better. Whether it's you or a friend who is suffering from a similar situation, it's important to let this scenario run its full course. You or they are simply dealing with and getting rid of a weak part of the personality. It's a tall order, but you have to be patient and available, at the same time as offering honesty and strength, if this is happening to a friend.

If you're the sufferer you must surround yourself with strong, truthful and caring people and take good care of yourself physically. Also keep reminding yourself that you won't be in this position or feel this way for the rest of your life.

STRESS AND FINANCE

There is so much fear surrounding this area because money is seen to equal status and success. The thought of being in irretrievable financial trouble is considered by many people to be a fate worse than death. Are any of these situations contributing to the stress in your life?

1. You constantly live close to the bone. At the end of each month you narrowly avoid going into the red, but only because you've become an expert at robbing Peter to pay Paul. Consequently, you're always thinking about money and planning your next evasive strategy.
2. You feel under immense pressure from your family, friends and peers to live up to a certain standard, in keeping with your so-called status. You find yourself in the position of working purely to maintain the house, send the children to the right schools, be seen in the right restaurants, belong to the right clubs and so on. None of it is what you thought you wanted, but now you're caught in the trap of having to keep up appearances and meet your commitments, even if it means working all hours for the sake of the mortgage and your lifestyle.
3. As a child of wealthy parents, you now find yourself financially dependent. They saw you through college, bought your car, gave you the deposit for a flat and so on. However, it seems that your gratitude is not enough. There are strings attached to these gifts, which basically entail you behaving exactly as your parents see fit. This may be in terms of your daily life, choice of career or choice of partner. In any event, you feel you are obliged to behave a certain way, and are completely unable to be open and honest with your parents about anything which may prompt disapproval and, of course, their continued financial support.

Money is frightening; sums and calculations about paying bills enter even our dreams. Make a point to get control of that aspect of your life. Be honest about what you have, your outgoings and what you can afford to spend. Then carry that honesty over to deal with anyone involved in your money problems – your bank manager, your

While we are being programmed to take in academic information during our formative years, we are not necessarily encouraged to understand the personal areas of our lives.

partner, the credit card companies, or even your parents.

Have a brainstorming session: mind dump all of your problems on paper and sift through everything – monthly expenses, what you owe, resources, where you could get more money and how you can lessen outgoings.

It is *not* the end of the world. Everything is resolvable. Get panic into perspective. Imagine the worst possible scenario that could result, and you'll see that you will still survive.

Pay a visit to your bank manager, or the Citizen's Advice Bureau and come clean. If you feel your life is becoming too tied to money, break some of the ties. Take a part-time course in another area that interests you. If you are feeling upset by the hold your job has over you – for example, working only for the money – enhance the other parts of your life for the time being. If you've always wanted to be a photographer and you're working in a bank, try taking some evening courses. There may come a point where you can actually change careers.

Money worries can always be sorted out. Relax and be honest with yourself and everyone around you. See a counsellor if you think they can help you sort it out. Practical, dogmatic and careful planning will eventually release you.

STRESS AND ADDICTIONS

Addictions don't just come in the shape of the obvious ones, such as overeating, anorexia, bulimia, drugs, alcohol and smoking. Addictions are everywhere. Addiction to work, to shyness, to a particular person, a relationship, to physically abusing ourselves and/or others, are just a few.

Almost everyone has an addiction in some form. Our addictions can be a way of seeking attention. Addictions that cause you and others pain and stress need tackling. Anything that is an ongoing situation in our lives could become a habit, which is a different way of saying addiction. The habit that is hard to break is usually there as a safety or comfort mechanism. What you must realize is that this safety or comfort is false, and you may actually be living in extreme discomfort.

Addictions are food for rocky relationships, if

> *Anything that is an ongoing situation in our lives could become a habit, which is a different way of saying addiction.*

we don't face up to them. Take a long, hard look at your life. Where do your addictions stem from? Under what circumstances did they arise?

How much longer are you going to fool yourself? Enlist the support of a friend, or sit down with a pencil and paper and try to face the problem, to understand why you do what you do. Agencies and support groups might be able to help. But take their help and support as it is intended – as advice and, often, an opportunity to share and compare your problems. Support groups and counsellors should *never* become a crutch. If you feel they are becoming a new habit, call back on your own resources to set yourself free.

Addictions do not have to be suffered; truthfully assess what you want out of life, and how these addictions might be preventing you from achieving that. In the end, you'll have sufficient food for thought, motivation and action.

STRESS AND CHILDREN

Having children is a ready recipe for stress. They look to you to learn how to behave, and therefore you feel responsible when they are naughty, or downright bad. There is the stress involved in bringing up children. If you're not worrying about their first walk home from school alone, or their GCSE results, you're nervous at their wedding or upset over their divorce. It never ends. Just because your child grows up doesn't mean your worries are any smaller.

Other factors can also come into play. Perhaps your child is problematic or a slow learner, disabled or prone to illness, insecure or lonely. Any of these will involve stress and heartache on behalf of the parents.

What we do with children will affect the next

generation. Treat them with respect; don't squash them. Remember what it was like when you were a child, and the manner in which your experiences are affecting you now.

Children are far more open to suggestion if you're straight with them. Forget about psychological games, bargains and bribes. Be open with them. Ask them if they want to talk about anything. Tell them when you're upset, but always let them know that you love them. Dealing with a recalcitrant child is ostensibly the same as dealing with an adult – you must use tact, honesty and prepare a well-thought-out argument.

Never accuse children; it's better to say, 'something you did upset me . . . .' Children do respond to honesty and respect, like any adult. Allow your child a point of view, and *listen*, don't just look for flaws in his or her argument.

By communicating and sharing we can learn a lot from children, and they will necessarily learn a lot from us. Always treat them as you would like to be treated, and you'll find the barriers, the antagonism, the malice, the unpredictable or selfish behaviour, and the arguments will disappear.

Don't waste energy battling through a temper tantrum or sulk. There are circumstances under which you should not bother talking or reasoning. Assess the situation, and the likely outcome. Talk to them about their behaviour and your fears, and ask them what it is about them that causes them to behave in the way they do. Teaching children self-appraisal skills will not only help your relationship, but it will better prepare them to understand themselves in the future. And we now know how self-knowledge is the first step to making changes towards a state of wellbeing.

MAKING LIFE EASY

These are only a few examples of situations that set up stress in our lives on a day-to-day level. They are so time and energy consuming that we don't even question their existence in our lives as, after a while, we take it for granted that that's just the way life is. When that happens we tend to take ourselves for granted without even

The energy it takes to worry silently, not to be open and honest with your partner, stay silent and skirt around sex, avoid communication, cling to your children and allow them to get away with things of which you don't approve, is exhausting, unproductive and, most of all, selfish, self-serving and self-indulgent.

realizing it and that puts us into a rut.

Do you get up in the same way every day? Give yourself reasons and excuses why you can't possibly say or achieve something? Do you sit down and ask yourself how you are? What you would like to have in your life that you don't have right now? Do you look after yourself, realizing from time to time that you need a treat? Or do you admonish yourself, saying it's time and money consuming, and selfish?

Do you ask your body if it needs a day off from rushing around, getting upset, and eating and drinking rubbish? When did you last change your daily and weekly routine, tell yourself how nice you look or what a good job you've done, bought yourself some flowers or a present? While you are taking yourself for granted, you are bound to feel that's the case with other people. When you are treating yourself right, you will find that you don't feel taken for granted. You know you are an incredibly important person in your life and until you sit down and take time off to work out exactly what you want from each area of your life, you will simply prolong and make worse any stressful situation. Remember what I said about choices in Chapter Three. If you say something is impossible and qualify it with a reason, then it will be, because you said so. If you say that something is impossible but you are going to take action anyway, then that's what you will do. The hardest thing to do in order to take stock of your life is to get off the merry-go-round that keeps you going around in circles.

What to do: Firstly, go somewhere different for a day on your own: go to a health club or to the country, or go on a day trip or visit an old friend who lives in another part of the country and with whom you know you can be sloppy and relaxed, feeling no pressure to put on any airs and graces. Maybe do something you have always wanted to do, but never got the opportunity – like parachuting, hot-air ballooning, ice skating, going out on your own for a meal, or on a mapped-out walk (walking is the best way of relaxing, getting the circulation of the mind and body going, and clarifying ideas and thoughts).

Watch your commentator come up with all the reasons why you can't do this. If there are none, he will slap a hard dose of apathy on you that will need an atom bomb to shift. This is just fear of the unknown. You may find that going away for a weekend to enact your plans will give you the time and distance to clarify what and how you are going to improve and make happier the quality of your life. You will also have a chance to get the molehills that you have made into mountains back into manageable size.

Once you have set that up, organized the kids, your partner, family, work, whatever, make sure to take a large notebook, pencil or pen. At some point during your day or weekend, when you have rested (and you must do that for at least the first half of your allotted time), sit down with your notebook and write out the following headings that are applicable to you: Relationships, Career, Living circumstances, Money, Children, Family, Sex, Parents, Physical wellbeing. Under each heading write down everything and anything that comes to mind. Particularly express your fear, anger and upset. Be as descriptive and uncensored as you can get. Nobody is going to see this stuff. You may feel at times embarrassed or irritated with yourself whilst doing this.

This is quite often the case because usually the person with whom we don't want to address things fully is ourselves, and we put up with situations because we have a motive that is more important than the dissatisfaction we are going through. These motives are the hardest aspects of ourselves to understand and be honest about because they can be quite selfish or upsetting. Here are a few examples.

A motive is simply a hidden factor that transcends the stress barrier and is a bigger consideration to you than the unsatisfactory situation. For instance, if I lose the house, I'll have to look after myself again. I'll have no one to cook for me. I'll be lonely. If I can't have him/her then no one else can. I don't want to be laughed at. I don't want to be rejected. I've put too much into this to risk losing it now (relationships and career and children). The list can go on and on. To give an idea of what I mean, there are two examples around relationships on the following pages.

When you have finished writing your thoughts and feelings, make a shopping list of what you want around the areas of your life that you want to change. Make your choices realistic and don't *not* put an idea or goal down because you believe you won't be able to achieve it. Put it down, then, as with all your other goals, write down shopping-list style what you have to do in order to achieve it.

*G*iven *technology, alternative education and science, our life span will start to increase to one hundred years or more. Could you bear to live that length of time in a bubble of semi-conscious, niggling dissatisfaction and constant stress?*

Gail and Nick

Gail is thirty-five, Nick is thirty-one. They've been going out for three years. She is attractive but slightly bitter and fairly insecure; nobody would guess, because she's got a tough-lady exterior. Their relationship is fairly volatile and he has affairs from time to time. They definitely see something in each other but they get bored as well. They don't talk about sex or about each other's feelings and thoughts unless they have a major argument, where she has been known to flaunt the most recent fling and bandy a kitchen knife in his face. Nick is not ready for marriage, but she is. Neither is wrong or right; they are just simply too scared or prideful to talk, be honest, change the rules of their relationship and again, state what they want and what they are prepared to give and not give to each other and the relationship.

So they co-exist but really know very little about each other and what makes the other tick. They just play on what aggravates and upsets each other in a never-ending contest. And when the right buttons are pressed, and both feel the hurt and connect with love, desire and whatever else, there is the big 'make-up' and then on to another merry-go-round of the same scenario. Gail just recently got pregnant and is delighted. As it was unplanned, Nick looks sad and defeated and is doing 'the right thing' by marrying her.

Her possible motive? Security at all costs, not losing the relationship. His possible motive? Not losing face, being seen to do the right thing. The result will be that he will always resent her and she will never feel secure in his love for her. If they are both willing to be absolutely truthful with each other and allow the other one to speak the truth, including all the fears, anguishes, upsets and and recriminations, then maybe they have the makings of a wonderful life together.

There would need to be great permission for this, with the condition that from now on they are going to air everything hurtful or otherwise in order to move forward happily, whether that be together or separately. In other words, no expectations, no conforming to shoulds and shouldn'ts, emotional blackmail or otherwise.

As it is, that hasn't happened and all those close to them can see what's going on, and what should be done, but no one has the courage to let Nick or Gail know what's what. Sad, isn't it?

Use the following points to help you plan this out:

1. Work out who you have to talk to;
2. What personal, hidden aspects do you need to take into account or check out that could get in the way;
3. What other aspects would have to be dealt with;
4. When you are going to do these things;
5. Write a list of all your major considerations and fears with plans for combating them;
6. Write a list of the resources you have that can help you. They can be inanimate objects or friends. You'll be surprised just how many resources and ideas you have at your fingertips; and
7. When that is done, write down what would stop you doing any or all of this.

Now you can begin.

Often we don't undertake this kind of behaviour or planning unless a major crisis hits. A bit like our health, we often leave things to the last minute. There are a whole bunch of skills that are invaluable to the job of making life easier. At first glance, employing them to start to clear out the debris of your life may seem a bit long winded. In actual fact, given how long we can keep unsatisfactory situations going, these skills greatly speed up the process. As well as that, they tend to stimulate your natural fascination and intelligence at just how differently you can cope with and affect derogatory situations.

HOW TO MAKE **YOUR** LIFE EASIER

While reading this, and the last two chapters, it has probably dawned on you that staying safe and not communicating for the sake of not rocking the boat, and, most important of all, thinking you are maintaining a comfortable existence, usually leads directly to the opposite. Time and energy spent in manipulation and manoeuvring around like a boxer usually results in bigger headaches than before. The energy it takes to worry silently, not to be open and honest with your partner, stay silent and skirt around sex, cling to

It is a known fact that if you can repeat the essence of a conversation in a moment, or refer to it at a later stage, the talker is always impressed, visibly more relaxed and easier to deal with.

your children and allow them to get away with things of which you really don't approve, is exhausting, unproductive and, strangely enough, selfish.

In order to make life easier, you first have to see your reasons for not communicating, and therefore staying safe. Try to realize that this will not get you the desired results. And as we have stressed throughout this chapter, honesty and action is the only way forward. Understanding yourself takes honest appraisal, and in order to

make changes in any other part of your life, your own self-knowledge must be complete – or on the road to being so. In order to communicate, and effectively decide what it is that you want, you must be honest with others, to garner trust and respect that is essential to every relationship – from work to children to partners to friends.

There are several key ingredients in the recipe for total satisfaction and wellbeing, and without these, your fight for happiness and contentment will be much more difficult.

THE INGREDIENTS

The common denominator: Whoever or whatever is to blame for any one of your predicaments, you are still the one who is being affected by the outcome of these events. If you are continually being hurt, disappointed, ripped off, or whatever, you must get to the point where you realize that you are the common element in all of this. Look at yourself – your character, your habits, your lifestyle. Do you see anything in them that you find unattractive? Or do you find yourself doing things out of character because you feel pressured by events or

David

*D*avid had been married to his teenage sweetheart for eight years and had the 'perfect marriage'. Three children – a five-year-old boy and two younger girls – a big house, two swish cars and a successful career.

On the surface you couldn't fault it. Slowly but surely David realized that he was deeply depressed. He realized he had married for the wrong reasons, that he had centred all his goals on material goods and possessions. He didn't blame anybody but himself and went around for three years in an internal turmoil. He felt he had made his bed and had to lie in it. He was never one to shirk his responsibilities. His wife never complimented him, never asked him questions about how he felt about

things, or whether he was happy. He, in turn, showered her with everything she wanted, but didn't look behind the scenes where she was concerned. When the children came along, he felt completely excluded and she went into her own little world.

It wasn't until he got seriously ill that he began to consider the implications of living the lie. To live out the rest of his life not being happy with a wife who was tight-lipped and also not happy, was indeed ridiculous.

To cut a long story short, he talked to her and it got worse. Eventually he divorced her and lived rough for five years, in order to give her everything. In fact, he went beyond the call of duty – still does in some ways. However, now he is back on his feet, he is happier than he's ever been, he gets on well with his children

and he has his whole life to look forward to. When I asked him what the hardest part was, he replied: 'I had to choose my satisfaction and happiness above my survival. I had to build my self-esteem back from having felt guilty and inadequate. I found out that my so-called friends were not and I had to back my decision, on my own, all the way.'

When I asked him if it was worth it, he gave me the biggest grin and said despite the pain, fear and loneliness, it was the best thing he had ever done. He disclosed that because he had learned the hard way, he didn't play games anymore and he didn't waste time pretending with people and, most of all, himself. He knows what he has to give and how to give physically, emotionally and verbally, and he is not going to settle for less back.

circumstances? Those are the things you must focus on. Changing anything that makes you unhappy, or leads to actions that will eventually make you unhappy, will call for some self-appraisal. Remember, you are the common denominator in every aspect of your life. If you want changes, you will have to perform them.

For starters, don't waste time and energy trying to deal with or blame other people in your life. Sit down with a pen and paper, and work out what it is you are doing to attract the outcomes and situations that are happening to and around you. Make a list of what you need to change in your attitude and/or communication, or choices,

Anne

Anne came to us about a year ago, simply wanting to lose some weight and get her body into better shape. She took hold of all the nutritional information she was given with a vengeance and really made a difference. She was consistent in class and slowly but surely her body changed, becoming sleek and firm and considerably thinner.

Then she began to slip. Her weight went up, her skin broke out in spots and generally she looked lethargic and lifeless, so we sat down with her one day after class and asked her what was going on. She burst into tears and told us how unhappy she was in the relationship with her boyfriend. Despite setting up home together after a few years of going out, her boyfriend refused to make any real commitments to her, hardly even acknowledging that the relationship was permanent. They were making love rarely and if she made any advances they were always rebuffed.

Basically, she felt that time was running out and that she really wanted to get married and start a family, but her boyfriend was totally against the idea. I put it to her that she had some real decisions to make and that her first priority had to be to sit down with her partner and let him know exactly how she was feeling and what she wanted, without being dramatic or hysterical.

It was apparent to us that somehow the idea of communicating her feelings to her boyfriend this directly didn't sit well with Anne.

Next time we saw her she seemed OK and she explained there had been no need to talk to her boyfriend as he had been more affectionate in the last few days and that they had even made love.

We sat her down at that point and were very straight with her, explaining that she must recognize that nothing had really changed. Putting off a difficult communication with someone cannot alter the inherent dissatisfaction. We were fairly sure that in a few days the situation would backtrack. We told her of our own similar experiences, trying to illustrate how easy it is for resentment and bitterness to pervade the relationship if he kept denying her own experience of feeling unloved and insecure. From a purely logical point of view, how could her boyfriend decide what he was willing to put into the relationship unless she was honest about how she felt? We were also very clear with her that she needed to be prepared to risk the whole relationship in order to do this, and that she must basically decide what she wanted first – the relationship as it stood, or marriage and children. The bottom line was that these were the only choices she had.

Over the next few weeks she wavered between the two. The only times she really said how she felt was in the heat of an argument with her boyfriend, arguments which she evidently managed to provoke. As a result, her boyfriend became more and more distant.

At this point, she withdrew entirely from us even though we'd established a strong friendship both socially and through Holistix, because

she knew we would always be truthful and honest about how we saw the situation.

She was soon back to her old weight, and tired and jaded, but she obviously did not wish to talk about things and kept her distance. She was drinking heavily and her nutrition had obviously deteriorated. Her current situation, about which I've learned through friends, is no better. She recently provoked a major argument with her boyfriend in front of a group of friends and remained sulky and moody for the next few days. She informed everyone that her boyfriend constantly undermined her, wouldn't give her what she wanted and refused to change. As far as I know, the situation is still much the same.

Basically Anne refused to take responsibility for what she wanted out of life, because of the risk and change that might be involved. She also couldn't acknowledge that her boyfriend, on the other hand, was doing just that. He knew what he did and didn't want, let her know this and then left her to make a decision.

At this point, it seems unlikely that things will change. Because Anne is actively going against what she knows she wants, she will continue to be dissatisfied with her life. She will become more possessive, argumentative and moody, and physically she will deteriorate, having less energy and enthusiasm for life and abusing herself by drinking and overeating.

Unless she is fully able to acknowledge this, I don't think she will ever turn the situation around.

when it comes to relationships, friends, work and other situations.

At the beginning of a personal relationship, you may have to be completely upfront about what you expect from that person, and also disclose what you think are your weaknesses. Take the time to develop a new relationship with yourself. Face yourself nose to nose in the mirror, and think thoroughly and carefully about what you have to do to change the unsatisfactory departments of your life. It will help you to be much more alert to the pitfalls you may walk into.

Expectations: These are fine, if you don't take them too seriously. We all have expectations about ourselves and others, and we often set ourselves up for disappointments and resentment time and again.

When you expect something or someone to be a certain way or to have particular traits, catch yourself thinking those thoughts and mentally take several steps back. Take a deep breath – in and out – and let go. You'll be surprised by the force of the physical energy that your body is holding when you catch yourself taking expectations too seriously.

Talk about your expectations to those that are involved, and don't hesitate to take risks just because you expect to suffer. Alternatively, don't hold overly high expectations, or you are bound to be hurt or disappointed. Many people set themselves up for this. Shattered dreams and melodrama are a part of life that a number of people thrive on. Forget the drama. Be practical, it's a lot more rewarding.

Be happy, pat yourself on the back when your expectations are fulfilled. But, when they fail, dig up your sense of humour; even the worst situations have some light at the end of the tunnel. Learn to calm down. Stop. Take inventory. You'll find that you *are* all there, in one piece. Don't let defeat of expectations defeat *you*.

Assumptions: When you are involved in a disagreement or an argument, stop, take a silent, deep breath, and think about the assumptions you are making on the other party's behalf. Consider whether or not you are determined to be 'right', or whether you want to reach an outcome that is satisfying to both parties. Also,

watch your imagination. Given half the chance it can make a mountain out of a molehill.

Communication means never assuming. Talk things out – talk about the common denominator, talk about expectations, and *then* find out what is really behind actions and words. Never ever assume anything.

Giving licence to yourself and others to express emotions, thoughts, opinions and feelings: This is a hard one. When our backs are against the wall, most of us are naturally defensive, self-protective, proud, judgemental and secretive by nature. You must try to allow yourself and others to be what they want to be when they are with you.

Forget all your pre-conceived notions about how men should act, or what women should do, or what the general opinion should be. Listen to others. Be honest with them and allow them to be honest with you. A natural expression of emotions, thoughts and feelings is the greatest relief of tension, stress, fears and any other number of things, that there is. Give the gift of freedom to your friends, partners, colleagues and acquaintances; it inspires trust, true friendship and honesty – something we all aspire to.

It is a compliment to be asked to listen to others' expressions of emotions, feelings and ideas. Whatever you do, don't squash that part of them because you are irritated or can't handle it. You will cause more pain than you can imagine, and stop that person from growing or trusting, and they will never be completely yours again until you redress the balance. And it is even more of a compliment for them to allow you to do the same back.

When listening, remember to breathe deeply and slowly, letting all the air out. Make sure you are not taking anything too personally, and continue to communicate, even if you feel hurt, angry or upset. Your turn will come later. Don't ever say you would rather they kept their feelings to themselves. Continue to invite them to say what they feel, whatever side of the fence you are on.

Giving permission in a personal relationship is the secret route to constantly expanding and learning more about each other. Quite frankly, it makes life a lot less complicated and dramatic. This is something we really should try to introduce into our sex lives, and with our subordinates and friends, with our children and with our colleagues.

SETTING A CONTEXT

I have had countless conversations with clients who find it difficult to express what they want to the following people:

Bosses	Partners	Friends
Children	Family	

Some of the reasons for not communicating are:
○ It's not my place;
○ It would hurt them;
○ I don't have permission to talk that way to them;
○ I'm frightened by what they might say or do in return; and
○ I never confront people, I don't think I could start now.

People's reasons and considerations are very real and large and they tend to take up most of a Consultation if there is an issue to do with not communicating. There is some very simple advice for dealing with communication problems.

1. Sit down and write out exactly what comes into your head about what you would really like to say to that person. Do not censor it.
2. Write a list of what you are worried about in terms of that person's reaction. Think of some good or fair points about that person so you have a balance of feedback, when communicating. Make sure they are true!
3. Work out what you would like to disclose about yourself, like the fact that you are scared of being angry or upset. State that you feel clumsy about the way you deliver your feedback, and ask them for their help by being patient with you until you have articulated the main points. By doing this, you take away the emotiveness in making this kind of communication, and you create co-operation and understanding.
4. It is wise to 'ask their permission', and in return tell them that anything they want to say back is fine by you.

Whenever I ask a person what it is they want to say to the person concerned, they are able to relate what they feel and think personally, and what their fears and ideas are. They then say to me: 'What do you think I should say to so-and-so when I see him?' 'Just exactly what you've said to me,' I say. They are always a bit surprised to hear me say that. If the truth has been told, there is no reason why they can't relate the same thing – and to the person concerned.

After reading this book, if this is the only point that sticks in your mind, and you use it religiously (avoiding lame excuses and communication), that alone will make this book worth writing.

Never keep to yourself what somebody could benefit from, even if it's critical feedback. All you have to do is take great care in the way you say what you have to say. You must allow people space to react. Be gentle, but firm. Encourage them to tell you what they think and don't complete the discussion until both parties are satisfied.

You have to be open to being completely wrong. And if you are worried about that, say so. That is also part of setting a context.

LISTENING

People in general are so bad at listening to one another. Because of our natural defence system, we tend to interpret too quickly what is being said, and are equally quick to start arguments, take offence and sometimes be thought of as stupid.

When you feel defensive, proud or hostile, take a deep breath and try to regain control.

Never keep to yourself what someone else could benefit from, even if it is critical feedback.

There are a number of things to watch for and then control:

1. Check what your facial muscles are doing. If they are tight physically, make yourself relax, uncross your legs and arms, and breathe so you can relax a bit.
2. Mentally prepare yourself just to listen, and ask them to repeat something if you find yourself scripting an answer back before they've finished talking.
3. When they've finished talking, give them a brief synopsis as to what you understood, so that you can clarify that you heard correctly. Likewise, make sure they heard you by asking them to verbalize what they've understood from your conversation.

You will find there is much more co-operation achieved as a result of this. The biggest war cry in relationships is that people are not being listened to.

In business, it is a known fact that if you can repeat the essence of a conversation in a moment, or refer to it at a later stage, the talker is always impressed, visibly more relaxed and easier to deal with. Try to carry that philosophy over into your personal life.

GOING TOWARDS YOUR FEARS

Have you ever stopped long enough to notice that you create more fear and considerations by not dealing with your initial fears? Fear and lack of confidence are compounded when they are avoided. Simply by going towards your greatest emotional and mental fears, and coming out the other side, generally unscathed and very much still alive, you will begin to eliminate your considerations and your fears will lessen. By confronting your fears before they get any bigger, you will find life much less frightening and complex. Here are some tips to help:

1. Make a list of all the fears that you have, and how they govern your life. For example, fear of being on your own, or of being dependent on someone and resenting it at the same time. Or, fear of losing a relationship so you will put up with

anything to stay in it, even if it makes you feel unhappy, with very low self-esteem. You will probably be completely preoccupied by this situation, and your work and looks will suffer as a result.
2. When you've made your list, work out how you would benefit if you went in the opposite direction, changing course.
3. Start to make contingency plans, and make sure you cultivate your relationships with friends and family, so you have people to fall back on.
4. Set up your home to be comforting and relaxing, and make sure you always have people with whom you can talk things through before and after the event.
5. Don't put off the inevitable, no matter how sick you feel; you will feel pretty extraordinary when you come out the other side. Make any changes you think you will benefit from. Don't be frightened; it's a lot more frightening to spend your life in misery.

DEVELOPING CONFIDENCE

Confidence to be the person you want to be is essential for personal development. We've talked a great deal about communicating, and about finding the power and the strength within yourself to do so. To be confident, you have to like yourself. In order for other people to like you, they have to know you, and that requires communicating. When people like you, you feel more confident. Does it sound like a vicious circle? It's not.

You are the key to your confidence. If you feel terror-stricken by the thought of communicating, don't push yourself over the edge. The whole point of communicating is to relieve tension, not to cause it. Relax, sit back and think about why you are shy, withdrawn or frightened. Develop a plan for yourself, with goals to strive for. For instance:

1. Look at the reasons why it is easier to stay shy. You might find that you will risk failure, disapproval or rejection. But then, if you don't take risks, you will not gain

David, Julie and Jo

A natural expression of emotions, thoughts and feelings is the greatest relief of tension, stress and fears that there is. Give the gift of freedom to your friends, colleagues, partners and acquaintances; it inspires trust, true friendship, honesty and relief – something to which we all aspire.

David and Julie came to see us as a couple very much in love, but very unhappy. She had been referred by the doctor, she was grossly overweight, drinking heavily, suffering from seriously high blood pressure, and their relationship was in jeopardy – mainly due to his weakness, particularly around women, which stemmed from a domineering mother.

His physical symptoms were seriously overactive bowels (colitis) and migraines. He was also a hypochondriac, moving swiftly from one bout of depression to the next. One inherent trait in his life seemed to be an inability to commit himself to anything one hundred per cent, which included his job, wife and children.

He was on anti-depressants and endless medication, and his mind was constantly on illness, failure and insecurities. The pattern of his life was to seek constant approval and attention.

First of all, David was adamant that he wouldn't change his eating habits, or cut down his medication due to his stomach and bowels. Because so much was awry with these two people, it needed great care and much time for any change to take place.

Julie was stubborn, difficult and depressed to begin with, particularly when it came to discussing her drink problem – to her mind she didn't have one.

It took a lot of talking before she finally had the courage to admit that she was an alcoholic, and from that point she was able to make some changes. Between us and AA, we helped to fight her addiction. She cut out alcohol completely, which resulted in radical changes physically, in terms of weight and blood pressure, and emotionally, in terms of her marriage.

David slowly changed his nutrition under the pretext of supporting Julie in her efforts, but eventually had to admit to feeling a great deal better.

Their relationship continued to improve as they became more and more open with each other, and when he got a fantastic job offer it was the icing on the cake. His migraines all but disappeared, he became less dependent and stronger around Julie, and, probably the loveliest of all, was that a sense of humour developed around his other ailments.

Meanwhile, it came to light during all this that their youngest daughter was also feeling physically unwell.

Jo had been traipsed from one doctor to the next, and each found nothing wrong despite symptoms such as spotty rashes, sulkiness, headaches, and bed-wetting. We advised that she be taken to a homoeopathic doctor, who could treat the symptoms to a degree, including handling the allergies, but who felt very strongly that Jo was suffering from stress, was withdrawn and depressed, and should have some counselling with us.

Basically, it became obvious that Jo was reacting very badly to her parents' trials and tribulations. Their time and attention was dedicated so much to themselves and their own problems that she had developed her own physical problems, as a subconscious plea for attention, just like her father had with his mother.

We decided the best plan was to get Jo and her parents together for counselling. Julie and David were able to acknowledge the part that they had played in Jo's state of being, and consequently, were able to formulate ideas for changing this. The basic plan was to involve the family congregating at least twice a day around the kitchen table. At these times it was important that they learned to talk tough, joke and be just like a family: allowed to air their views, disagree with each other, and kiss and make up.

It worked.

anything, either. What is the worst that can happen? A snub has never hurt anyone irretrievably.

2. Look at those around you – people with confidence, people you admire, people that handle themselves well. Study them, and see if you can pick up any tips. Are they well-groomed? That certainly inspires self-confidence. Are they relaxed? Do they breathe deeply and properly? Do they listen carefully, and soak in everything around them? Truly confident people have plenty of time for those around them. They have mastered their own security, by taking care of themselves and liking who they are. Those tips are invaluable.

3. Develop your sense of humour (everyone has one). See the funny side to situations. Don't be afraid to laugh out loud. Express your emotions and opinions. People will be flattered by your openness and honesty.

4. Make a point of dressing comfortably, in something you feel confident that you look well in. Force yourself to talk to people – maybe one at a time, at first. Listen to people. Speak clearly and with animation when you have something to say. If you don't feel confident, fake it. People will rarely know the difference. Soon you will find that confidence and communication comes naturally.

5. Set goals for yourself. For instance, I will go to two parties or social events this week. I will talk to five people at each. I will go alone to test my new communication skills, and I will smile and have a good time no matter what happens.

6. Jump right in. Start wearing different clothes, doing things out of the ordinary, don't even think about it. Do whatever interests you. When you are interested, you become interesting.

7. Try to avoid situations that could be disappointing. Develop peripheral vision and don't try too much at once. Confidence develops, it does not just happen overnight. Once you appear willing to get involved to others, you'll feel confidence developing within yourself.

Trust yourself – like yourself and be honest with yourself. Summon up the energy and willpower within you to develop self-confidence. Start today.

CREATING HAPPY RELATIONSHIPS

Being happy with yourself. What does this mean? When you are happy in your own company, and have your own interests, you will find solace *and* stimulation. And getting to know yourself is as interesting as getting to know a stranger. Once you have accomplished self-knowledge, you are ready to enter into a relationship that is satisfying and productive.

Look at what you've been like in the past, and what hasn't worked. Be aware of the games you play in relationships – whether it is to interest, inflame or fool your partner. And remember, at all costs, to communicate and to be honest.

Remember what you have to offer (you learned this when you got to know yourself), but also realize what is destructive about yourself in a relationship. What are your expectations? Are they realistic? What do you like in a man or woman? Challenge? Romance? Make sure that whatever you like is a part of any relationship you choose, and that you don't rely solely on the other person to provide your likes for you.

In a relationship, tune into what really interests the other person – you may develop new interests as well. Communicate what you are like; for instance, you might be very greedy sometimes. Arrest each other's expectations by being straight about yourself, and avoid the need for assumption.

There is an enormous difference between being overly serious or heavy, and being direct.

*F*ully getting to know yourself is as interesting as getting to know a stranger.

Forget about long-term plans when you begin a relationship. Don't say you want marriage straightaway, but disclose your future plans and ideas, and ask questions about theirs. If they don't want to answer, don't take it personally. It is not a personal slur, everyone has different ideas of what they want their lives to be, and it is important to respect that. Never manipulate to get what you want.

Listen when they say they like things (for example, open-air theatre in summer). Remember little things and act upon them. It is always flattering when people remember tiny things about your likes and dislikes; why not return the favour?

If you are feeling needy or down, express that feeling. Don't just be needy. Say, 'I'm feeling a bit weak tonight, can you cope with that?' If they can, they will. Don't be disappointed if you are not pampered. The best pampering we can ever get is the pampering we get from ourselves. Spend a little time alone if you are feeling weak and vulnerable. Or do something independent of one another, but in the same place. Little hugs and sympathetic looks can make all the difference.

It is important to be provocative sometimes, warm and cuddly others. Try to match your emotions to what your partner is feeling. If they seem withdrawn, bad-tempered, or waiting to be irritated, don't feed it. Walk away and indicate that you are available to talk, or for support, when and if they want it. Don't get angry with yourself or them. Other people's bad tempers are rarely the result of you.

Like yourself, and continue with other interests and friends. These things feed every relationship. As we said earlier, interested and fulfilled people are interesting. People are always evolving; never let yourself stop. Continue to disclose new things, new ideas, or things you wouldn't normally reveal. You will add stimulation to any relationship

PROBLEMS WITH SEX

Sex is a much talked *around* subject. I use the words talked around, because this is the area where I have witnessed more fear, lying, lack of understanding and dissatisfaction than any other.

In short, many men think that women should be satisfied simply with penetration, and women feel pressured and obliged to achieve climax in order not to lose face and, even more important, not to hurt the man's pride. As well as all this, the majority of men and women feel uncomfortable with the appearance and feel of their bodies.

It is not a man's job to satisfy a woman with his penis inserted in her vagina. Although it is immensely pleasurable, it is not the thing that most often leads to orgasm. Stimulation of the clitoris provides women with orgasm.

Women should take time explaining where it is and how she likes to be stimulated. She has to explore with her partner. Some women can climax through penetration because of the position of their clitoris. Others cannot. It certainly takes courage to express what will give you pleasure, but a relationship is the best place for this to happen. No one will take offence, and a little embarrassment suffered for pleasure may be well worth it.

Men should take time to find the clitoris. Ask, don't guess. Take the pressure off the woman by telling her you know it's perfectly normal not to have an orgasm every time. Encourage her to open up to you by talking or expressing herself physically.

Men and women *both* fake orgasm. Providing genuine pleasure is much more satisfying for both partners, so why suffer through unsatisfactory sex – on both sides – when you can discover what truly does turn you on. Explore each other's bodies, be honest with each other. Never ever bother to fake an orgasm. Nothing will ever improve, if you don't take steps to change it.

There are still many taboos around the sexual act. People are frightened of looking stupid or getting it wrong, of doing something that displeases their partner. For many reasons there is often guilt involved and a fear of discovering a 'baser' part of your nature.

I wrote earlier about the body sensations you had as a child, and how that led you to articulate what you were feeling quite openly and directly.

You've also seen that as you get older you get further and further away from using that skill, and go more and more into your head about life in general. When body meets body, we are thrown straight back into a heightened body sensation, and the only direction our commentator thinks is safe, is the one of pretence or cut off – or to be loudly extrovert.

The thought of communicating intimately and honestly about our fears, our likes and dislikes and fantasies, is horrifying to many people. The things we find hardest to communicate are: a) The fact that we don't know what satisfies us, and asking our partners to help us explore that; and b) Telling our partners what does satisfy us; c) Communicating what we want out of sex (and when we don't want to have it). For the most part, sex can be a clumsy romp in the dark.

For those of us who suffer from an unsatisfactory sex life, there are a number of strategies that can help ease the problem. And, as we keep on stressing, honesty is the very best policy. Confident action can always conquer embarrassment – even if it's admitting self-consciously that you are shy and scared.

Ask your partner to get into bed with you, hold you and talk to you. Or, set up a relaxed, intimate evening. Speak softly, with humility, and don't be afraid to allow your vulnerability to show. Set it in the context of self-disclosure. Say 'I feel really shy . . .', 'I really fancy you and I think you're very sexy . . .' or 'I like that, I like it when you. . . .' Communicate what it is about

---

*I*nterested and busy people are interesting. Don't ever let yourself stop evolving. Continue to disclose new things, new ideas, or things you wouldn't normally reveal. You will add stimulation to any relationship.

---

him or her that you like – their skin, the way they touch – and say, 'I'd like more of that'. You don't have to sound critical. It can be a real turn-on to talk about sex; invite back what the other person wants. Ask – even in the middle of the act – breathe, and touch.

Non-verbal communication will help: move their hand and encourage them to do the same. Sexual communication can be fun and rewarding; experiment and treat your partner with respect. Who knows what will come up?

MAKING LOVE

Personal hygiene and taking care of yourself are essential to a healthy sex life. Feeling good about yourself will always make you feel more sexy, and therefore more desirable. It will inspire confidence in you, and make love-making that much more interesting and abandoned. Choose sensual fabrics, rub your body with an erotic oil or scent. Put yourself in the mood.

Women need to know that men need foreplay as much as women. There is a general consensus among men that women treat them as 'cocks'. That is certainly not sensual. Take as much time over your partner's body as you would like spent on your own. Sex is a shared act, and intercourse is a culmination of emotions and sensual feeling. Don't deprive the act of intercourse of any of these things.

Run your fingers through your partner's hair, stroke his or her back, face and back of neck. Nothing should ever be of just one pace – different intensities, faster, slower, faster, slower, will increase excitement and enjoyment. Never take it personally if they lose their 'excitement'. Give them a little bit of distance and wait.

Breathing is terribly important. When you are fully relaxed, and literally pounding with freshly oxygenated blood, your sensual feelings will heighten enormously. Breathe out slowly close to your partner's ear. Let him or her feel and hear the sound of your breath. Eye contact is provocative, and can be very warm and loving. If there is any fear or pain, this is the way to ease it away.

If you are frightened of trying new things,

take it slowly. Imagine how your partner would like things. Ask questions in a very soft voice. Make your touch light to begin with, and alternate it according to the reaction. Don't be afraid to giggle, if the moment strikes. Sex should be natural and at times playful. Tense situations may well be relieved by a giggle.

Always look for new things to add to your sex life – new, sensual sheets, aromatherapy oils, new positions or different methods of approaching the same ones. But build up a library of things your partner likes:

○ Does he or she like to be adventurous? Get involved with your own sensuality and fantasies. Read books. It is nothing to be guilty about. Be comfortable with your own body.

○ Does he or she like to play, or be mischievous? Experiment. Laugh and enjoy love-making. It is one of the best ways to express emotion and to release tension.

○ Does he or she like variety? Learn what he or she likes and try to adapt your own fantasies and erotic experiences around those. Play games together and share. Each partner should leave the experience equally fulfilled.

FINISHING THINGS

Calling it a day in a relationship is very difficult. After trying and failing to communicate, there is very little else that can be done. You should almost certainly give it up if:

○ You are more unhappy than not, most of the time;

○ You constantly argue;

○ You have become destructive;

○ Your health and work is affected;

○ You are losing concentration; or

○ You've tried and failed to make things right.

Even if you get back together eventually, you must be able to give it away. There is a beautiful adage which expresses this point: 'If you love something, set it free. If it comes back, it was yours. If it doesn't, it never was.' We couldn't express it better ourselves.

No relationship actually *ends*, it just evolves into a different form. Friendship or even just acquaintanceship can always follow. Don't panic about not being in a relationship, you'll find that things fall into perspective when you are out.

Unless you are very mature, it is a mistake to rebound too quickly after finishing things. We tend to use rebound relationships as crutches, and that, as we know, can become a bad habit, and even more destructive for the people concerned. You can never expect happiness in a relationship that you didn't help to create. Rebound relationships tend to offer total dependence to the wounded party. And that's not a relationship at all.

Take some time to analyse where things have gone wrong, and to mourn. Only with foresight and careful thought can you avoid them happening again. Be dependent on yourself only, then you'll have everything to give.

CHANGE

Everything that we are talking about in this book involves change of some sort. It can be:

Physical	Psychological
Emotional	Ideological
Intellectual	All of the above

Change usually involves taking risks, going towards the unknown. Some people purposefully design their lives so that risks are minimal. That is not a bad thing, and you are certainly safe from anything but the ordinary happening if you take this course of action. But really, satisfaction and self-esteem must suffer. There will be no exhilaration at achieving something unexpected. There will be no lessons to learn through failure. Emotionally, a risk-free life must be pretty empty.

Change can be difficult if only one person in a relationship evolves and moves on. Change makes a person more exciting; it creates new situations, opinions, talents, influences and experiences. Where one person wishes to remain in his lot in life, his or her partner will necessarily notice a stagnancy – or, more importantly, a lack of common interests.

Liz

When Liz first came to us she was dreadfully overweight and always tired. Her whole life centered around her job, which was demanding and often involved her working late into the night. Although her upbringing and family life had been good, her parents had just split up and she was dreadfully upset.

Her history revealed that she had consistently overeaten. Now, although she rarely ate proper meals, she also never stopped eating. Liz's usual pattern was somehow to opt out of relationships, either with friends, family or boyfriends, and not to get involved. Instead, she would retreat into herself using food as a comfort.

The very fact that she had got herself to us was a step in the right direction, and the trauma of her parents' separation was to be a real test for her.

We spent quite some time with Liz talking about the type of food she now needed to eat and emphasizing that she needed to eat balanced, regular meals and not constant snacks. On the psychological side, she was soon able to see how she was addicted to using food to see her through any crisis or drama in her life, and that she also used it as a substitute for having people in her life.

So it seemed that one of Liz's main objectives had to be to get more involved with people. We encouraged her to rebuild her relationships with friends and talk to her mother and father about how she felt about their separation, letting them both know that although she wouldn't be taking sides, she very much wanted to spend more time with them, and so on.

Coming to class regularly helped enormously. There Liz had no choice but to make contact, not only with us but also with the people around her.

During her first course Liz came to class, kept to herself, addressed her nutrition and began to lose weight. On the second course, however, things really started to shift. She'd begun to build up her social life over the recent weeks, and had spent time with her parents. The physical change in Liz was amazing. She was still losing weight and, more often than not, was smiling and happy, instead of miserable and isolated.

If you plan to make changes in your life, don't make too many hard and fast decisions; you will need to be patient and observant, without being obsessive. Above all enjoy yourself. Because our imaginations often run away with themselves, you have to be strong and stern enough to bring your fears into perspective. Remember not to make assumptions or to dramatize a situation.

If you honestly want to 'survive', and be 'safe' and 'comfortable', you will realize that going in this direction – making changes – is actually a short cut.

There is a saying that deserves to become famous in the nineties: *What you resist persists*!

We have looked at a handful of personal issues and ideas, and it is important to reiterate the diverse effects that these situations can have on your health and your body, if they are not checked. And checking fears, worries and weak points in your life requires some work: some personal and intimate appraisal of your life and the influence of those around you, and of what exactly you are most afraid.

Obviously it's not that easy. In an ideal world, believe it or not, the best way to be is completely honest about what we think, feel and want, one hundred per cent of the time. The sense of personal satisfaction and freedom in living this way is enormous. Scary, but great fun and very exciting. Didn't you always want a little stimulation in your life? It is also the easiest way of achieving long-lasting happiness and satisfaction.

This way of life means that instead of punishing or judging each other silently, we stand back and look at things from our standpoint – for instance, the common denominator aspect – communicate immediately and directly, set a caring context, and acknowledge upfront what we are thinking and feeling.

HOW YOU COME ACROSS

When talking to someone always pay attention to your delivery. Watch for tones in your voice that sound whiney or uptight. You could be saying something really intelligent or useful, but if your voice denotes something else, like irritation, the essence of what you are saying will be lost, and you actually *will* end up being very irritated and losing patience.

Tape yourself on the phone so you can listen to how you come across. By doing that, your delivery will automatically start to improve, and you will develop antennae for when your communication sounds strange or contradictory.

CREATING A BETTER LIFE FOR OURSELVES

By starting to put all that you have learned in this chapter into action, you will find that the quality of your life will increase and that the fun factor will shoot right through the top of the barometer.

If you are in therapy, use this chapter to speed up your process of understanding. If you suddenly react to your therapist adversely, it is probably because they have hit a sore point; in fact, that sore point may be the crux of all your problems. Stay with it until you come out the other side. Remember, it often hurts to face issues in our lives. If you are particularly wary of a subject or an issue, it is probably because you are frightened by its consequences. In the end, a little suffering is worth it.

On the other hand, check to see if you are using your therapist as just another crutch, perpetuating more of the same – which ultimately can be described as the best way of not taking responsibility for yourself.

There is much to learn around these areas; the world of living becomes your playground. Because you've set a context that problems, negative emotions, and difficult people are all part of your personal game plan, there then ceases to be the immense effort, drama and blame. Instead, that childlike curiosity and simplicity begins to creep back into our lives slowly but surely.

THE IMPORTANCE OF WHAT YOU HAVE TO SAY

One final incentive to get you going is to remember that there are often severe consequences to other people's wellbeing, as well as your own, when you don't communicate within a relationship. See the story of Cathy and Derek on the next page.

My point to you is that when it comes to other people's predicaments, you have an innate ability to sense what's going on deep down. If you don't state as much as you can about what you see and think, two things will happen:

1. You will always have a niggle, and that niggle will unconsciously build, leaving you feeling dissatisfied as a result. So staying safe for whatever good reason isn't the answer.
2. That person will miss out on having the opportunity to change things for the better.

We really don't give ourselves and others much credit when it comes to our ability to help one another. When we give advice, we are rarely certain that it will be taken on board. In the case of Cathy and Derek, his response, or rather lack of it, is a perfect reflection of Cathy's communication. Unless she was willing to take the risk of his rejection, their relationship was going to become more strained and distant.

So don't be a stranger or a coward. Use all the information in this chapter about setting a context, watching the tone of your voice, disclosing your weaknesses and fears, and really start to get involved. I suspect that everyone, including you, will benefit increasingly. Just remember to realize when enough is enough. Bombarding someone and going to the other extreme isn't the answer. Just be watchful; maintain an overall balance and take things slowly at first.

ENERGY

The following details the essential parts of every day – even before we can get around to doing anything for ourselves:

○ Get up in the morning;
○ Go to work; whether it is in the home or at an office;
○ Listen to people's problems;
○ Eat;

*M*yth: *That the penetration of a man's penis alone should do the great big joy.*

Cathy and Derek

A friend of mine has a very close male friend who is diagnosed as having ME. When Cathy talks about Derek, she always seems slightly agitated. One day I asked her to explain to me what exactly was bothering her. She said she realized that ME was a serious and debilitating illness and that she had done everything she could to help Derek.

She then went on to say that she had a strong sense that Derek contracted ME at a time when he had been on a roller coaster of success. She had visibly witnessed him becoming increasingly withdrawn and fearful (and trying desperately to mask it) at prospective challenges being thrown his way. She watched him go downhill from there on.

Cathy didn't feel that she could tell him truthfully what she thought: she didn't feel it was her 'place' to do so. She then came across an alternative practitioner who had an incredible track record of helping the most hard and fastened illnesses from all the varying aspects. She spoke to him about Derek and he told her to bring him with her the next time she visited.

Cathy was really excited and couldn't wait to tell Derek. She rang him as soon as she got home, and told Derek about her discovery. Derek replied that he had tried everything and wasn't interested in seeing yet another person. Cathy let him talk and didn't say much back. As a result, she got to the point where she was very angry and upset.

When I pointed out to her that she wasn't exactly being direct with any of her thoughts and feelings about her 'close friend' Derek. She said that the way she liked to communicate was by giving people enough rope, and if they didn't catch on, she just got on with her life. I very directly told her that that was why she probably ended up feeling disappointed, angry or let down so often. She looked at me quizzically, and I explained that if she was willing to be honest about how she felt, and to imbue her communication with the passion and energy that she felt, at least she would know that she'd done everything in her power to help. As long as she set a thorough context in herself and for Derek – in terms of why she was telling him, and her fears around it – she would walk away feeling complete and satisfied that she had let all the cats out of the bag. If you claim to be close to someone and care about the outcome of their actions or non-actions, it is essential that you communicate everything you think.

All she had to do was take a deep breath and be prepared to risk Derek's wrath for a while . . . or not!

○ Shop for food, clothes or personal items. There is rarely a day that we do not enter a shop;
○ Address personal and work-related problems;
○ Keep up to date with everything;
○ Be social;
○ Be understanding;
○ Give feedback; and
○ Get results.

It takes a lot to get through a day, even before taking on any additional needs or requirements. When your energy is low, it is either because you are generally tired or because you have got a negative emotion digging you in the back. If it is the latter, go forwards at full steam, even if you are practically snoring at first. That pushing creates a momentum of its own, and suddenly you find that your energy is much higher. In any case play with your energy levels; they are a useful toy as long as you don't waste or abuse them on other people and activities that are detrimental or transitory. You will have found a very useful tool to have around you at all times.

Energy is derived from all aspects of our lives: from the food we eat, the exercise we take, the amount of water we drink, our sense of wellbeing and our happiness. Rest, relaxation,

You can never expect happiness in a relationship that you didn't help to create. Rebound relationships tend to offer total dependence to the wounded party, and that's not a relationship at all.

the avoidance of dietary toxins (see **Nutrition**, chapter six), deep, healthy breathing, plenty of fresh food, water and exercise will create unlimited sources of energy. By avoiding situations that cause you stress or unhappiness, you will reduce energy-depleting tension.

Energy feeds on energy. The more energy you put into life, the more energy your body will produce. Encourage yourself to be active, drag yourself up when you're down. You'll feel enormously better for it.

Jumping the gun a bit, I will stick out my neck and remind you that the next century is steadily creeping up on us. Let's not waste any more time scrabbling around, staying safe, constantly moaning about our weight and spotty bums. With or without our co-operation and wisdom, it is possible that we are actively heading for more peaceful times. Given technology, alternative

When your energy is low, it is either because you are generally tired or because you have got a negative emotion digging you in the back. If it is the latter, go forward at full steam, even if at first you are practically snoring.

education and science, our life span will start to increase to one hundred years or more. Could you bear to live that length of time in a bubble of

Susan

Susan had been bulimic for a number of years, was very prone to depression, and had attempted suicide on two occasions. Physically, her weight was very unstable, her skin pale and blotchy. Her hair was dry and flyaway, her nails flaky and weak. Generally, she felt very rundown, weak and lethargic.

We asked her to describe in detail exactly how she felt and somehow by putting her feelings into words, she was able to see just how revolting she felt most of the time, and that she really did want things to be different.

So, because of the nature of her problems, we had to do some digging around in her past to find some explanation for her behaviour. Between us, we unearthed three generations of people who had been unable to sustain normal everyday lives and, instead, constantly created dramas and crises; people who couldn't handle any type of stress and who instead turned to some kind of

crutch, be it alcohol, love affairs, wife beating, food abuse – anything to avoid the situation at hand.

The scary part, as we pointed out, was that Susan was in danger of beginning the whole cycle again. We talked this through long and hard, until she could really see the pattern unfolding. Once she'd reached that stage, we then told her that perhaps she needed to develop a sense of humour around it or she really would go nuts.

She was living in a situation where her parents were both alcoholic and would row endlessly. Her mother was suspicious, and if Susan spent time alone with her father, she was accused of having an affair with him.

Anyway, we sat down and between us worked out a plan of action around her eating habits, her situation at home, how she dealt with her brothers and sisters, her boyfriend and her parents. After a fairly gruelling morning, she felt scared but very optimistic about the future.

Over the next few days, she was in constant contact with us. Sometimes she lapsed back into confusion and

depression, but mostly she remained optimistic and open to suggestions.

She then came back for a second consultation at which we really addressed the whole business of food and eating. We encouraged her to eat three meals a day and to eliminate any junk from her diet, sticking to fresh whole foods and substituting fatty and dairy products with soya and vegetable products. We also worked out a set procedure for her to follow whenever she felt a bulimic attack coming on, which involved getting on the phone to us – no matter what the time, day or night. When she left, she was armed with a mass of information and she felt inspired enough to put into practice the various ideas on offer.

One of her first tasks, which we had led her to see was necessary, was to address her parents and their behaviour. Susan actually found the courage to go straight home and talk to them. The first step has been achieved: her father is going to see a marriage guidance counsellor, and Susan didn't turn to food to help get her through the ordeal.

semi-conscious, niggling dissatisfaction and constant stress?

No.

Well then, let's have a toast to you getting exactly what you want, resulting in peace of mind and happiness. Crack open the bubbly (mineral water, of course!) and start celebrating the first day of the rest of your life. Getting exactly what you want is a lifetime's work. In the process of doing just that, have a bloody good time along the way.

Chapter Five will give you some incentives to begin the fight, because it begins with our bodies – how they work and how to keep them healthy.

Staying Healthy

IN CHAPTERS TWO, Three and Four we looked at the emotional reasons for the health problems you may be suffering from. In this chapter, we will look at the physical symptoms and the practical ways you can deal with them. We will cover some of the most common problems that our patients discuss with us, and the solutions we have found most useful. For further information we recommend in-depth books on the subjects (see page 191, **Further Reading**).

The body is like a finely tuned machine and, like a machine, if one part is not operating efficiently, it places more load on other areas. If this carries on unchecked, more and more parts will become affected and that will eventually lead to a complete breakdown of the machine.

The good news is, however, that when it does break down, the body – given the right conditions – has the inherent capacity to heal itself, with a little help from you.

Go through the following list to see which of these symptoms apply to you, on either a regular or occasional basis:

- Headache;
- Backache;
- Migraine;
- Skin problems;
- Respiratory problems;
- Bowel problems;
- Urination problems;
- Vaginal discharge;
- Thrush;
- Cystitis;
- Lethargy;
- Continuing debilitating illness, such as ME;
- Glandular fever;
- Colds, sore throats or flu;
- Swollen glands;
- Pre-Menstrual Syndrome (PMS);
- Period pains;
- Bruising;
- Circulatory problems;
- Cramps, aching joints, slow reflexes;
- Nausea; or
- Feeling over-emotional.

Examining your personal medical history is important when it comes to tackling these symptoms. You need to take into account each of the following:

- Major illnesses suffered;
- Operations undergone;
- Antibiotics taken (in the past or on a regular basis);
- All other medications taken (in the past or on a regular basis);
- Steroids taken;
- Anti-depressants taken;
- Pain-killers taken;
- The regularity of recurring minor illnesses;
- Long-term emotional stresses and traumas;
- A history of poor nutrition;
- Consistency of bowel movements;
- Colour of urine;
- Mood swings;
- Viruses suffered; and
- Accidents causing personal injury.

We have seen so many people who have – either in the past or on a regular basis – taken a huge number of prescribed drugs and over-the-counter medications. Antibiotics, while they can be essential and life-saving, have often been overprescribed in the past, and in many cases they still are. Antibiotics disturb the enzyme actions in the stomach and create that well-known sensation of feeling the side-effects of the drug far worse than the symptoms of the disease

Anne

Anne had one major problem which made her feel grossly uncomfortable with herself. There was a family history of three generations of problems in the chest, nose, throat and skin areas. The result was that she suffered asthma, hayfever and countless allergies, which meant she breathed through her mouth most of the time, her co-ordination and balance were appalling, and her nose and cheeks were usually swollen and unattractive. Her skin was also blemished, and she suffered chronic acne.

She had been through countless drugs and treatments in her time, none of which really had any great effect.

The first step was to give her a more thorough understanding of a condition which she had genetically inherited from her family, with its history of TB, asthma, lung cancer, and so on. Then we began to give Anne suggestions which would improve her condition.

Nutritionally, her history was appalling and so we explained that in order to rid her body of toxins, and thus prepare it be in the best possible condition for dealing with her breathing problem, it was vital that she eat only the freshest and most nutritious foods. We also took her off most dairy products, which could have aggravated the problem.

In terms of the classes, we spent quite some time working with Anne on her breathing. By breathing into her stomach, using her nose when possible to breathe in, opening up her chest in the process, her circulation began to improve. She began to concentrate on breathing correctly as much as possible, and gradually, as she became more confident with the exercises, her balance and co-ordination improved. She was then able to use her breathing in time with the exercises to enable her to go further.

For Anne, the biggest benefit is simply an overall feeling of being more at ease with herself. Her problem hasn't gone away, but through some constructive action she has reduced drastically the effect that it has on her everyday life. Her balance and co-ordination keep improving, the swelling on her face has gone down and her skin has all but cleared up. Physically, she feels able to move with more grace and confidence.

– both during the course of taking them, and often for a protracted time after. Acidophilus and bifidus supplements are recommended if you are taking antibiotics, for antibiotics tend to destroy beneficial intestinal flora, causing numerous intestinal disorders, including diarrhoea and an overgrowth of fungus infections. Acidophilus will act to clean the intestines; it is commonly known as the 'friendly' bacteria.

Of the many effects that these drugs have on the body, the digestive system and bowels suffer particularly, and the immune system can be adversely affected. Wherever possible, more natural alternative therapies and remedies should be used. Leaving the work to be done by drugs and handing over responsibility to your doctor is not always the answer. Get to know your body; eating a healthy diet and understanding the roles of various food substances in combating disease can eliminate much of the need for prescription drugs.

If you are taking tranquillizers or sleeping pills you *must* aim to cut down, but always under supervision. There are numerous natural sleep-aids available on the market today – with no addictive properties or harmful side-effects. If you have been taking diuretics on a long-term basis, take a close look at why you need them, and consider whether improving your overall nutrition will help. Whatever drug you may be on, ask your doctor about the possibility of lowering the dosage. A slow decrease may be possible.

With your medical history and list of common symptoms in mind, take a look at the various orthodox and alternative therapies available (see pages 68–73). You might be surprised to find a simple cause for your symptoms; one which can be rectified with little fuss.

FINDING YOUR WAY IN THE ORTHODOX AND COMPLEMENTARY MEDICAL PROFESSIONS

When you are ill or need to seek medical help, the essential point to remember is that you need to be treated uniquely. Ill health affects each person differently, even if the symptoms are identical. So just treating the symptoms using methods and concepts is not enough to accurately and thoroughly deal with the problem.

The success of all treatments depends on the individuality of each person concerned.

My advice to people in all areas of ill health is to consult an orthodox doctor, get a diagnosis and prescribed treatment, and then consult an alternative practitioner and try the natural form of treatment before embarking on any type of antibiotic or other form of drug. Talk to your GP about alternative sources of relief; you may find that he or she can offer a drug-free cure. But be sensible – serious illness demands immediate attention, and trying various methods can be time-consuming and therefore, in the case of very serious health problems, dangerous. Always tell your GP what you are doing, and make sure that any forays into alternative therapies will not lead to delays in treating the problem. You can get alternative help at the same time as being treated by an orthodox practitioner.

There needs to be a more open-minded and co-operative attitude between practitioners on both sides of the orthodox and complementary medicine fence – as well as between practitioners on the same side of the fence as peers (they are just as mud-slinging between each other, as they are with rivalling philosophies). It is still rare for the different practitioners to share insights with each other.

A deeper understanding would then develop, which would increase mutual respect and improve the standards of treatments. Then we, as patients wouldn't feel 'conned', 'experimented on', 'cynical', or generally in the dark when it comes to choosing various treatments and therapies.

Getting to know your body, eating a really healthy diet and understanding the roles of various food substances in combating disease can eliminate much of the need for prescription drugs.

Therapists and medical experts must be able to admit when they can't take your treatment further. In the complementary field, it is *vital* that they have enough knowledge to know when to refer you to a different practitioner.

Furthermore, it is an extremely good idea to choose an alternative therapist who has qualified and practised in orthodox medicine. You may feel safer getting a well-rounded and sound diagnosis – based on both orthodox and alternative precepts.

The constraints of time on a doctor and patients leads to frustration on both sides, and therefore needs to be acknowledged. Beware of doctors who take short courses in alternative therapies. Likewise, beware of the alternative practitioner who hasn't had in-depth training. When consulting an alternative therapist about a serious health problem this is absolutely essential. To ensure that the practitioner from whom you are planning to seek attention is properly qualified, contact the registered society for that particular therapy. Some numbers to try are listed below the details of each therapy available and also on page 190.

No one form of medicine contains all the answers to the problems of ill health. Practitioners today don't know everything, any more than they ever did. There are unnecessary operations performed, and there are alternative remedies and therapies that have turned out to be a waste of time, inaccurate or dangerous as a result of a potentially serious problem not being recognized or correctly dealt with. The following are some of the natural alternatives to orthodox medicine. Some or all of these therapies may be applicable to you and your symptoms. All alternative therapies are based on individual prescription; don't try to self-diagnose. Take a look at what's available, and get in touch with a registered practitioner to see if he or she can help. If in doubt, there are numerous books available on complementary therapies (see **Further reading**, page 191, for details).

Alternatively, you can contact the British Council for Complementary and Alternative Medicine, Suite One, 19a Cavendish Square, London W1M 9AD (071-409 1440), for advice.

ACUPUNCTURE

Traditional Chinese acupuncture sets out to restore health and prevent further illness by maintaining a person's vital energy (*ch'i*) in balance and harmony. In this way, a person is less likely to succumb to disease. Treatment comprises the insertion of very fine needles into any one, or several, of over 700 points on the body, to stimulate or sedate the flow of energy. Sometimes a herb, *moxa*, is used to assist in the treatment.

Contact the Council of Acupuncture, Suite One, 19a Cavendish Square, London W1M 9AD (071-495 8153) for details of a registered acupuncturist nearest you.

ALLERGY TESTING

A growing amount of evidence links many physical symptoms with an intolerance of food (see **Nutrition**, chapter six) and other substances. Hyperactivity in children, skin complaints, and respiratory problems may all be reactions to allergens. In identifying these substances the patient may avoid his or her known allergens and hence enjoy a better quality of life. (See also **Radionics**, below.)

For more details of allergies, and the kinds of effects they can have on your wellbeing, contact: Action Against Allergy, 43 The Downs, London SW20 8HG (081-947 5082).

Daniella

The daughter of a friend of mine had always been sullen and lethargic, suffering from psoriasis. At the age of eight, and after many visits to doctors, Daniella was tested for allergies. They found that she was allergic to yeast. Within four weeks of cutting it out of her diet, she became a naturally bouncy and playful little girl. All of her symptoms disappeared and, previously an average student, Daniella soared to the top of the class.

AROMATHERAPY

Aromatherapy uses essential oils, either topically (ie massage, compresses, or in the bath) or by inhalation, to induce relaxation, heighten energy

*N*o one form of medicine contains all the answers to the problems of ill health. Practitioners today don't know everything, any more than they ever did. There are unnecessary operations performed, and there are alternative remedies and therapies that have turned out to be a waste of time, inaccurate or dangerous, as a result of a potentially serious problem not being recognized or correctly dealt with.

levels and restore your body's natural balance. The oils are pure aromatic substances extracted from natural sources: trees, fruits, herbs, flowers, etc.

There are many antiseptic and analgesic properties to the oils, and they are excellent agents for treatment of stress or nervous exhaustion. Other conditions which can be relieved include: respiratory problems, cystitis, high blood pressure, nausea and insomnia, among others.

A list of aromatherapy essential oils, along with their practical uses, can be found on pages 174–176.

Contact the Tisserand Aromatherapy Institute, 10 Victoria Grove, Second Avenue, Hove, East Sussex BN3 2LJ (0273 206640) for books and self-help details; or the British Council for Complementary and Alternative Medicine (address on page 67).

AURICULAR THERAPY

This is a form of acupuncture without needles. A

large point (which does not pierce the skin) conducts an electrical pulse, which stimulates the meridians that correspond to different parts of the body. It is effective for both mental and physical conditions, especially nervous disorders, bladder and kidney problems, digestive disorders, skin problems and fatigue.

Contact the British Acupuncture Register and Directory, 34 Alderney Street, London SW1 4VE (071-834 1012) for a practitioner nearest you. Or contact the Council for Acupuncture (address above).

BACH FLOWER REMEDIES

In the 1930s, Dr Edward Bach discovered that a number of plants had specific properties that could help patients overcome mental and emotional problems. These flower extracts provide a safe and simple means of helping people cope with many of today's stresses.

These remedies are prescribed according to a patient's emotional rather than physical make-up, and are based on the belief that physical problems can be healed by first improving the spiritual or mental state. Bach flower remedies can be taken by people of all ages, with no danger of over-dose or side-effects. Animals and plants will also benefit from this treatment. Rescue Remedy, made up of Cherry Plum, Clematis, Impatiens, Rock Rose and Star of Bethlehem, is an excellent, all-purpose emergency remedy for anguish, distress or fear. It is comforting and calming to anyone suffering shock of any kind.

Clare Harvey Thompson is also well known for her work with flower remedies, and crystals, for which she has devised her own method of diagnosis and treatment. She uses Bach flower remedies for the emotional level, and crystals for spiritual or auricular healing. She also uses new flower essences, imported from Alaska, California, Colorado and Australia. She has hundreds of remedies, as she says that life is more complex now (Bach had thirty-eight).

For details, contact: Clare Harvey Thompson, Middle Piccadilly Healing Centre, Holwell, Sherbourne, Dorset (0963 62466). Or, Bach Flower Remedies Ltd, Dr Edward Bach Centre, Mount Vernon, Sotwell, Wallingford, Oxon OX10 0PZ (0491 34678).

CHIROPRACTIC

The theory behind the practice of chiropractic is that illnesses are caused by misaligned spines, and treatment is based on the manipulation of the spine and neck. A careful analysis of your medical history, along with, possibly, a series of X-rays, takes place before any treatment is offered. Backache, neckache, shoulder, hip and arm pains can often be the result of tightened muscles surrounding an inflamed nerve – the result of one of more vertebrae being misaligned.

Chiropractic treatment can also relieve problems resulting from poor posture, as well as some arthritis and rheumatism. Migraines, digestive troubles, asthma, sciatica and period pains can also benefit from this therapy.

For more information, and a list of registered chiropractors, send £1 and an SAE to the British Chiropractic Association, Premier House, 10 Greycoat Place, London SW1P 1SD (071-222 8866).

CLINICAL NUTRITION

Although in today's society people do not have outright vitamin and mineral deficiencies (manifesting themselves in scurvy, rickets, or the like) many people have what are called 'sub clinical deficiencies' which cause fatigue, minor illnesses, susceptibility to colds, flu and other viruses, and aches and pains.

The clinical nutritionist will analyse your diet, spotting any deficiencies which are causing your ill health, and suggest a diet (perhaps with supplementation) to alleviate this. A healthy diet is essential to total wellbeing, and it is often deficiencies of trace minerals and vitamins which can play havoc with an otherwise healthy and fit body. Chapter Six has further details of the role nutrition plays in our life, see page 93. To contact a clinical nutritionist (or dietary therapist, as they are often called) try: the Dietary Therapy Society, 33 Priory Gardens, London N6 5QU (081-341 7260); or The Institute for Optimum Nutrition, 5 Jerdan Place, London SW6 1BE (071-385 7984).

COLON HYDROTHERAPY

Colon hydrotherapy is simply cleansing of the bowel by the safe, natural infusion of purified warm water into the colon – using no chemicals or drugs. It is a pleasant, relaxing experience involving neither embarrassment nor discomfort. By cleansing the bowel of unwanted faecal matter and debris, normal absorption and bowel function return, thereby alleviating many symptoms not related to the colon, such as fatigue, headaches, bloating, liver disease, abnormal blood pressure, pain in the joints, halitosis and candida. It is also the natural solution to such conditions as constipation, colitis, diverticulitis and irritable bowel syndrome.

As a result of the treatment, you can expect a feeling of wellbeing, clearer skin and eyes, more energy, and the relief of allergic symptoms. For details, contact: Life Works, 11 Southampton Road, London NW5 4JS (071-485 7122).

HOMOEOPATHY

For over 150 years, homoeopathy has been successfully dealing with many problems that have proved resilient to allopathic (or orthodox) medicine. The patient is treated by administering a remedy which mimics the symptoms the condition is manifesting, following the principle that 'like cures like'. In other words, minute quantities of whatever is causing the symptom will be given to the sufferer so that the body's defence system will be stimulated, and therefore naturally make it well. For example, someone suffering from hay fever or rhinitis will be given small quantities of the allergen, which will aggravate the body into defending itself, thereby curing the principal cause of the symptoms.

Homoeopathic drugs are diluted to such a degree that side-effects are rarely experienced. Furthermore, whereas orthodox medicine suppresses symptoms, the homoeopath would see them as a good sign – an indication that the body's natural healing ability is at work.

All remedies are prescribed according to individual requirements, and this is based on all aspects of a person's mental, physical and emotional state. Homoeopathic remedies are very often safe for children.

For more information and a list of registered practitioners, contact: the Society of Homoeopaths, 2 Artisan Road, Northampton NN1 4HU (0604 21400), or the British Homoeopathic Association, 27a Devonshire Street, London W1N 1JR (071-935 2163).

KINESIOLOGY

Systematic Kinesiology embraces techniques which use the response of muscles, when gently tested, to access the 'computers' controlling the body. Kinesiology enables the practitioner to investigate what is happening in the body without intrusion, and find the underlying causes and the nature of problems. Energy balance is restored to the whole person mentally, physically, chemically; natural healing is enhanced, health and wellbeing improve. Using the changed muscle response as a guide, the specific problems located may be swiftly corrected in the priority order the body indicates it prefers. Changes are usually very quick to take place and problems which have persisted sometimes for many years are often resolved in two or three sessions.

Kinesiology can test for allergies and deficiencies, strengthen the immune system, remove acupuncture energy blocks without needles, help resolve phobias and fears in minutes, reduce anxiety, tension and

When you have found a good practitioner or team of practitioners, you must back them up by explaining everything you can think of medically, emotionally and physically, past and present. The more you disclose about yourself, the more you allow the practitioner to help you.

hyperactivity, deal with stress and drama, correct postural aches, imbalances and pain, correct digestive disturbance, and lift depression without drugs. Contact: Middle Piccadilly Natural Healing Centre, Holwell, Sherbourne, Dorset DT9 5LW (0963 23468).

ORTHO-BIONOMY

Structural problems of a skeletal nature are often an undiagnosed source of pain. Ortho-bionomy is a safe, easy and gentle method of regaining structural integrity. By releasing the muscular spasms at well-defined trigger points, the body can re-adjust naturally.

Contact the Institute for Complementary Medicine, 21 Portland Place, London W1N 3AF (071-636 9543), or the British Council for Complementary or Alternative Medicine (address on page 67), for details.

OSTEOPATHY

Osteopathy is based on the theory that spine misalignment can cause muscular, circulatory and nervous problems in the rest of the body – that the skeleton and the organ systems are inter-dependent. Therefore, by correcting structural imbalances in the spine – and muscles – by manipulation and adjustment, bones, blood supply, ligaments, nerves and muscles will be able to function at their best.

When bad posture, or even just posture changes, take place, muscles shift to trap nerves, soften ligaments and bind joints. Manipulation alters this shift so that fluids can circulate more freely, and joints can resume their flexibility.

Osteopathy can relieve neck, back and joint pain, and also help asthma, bronchitis, constipation, digestive problems, chronic headaches, sinusitis and sprains.

Cranial Osteopathy is based on similar principles, but refers to the bones of the skull. By careful and gentle manipulation, the cerebro-spinal fluid – in which the entire nervous system is bathed – can attain a state of excellent circulation and balanced pressure.

Not all osteopaths are qualified to practise cranial osteopathy, so if you wish such treatment, check first to ensure your osteopath can undertake it.

Osteopathy in pregnancy is superb for helping control stretch marks, prevent damaging posture changes, relieve muscle cramping and the aches and pains associated with increased stretch and strain on soft tissues. Osteopathy is ideal for the preparation for labour, and for after labour, to help return the joints of the pelvis to normal. Osteopathy can be of great benefit during pregnancy, both in terms of treatment *and* reassurance. Labour can actually be less painful when your body is working smoothly.

For details of registered practitioners in osteopathy and cranial osteopathy, contact the Cranial Osteopathic Association, 478 Baker Street, Enfield, Middlesex EN1 3QS (081-367 5561), and General Council and Register of Osteopaths, 56 London Street, Reading RG1 4SQ (0734 576585).

HYPNOTHERAPY

Therapeutic hypnosis is a valuable treatment in dealing with many nervous, emotional and psychological disorders. It can shorten the time taken in conventional analytical therapies and is effective as an anti-smoking and slimming treatment. Lack of confidence, stress, anxiety and phobias are examples of other problems that also respond well to this therapy.

This therapy is based on mental relaxation, which encourages the release of tension, allowing your unconscious mind to become more open to suggestion; for instance, to giving up smoking or alcohol.

Contact the British Society of Medical Hypnosis, 42 Links Road, Ashtead, Surrey KT21 2HJ (0372 273522), the British Council for Complementary and Alternative Medicine (address on page 67), or the Natural Healing Centre (see page 190 for address).

MEDICAL HERBALISM

This therapy is based on the principle that the healing properties of plants (fruit, vegetable and herb plants) are sufficient to ensure total wellbeing. It is, perhaps, the oldest art of healing, and can, in general, benefit your health,

Becoming healthy or fitter is not affected by how old you are – rather, it is simply to do with how long you have had your bad habits. Even if there is longevity involved, your body has the most incredible ability to heal itself and to revert back to a strong and healthy state.

stimulating your body's ability to heal itself. Herbalists believe it is safer to use the whole (or part of the whole) of a plant, rather than extracting and synthesizing the active part, as orthodox medicine does.

A number of remedies can be purchased over-the-counter; for instance, chamomile and lime flower for inducing sleep, calendula and arnica for cuts and bruises, fennel, peppermint and slippery elm for digestive problems, and raspberry leaves and rose hips for PMS or muscular cramping.

Herbs can be prepared in a number of different forms: as tinctures (suspended in alcohol), lotions, liquids, tablets, infusions (teas or coffees), or even for bathing.

Hay fever, headaches, depression, fatigue, stomach upsets, insomnia, arthritis, skin problems and a large number of other complaints can be relieved by medical herbalism. Contact the National Institute of Medical Herbalists, 41 Hatherly Road, Winchester, Hants SO22 6RR (0962 68776), or PO Box 3, Winchester, Hants SO23 8AA, for a list of registered practitioners.

PSYCHOTHERAPY

Within psychotherapy there are many techniques that can be applied to help bring about change in a patient's perception and awareness, allowing that person to achieve mental and emotional stability. These techniques may be drawn from behavioural, or Rogerian methods, Transactional analysis, or some other modality. All treatment is based on individual requirements – on both a physiological and psychological basis.

Counsellors are usually specialists in one area of psychological health; for instance, marriage guidance and relationships, or trauma, stress and phobias. As discussed in Chapter Four, adult crisis or ill health can often stem from childhood experience, and can manifest itself in a number of physical disabilities. Counselling is an excellent method of facing any emotional difficulties or traumas, allowing for complete mental and physical wellbeing. The importance of the balance between mental and physical health cannot be stressed enough. If there is any past or present difficulty which is causing you physical pain or discomfort, counselling is an ideal route.

Only when you are psychologically ready to change your life can you successfully do so, and that means starting with a clean slate.

For information about psychotherapy, and a list of registered practitioners, contact the British Association for Counselling, 37a Sheep Street, Rugby CV21 3BX (0788 78323).

PULSORS

Pulsors, which are small magnetic discs, provide the means to balance out the body's polarity and amplify the aura, or energetic field. Following treatment, patients report a feeling of deep relaxation and wellbeing, and a sense of having got rid of unwanted negative energies, thoughts, tensions and stress. Contact the Natural Healing Centre for details (see page 190 for address).

RADIONICS

By tuning in to a patient's fundamental ray through a 'witness' (usually a hair sample), accurate diagnosis and treatment of that person is possible. A radionic computer analyses conditions at various levels and may then be used to formulate a remedy or treat at a distance.

This practice is used to diagnose allergies and various deficiencies as well as illnesses (both minor and serious) which may not show up in orthodox testing.

For information, contact The Institute for

Complementary Medicine, 21 Portland Place, London W1N 3AF (071 636 9543) or your GP.

REFLEXOLOGY

Each part of the body is reflected at certain points on the feet and hands. Pressure or massage of these points activates the vital force of each organ. This also breaks down any unwanted crystalline deposits in the feet, which may then be eliminated from the system, restoring the natural flow of energy to the body.

If an area on the feet or hands feels painful or sensitive, the organ to which it is connected may be weak; therefore, massage of that portion of the foot will help to heal the affected organ.

Reflexology is effective as treatment for a number of common complaints, including stress, headaches, digestive troubles, backache and breathing problems.

For more details and a list of registered practitioners, contact the International Institute of Reflexology, 28 Hollyfield Avenue, London N11 3BY (081-368 0865), or the British Council for Complementary and Alternative Medicine (address on page 67).

SHEN TAO

Shen Tao is a form of acupressure, but the process of touching is much lighter. It harmonizes the total being, treating deep-seated imbalances and relieving current symptoms of distress at source.

Shen Tao is a powerful, yet subtle therapy, activating meridian points to move the *ch'i* energy. This promotes deep relaxation, natural healing and revitalization of the mind and body. If organs of the body are either congested or deprived of their vitalizing energy (*ch'i*), for any length of time, it predisposes them to a condition of disease or malfunction.

Some of the conditions that Shen Tao can help include: asthma, backache, digestive problems, arthritis, fertility problems, PMS, migraine, insomnia and allergies.

For details, contact: the Shen Tao Foundation, Middle Piccadilly Natural Healing Centre, Holwell, Sherbourne, Dorset DT9 5LW (0963 23468). Send SAE.

SHIATSU

Also known as acupressure, this form of Japanese massage is quite different to regular body massage. Using their hands or feet, and sometimes elbows and knees, the therapist applies pressure to acupuncture points in order to restore the flow of energy around the body. It is highly effective and increasingly popular, but it is well to be aware that there is a lot of physical contact between you and the therapist, and you have to feel confident in him/her to allow them to move you to different positions.

Shiatsu can alleviate a number of common ailments (like acupuncture or Shen Tao), and is often an alternative for those who have trouble facing the acupuncturists' needles.

For information and a list of registered practitioners, contact the Shiatsu Society, c/o Elaine Liechti, 19 Longside Park, Kilbarchan, Renfrewshire PA10 2EP (05057 4657).

Over-the-counter treatments using natural remedies, vitamins and minerals, can only ever be of limited value. You must do your own reading and seek several professional opinions for serious or long-standing problems. However, there are some excellent herbs, essential oils and natural remedies and creams available for: spots, colds, flu, sore throats, swollen glands, diarrhoea, shock, nerves, bruising, recovery, insomnia, fatigue, digestive troubles, headaches, backaches.

Most chemists and, in particular, healthshops, like Holland and Barrett, stock a wide range of these products.

When you have finally found a good team of therapists, you must back them up by explaining everything you can think of medically, emotionally and physically, past and present.

The more you disclose about yourself, the more you allow the practitioner to help you. If you are sceptical, then say so. Don't waste your or their time by being dissatisfied or difficult. If you sense they are not right in their decisions, then tell them why, or ask more questions. If you don't do this, you simply will not learn to discern between what's best for you and what's rubbish.

You *must* feel fully confident in your practitioner and the recommended treatment, as this will affect your mental attitude and, therefore, the success of the treatment. Be very specific about what results you want or expect and ask if they are realistic. On the other side of the fence, don't believe blindly and ecstatically that something or someone is supreme in the art of healing. Often people can be misled, with no actual benefit taking place.

Your practitioner should examine all the symptoms you complain of, from all the sides, not just the weight problem, for instance, or the headache.

When going to a practitioner, or when considering why you suffer from something, it is important to: (a) go back to when you first suffered the symptoms so that you can begin to decipher where and when the cause arose; and (b) also look at what else you suffer from regularly. For example:

○ I don't sleep when I've had an Indian meal;
○ I get flatulence regularly;
○ My skin is always slightly oily and spotty, no matter how much money I spend on products; or
○ I always suffer from back trouble.

There are many establishments that offer many diverse therapies. I'm going to make myself very unpopular here by saying that you really have to shop around – some therapists are better than others – and make sure you are not going week after week with not much to show for it.

Participants of Holistix and I have gone through our 'flavour of the month' therapies, and at times have experienced becoming dependent on their thinking. No crutches, please. You must have a definite plan for the beginning, middle and completion of your treatment and arrange periodical check-ups.

If your practitioner is caring and professional, he or she will want to become redundant as soon as possible. It is an important part of their job to set you on your way to feeling better, more knowledgeable and able to cope.

We have tried hundreds of different types of centres, therapies and therapists, and orthodox

*U*nless you are crippled, deaf, dumb, blind or impaired in a serious way – and sometimes even then – there is no excuse to be unwell, and not to feel normal, full energy and functioning at your optimum.

practitioners, and have, after fifteen years, found one in each area that has the qualifications, high standards, caring approach and the ability to communicate with the patient. An example is the Natural Healing Centre in Ruislip, Middlesex, which provides a wide range of therapies to treat the cause of illness with natural methods. As no drugs are used, there are no harmful side-effects.

Treatments include: Pulsors, Radionics, Acupuncture, Ortho-bionomy, Bach flower remedies, Allergy testing, Psychotherapy, Homoeopathy, Reflexology and Hypnosis.

All the practitioners at the Natural Healing Centre have undertaken extensive training in their respective therapies, and all adhere to strict codes of practice and ethics, as laid down by the various professional associations.

Each initial consultation involves taking a detailed case history and for some therapies a physical examination, where appropriate. A first consultation for acupuncture can take up to two hours; for other therapies it is generally fifty minutes. Most treatments thereafter take between thirty and fifty minutes.

When you go for any alternative therapies, especially acupuncture, do not drink or eat anything for three hours beforehand, if possible. Therefore, your body will be free of having to digest anything, and the therapist, when examining and treating you, can really feel what is going on, with no interference or false reading from the digestion of food and drink.

TAKING ACTION

You have to ask yourself if you really and truly want to be totally well. Earlier in the book we looked at the common attitude 'better the devil you know than the devil you don't', plus all the excuses we might use in order to avoid getting started.

The biggest problem we have come across at Holistix is that it takes an enormous amount of energy to get most individuals to shift from doing nothing about their health problems, or physical dissatisfaction, to actually doing something.

Most of the conversations centre around a person complaining about this and that, stating how bad it all is, they've seen this person and that practitioner, but nothing has made a difference. Comments like 'Well, I'm not going to do that all the time' and 'I have to eat such and such sometime, don't I?' are so common, I could write a book on it!

Surely you can see that if it's taken you ten, twenty, thirty, forty, fifty odd years to get to the point you are at now, it follows that you are going to have to address your habits and actions straight on, with discipline, and no messing around, once and for all. And you can expect to have to spend a little time getting there!

Don't you think it's extraordinary that between approximately three months and one year (or less, depending on the extent of your problems) of doing what works can completely transform the way you look and feel emotionally and physically. I often find that Holistix clients are almost unrecognizable after a short period of time; no matter what age they are, their lives have taken a huge upward swing, and the lessons they learned along the way gave them strength and integrity. Reach this point and it is highly unlikely that you will ever go backwards – or that you will accept less than one hundred per cent from yourself and from others.

Those of you that just scoffed and hooted loudly with laughter and unhealthy disbelief: have a look at why you react in this way. If you think that you are too old, or that age makes everything worse and there's only so much you can do, let me put a different slant on things: *Becoming healthy is not affected by how old you*

are – rather, it is simply to do with how long you have had your bad habits.

The minute you begin to address these bad habits, and replace them with good ones, you can sit back and watch your body respond. Over time, the good habits will take hold. It is quite extraordinary to witness your body changing – to see its incredible ability to heal itself when pointed in the right direction. The only elements that get in the way are our own impatience and anger when we don't get results immediately. Our bodies may have spurts of good responses, and then there is a plateau, or lull in improvement. You must give your body time to change. Be even more disciplined with yourself when you hit your anger patches, and treat yourself to pampering.

Unless you are crippled, deaf, dumb or blind, or impaired in a serious way, there is no excuse to continue being unwell; feeling normal, full of energy and functioning at your optimum could be easier than you think, if you are prepared to do what works. Think about it.

You cannot expect practitioners or friends to have an effect on your predicament without your input. The only person who knows which buttons to push is you. When you are ready to agree to this, you will be in a position to make a start. You must just remember that no one promised that what you want to achieve can happen overnight,

---

Breathing is very important when you have to contend with pain – breathing into the pain releases it, while holding your breath, which is what we usually do, increases it. Breathing deeply will help release tension both physically and mentally.

Laura

A boyfriend invited me to stay with some friends of his in the country. I knew very little about them, apart from the fact that the husband had been really down in the dumps. After introductions, and jovialities, the men went off to the pub and left us girls in the kitchen. Needless to say, we got on to the subject of Holistix. It turned out that Laura had several excellent alternative practitioners she was seeing and expounded about their brilliance for about five minutes. She then revealed that she was very upset about her weight, which was increasing rapidly.

I didn't interrupt, but just let her talk on. It was as though she were talking to herself as she kept saying how healthy she was, and that she was really good nutritionally, given that she was a cook and knew about food values, healing herbs and so on. She then switched track to disclose about the rashes, blotches and spots that were increasingly affecting her skin. Next she hitched up her skirt to reveal what looked like a pitted gravel effect from her calves up. She went to bend down, her knee gave way, and she had great difficulty moving it. She gasped, made a worried comment, and then two seconds later said, 'nothing to worry about'.

She absently went through a list of when and why her weight had begun to increase, including how aware of her worries she had become, and she went on to say that there was nothing she could do. At almost the same time, she said that she couldn't let this go on for another day.

She showed me a picture of herself in a bikini, when she had been at her previous, normal weight, and she looked terrific. The worst thing about Laura was that she looked as if her body and face were going to explode. Her body was breaking down, she was completely unaware of her rambling, and she was becoming totally frenetic. Apart from her bowels, nothing physically was working to order, and her description of what she called nutritious small meals turned out to be an abundance of all the worst substances!

As her whole life, from her relationships to money, from food to emotions, was involved, I did not try to give her advice. She admitted that, for the first time in her life, she was aware that all these problems were contributing to her state of ill health. She only had one thing left to do – to reconcile herself to the fact that she had to change everything for at least six months, and first to tackle her emotional and relationship problems.

When Laura started to address her problems, she started off by seeing an alternative practitioner who was highly skilled in allergy testing and individual nutrition, as well as Bach flower and homoeopathic remedies. The outcome was that what she had been suffering from – severe allergies, excruciating PMS and heavy floodlike periods – eventually disappeared, taking with them her excess weight.

I don't think at this point I need to explain how her personal life was affected for the better.

---

or that results come in a neatly wrapped package with a pink bow.

To ensure total health, it is recommended that we have an orthodox medical check-up once a year, as well as consult a registered alternative practitioner, and see a well-trained osteopath (preferably someone who has training in cranial osteopathy as well). The help that they can give us on the routine and mundane gripes we have, such as lack of energy, bad circulation, or not being able to relax, is enormous.

It is also important to have a gynaecological examination once or twice a year, a dental check-up two to three times a year, and to see a hygienist three times a year. Most of the time we don't know what is happening with our bodies and we don't register the stresses or problems we are accumulating.

Take the Pill, for example. Its function is to stop you getting pregnant. It is prescribed for that, but also for irregular bleeding and acne, sometimes from a very early age. It provides you with a false body clock and you can't really tell what's going on internally, because the Pill makes you regular and very often has you feeling very good, especially if you suffered from problems in the past. Taking the Pill month after month, year after year, is pretty unnatural and taxing on the body. Without always knowing it, people become weak, suffering many side-effects such as weight gain, nausea, depression and frequent headaches.

There are numerous other factors which unnaturally stimulate and depress our body functions. Antibiotics, tranquillizers, tobacco, alcohol and caffeine all produce unhealthy and unnatural body functioning. It is important to cut out substances that produce poisons, and toxic waste which can weaken internal organs. For instance, if you suffer from bowel problems, headaches, broken capillaries, cellulite or fatigue, cutting out alcohol, tobacco, coffee, red meat and dairy produce can be very effective. Don't bother wasting too much time looking for reasons to justify your having these health problems. Take it as a sign that you have to address any internal imbalance.

HOSPITAL CARE

An operation may be necessary for a number of health reasons. Whether you are having a hysterectomy, an appendectomy, or even a vasectomy, a healthy body will be able to deal more quickly and efficiently with recovery, and avoid complications. Preparing for an operation is very important. Don't wait until the day you go into hospital to prepare yourself. Take action to ensure that you are as strong as possible in order to make a speedy recovery.

First, for women, it may be necessary to stop taking the contraceptive Pill, according to the advice given by your anaesthetist or doctor. You may be told to complete the month's supply and then to stop (as you should not break off during a month). This will help you avoid the need for drugs to prevent blood clotting.

Clean up your nutrition: at least three weeks before the operation, cut out alcohol and all foods that are hard to digest, such as red meat, nuts, wheat and yeast, saturated fats, chocolate, caffeine and sugar. By doing this you immediately alleviate unnecessary irritation of your condition. Replace these foods with nutritious vegetables, fish, pulses, soups, chicken, and plenty of water and no other liquids. Avoid fruit juices, which might be too acidic, or dilute them with water. In addition, your attention to your bowels working regularly is vital for your comfort and wellbeing.

During an operation, your digestive system is turned upside down, so looking after yourself in these ways, and getting enough rest, sleep and nutrients will help your body to heal.

Make sure that you organize in detail all household and domestic affairs, paying special attention to bathroom and kitchen goods, and leaving the bedroom uncluttered and fresh, stocked with magazines, videos, books, your telephone and fresh water, all within comfortable reach of your bed. Also ensure that you have all you need for your room or bed in hospital.

There is a specific homoeopathic remedy called Arnica that is now widely used by both orthodox and alternative practitioners, before and after hospitalization, for speeding up the healing process. It is also used for shock, nerves, skin disorders, upsets and trauma of any kind, and comes in various external and internal forms. Ask your GP if it will help you.

Ask your practitioner which vitamins and minerals would be appropriate for you – for both before and after hospitalization. Always take the supplement with or after food, unless stated otherwise. On an empty stomach, some supplements may cause nausea. Over the past fifteen years, a number of studies have shown that a surprisingly high percentage of hospitalized patients suffer from malnutrition. Pay special attention to your diet before you enter hospital, and ensure that correct supplementation is prescribed for you. Zinc, for instance, has been found to be useful in patients who tend to heal slowly, especially when given in high doses. Natural sources of zinc include: wholegrain products, seafoods and wheatgerm and bran. Vitamin A will also promote healing.

HAVE AN UNDERSTANDING OF WHAT IS HAPPENING TO YOU

Ask your doctor to explain what is going to be done – how long you will be in hospital, and how much pain and discomfort to expect. Knowing

Any alternative or orthodox therapy must be backed up by good nutrition, exercise and breathing techniques. Otherwise nothing will remain effective. A poor body image, bad posture and habits compound the problems.

these things helps to take away some of the fear and unnecessary expectation of pain. You may want to make a list of questions. For instance: How long will the operation be? How long will you be hospitalized? When can you expect to go home, return to normal, and go back to work? When can you return to exercise, making love, travelling to work or, even better, go on holiday to recuperate?

Ask your doctor what he thinks you should eat, then check out the standard menu at your hospital – you will usually find that it is either very rich food or aeroplane-type food. Neither is conducive to feeding you the nutrients you need to nourish your body. You will need light, fat-free, easily digested food, such as fish, steamed, grilled or baked, very little minced chicken for the first meals after surgery, with light vegetables such as a little mashed potato. Cauliflower, broccoli, and carrots can be puréed, or try a lightly scrambled egg or omelette. Remember, foods can be liquidized if you have had plastic, dental or heavy surgery. The ingredients must be pure. You can take your own muesli, made the Holistix way (see page 122, for details) – then you can be sure that there is no wheat or sugar to aggravate your digestive system. Soft fruit, such as apricots, pears, grapes, peaches and nectarines are easy to eat, nutritious and not too acidic.

You may keep up these eating habits during and after hospitalization. You will have to stipulate your requirements before going in. You may have to be tough with them, but stick to your guns and arrange for your food to be prepared specially for you – or for a friend or a nurse to deliver dishes you have prepared earlier.

HINTS AND TIPS

Stimulating your bowels to work as soon as possible after surgery is essential. You may feel resistant to this idea, but an empty bowel means a release from discomfort and pain. Usually, with any stomach surgery, pain is due to wind, rather than to incision, and wind can be really nasty.

Breathing is very important when having to contend with pain – breathing into the pain (breathe out fully) releases it, while holding your breath against the pain, which is what we usually do, increases it. Breathing deeply will help release tension, both physically and mentally.

Stretching out your arms, hands, and any other parts of the body which you can move also helps to make you comfortable. Don't tense against the pain. See the exercise for breathing on page 138, and practise well before you enter hospital.

Very rarely do hospitals provide bottled or

Catherine

*W*hen we first saw Catherine, she was something of a wreck. Her energy and emotions were all over the place, swinging between depression and euphoria, although her main tendency was towards depression and lethargy. She was rather underweight and the quality of her skin and hair was very poor.

We suggested that she should see a specialist gynaecologist, as we suspected a hormonal imbalance, but even if that were the case, she still needed to seriously address her nutrition.

It was fair to say that she was sure she was eating a very healthy diet – nearly all her food intake was raw or cooked vegetables, or salad, supplemented by minerals and vitamins.

We then went into food with her, in great detail, explaining how a balanced diet was essential. She needed to add protein and low fat carbohydrates to her daily diet, and her intake of water needed to increase, in order to keep her system flushed clean.

She was rather sceptical, still half-believing that her diet was faultless, but agreed to a one-month trial period. She was to be pleasantly proved wrong.

She received Hormone Replacement Therapy from a gynaecologist, which went a long way towards stabilizing her moods. As a result of this, and the change in her eating habits, she now looks and feels amazing. Her skin and hair look healthy and alive, her body is now shapely and defined, and her energy is good and constant.

Of course, one added bonus was that suddenly food became interesting, much more delicious and satisfying. Whereas before she had stuck rigidly to her extreme 'healthy' diet, now she really could eat well and nutritiously, while actually enjoying her food. And that was a whole different ballgame.

purified water, so make sure you take your own, or a filter jug with your name clearly marked on it. (Ask the nurses to keep it filled.) In terms of food, it will depend on the type of surgery you are having – stomach, orthopaedic, dental, internal, plastic or gynaecological.

Whatever the operation is, after any anaesthetic, you must not consume anything until you are given permission. You may rinse out your mouth, but even a sip of water could cause you to vomit if taken too soon, so no matter how much you want a drink – be patient, rinse and don't swallow until allowed.

HOW TO COMMUNICATE YOUR NEEDS

Hospital staff and nurses are a mixture of kindness and officiousness, and when you are feeling low you will be more sensitive to whatever is going on. Nevertheless, you don't have to be frightened to ask your questions, whatever they are. You don't need to drive anyone mad, just be clear about what you want. Making a small list of needs will help, so you don't continually ring your bell. You will find your world becomes the size of your room or bed in hospital, and small inconsequential things become amazingly important.

You'll need the newspaper basket near enough to chuck in used tissues and papers. The television remote control should be to hand for a daily TV programme. Treat yourself to a humorous book – it's guaranteed to lift your spirits.

GOING HOME AND RECUPERATING

You need to adjust mentally to the outside world. A hospital stay is rather like living in a greenhouse – you have been looked after, cooked for, waited on, and it's quite a shock to have to go it alone now.

So arrange to have a good friend prepare your kitchen, with food, hot water and the heating turned up, the electric blanket on if you're going to bed, and everything to hand that you'll need for the first few days.

Your eating habits slowly must be allowed to return to normal gear, and regular meals, rest, sleep, bathing and pampering are all important to

Today there are cures for almost every common ailment, and by preparing your body and mind to become entirely fit and healthy, most of these ailments can be prevented altogether. When you become ill, your newly healthy body will be able to heal itself more quickly than you ever imagined.

full recovery. Get your balance of life back. The post will have built up (unless someone has brought it to you in hospital), but resist opening before day one is over; the following day is soon enough for that. Stay calm when confronted with any aggravation; for instance, a final reminder for the phone bill. Ring the accounts office and explain your situation.

POST-OPERATIVE NOTES

After any type of abdominal surgery, the patient is asked to get out of bed and to take a few steps. This can be a daunting and frightening event. There are techniques for you to remember to use, should you have the need.

From a lying position, take your elbows back, in order to start propping yourself up. Put the palms of your hands on the mattress and lever your weight and your body up on your elbows and hands. Keep one hand behind you and grab your opposite leg, under the knee. Take the weight off your leg in your hand and bring your knee up, so your foot is flat. Take your right hand up behind you and take your left hand under your left knee and bring it up so both feet are flat now. Then you can push on your feet and your hands and straighten your body into a more comfortable sitting position, and start to ease and shift to one side of the bed, inch by inch. Then you take one hand under your knee and lift your leg over the bed, and then take the other leg over the side of the bed. So then you are in a sitting position on the side of the bed, legs dangling towards the floor.

Shift to the edge of the bed, both feet touching the floor, and grab hold of something steady or solid. Now comes the most important part. Your aim is singular – you are now going to stand straight. Never mind the walking, straightening your body at this stage, no matter what your surgery, will be of the greatest importance in your recovery and healing process. So using your breathing, literally start straightening up your spine, inch by inch. This achieved, you've really won a huge battle. A couple of steps and you'll be in the chair.

The next time you get up from that chair, stand straight and walk straight. The biggest instinct is for you to fold in towards your pain. Both physically and mentally, this will result in feeling and looking the invalid. This technique applies to most surgery.

FOLLOWING RECOVERY

Now is the time to take your life back into your own hands. Operations and illness are frightening, but they often provide us with a new lease of life – if anything, to avoid their future recurrence. Turn to page 92 and follow the guidelines for staying healthy. It's never too late to begin taking care of yourself.

COMMON COMPLAINTS AND CURES

The following ailments are common to many of us, and research has proved that most can be prevented and/or cured, by simply taking care of our bodies. As we said earlier, the body is very much like a machine – when that machine is well-oiled and working in peak condition, very little can go wrong. Protect your body and work with it to prevent disease. You'll be amazed at how much better you'll feel.

This is not intended to be a DIY guide to curing complaints from which you may suffer, just simple guidelines to achieving optimum health, relieving symptoms and, through preventative measures, achieving a cure. If you suffer from any of the following on a regular basis, please see your doctor or alternative practitioner.

ARTHRITIS

There are generally two types of arthritis – Rheumatoid arthritis and Osteo-arthritis. Rheumatoid arthritis is a destructive and inflammatory condition of the joints, which is more common in women and young people than in men. There is no confirmed cause, though the theories as to why it occurs are numerous.

Some foods may aggravate the condition, or be partly responsible, through allergic reaction. Try the food allergy tests listed on page 99, and try to cut out dairy produce, wheat, oats, eggs, chicken, caffeine drinks, beef, pork and foods containing yeast.

As with any inflammatory ailment, drinking plenty of water will cool down the body and flush out toxins produced by your body fighting the disease. Evening primrose oil, green-lipped mussel extract (beware if you are allergic to any shellfish, a common allergen), extra niacin and pantothenic acid, along with Vitamin A and C, can help relieve symptoms by fighting deficiency – always a problem with arthritis sufferers because of the wear and tear on the body.

A wide variety of complementary therapies, including osteopathy, Shen Tao, homoeopathy and aromatherapy have all shown positive results. Orthodox treatment may involve the administration of painkillers or medication to reduce/relieve suffering. For further information, contact: Arthritis Care, 4 Grosvenor Crescent, London SW1X 7ER (071-235 0902).

Osteo-arthritis is a degenerative condition, and part of the ageing process. It is different from rheumatoid arthritis, as there is no inflammation and it begins in middle age. Some of the predisposing factors include: being overweight, uneven stress on joints, lack of exercise, bad nutrition, previous surgery for removal of any knee or joint cartilage, repetitive trauma, and previous degenerative disease, such as rheumatoid arthritis.

Nutrition is essential in the prevention and treatment of this condition. Try taking green-

lipped mussel extract, Vitamin E (400 IU daily), fish oils, and extra Vitamin C (1000 mg daily). A number of the above complementary therapies can ease your pain.

ASTHMA

Asthma is a chronic allergic reaction which affects the upper respiratory system, particularly the bronchial tubes. Allergies, emotional stress and heredity have all been pinpointed as key causes, and poor nutrition will increase the symptoms.

Try evening primrose oil, extra Vitamin C, Vitamin B15 and adrenal glandular concentrates for relief. Acupuncture, cranial osteopathy, homoeopathy and clinical nutrition are all therapies which can be of partial or total help.

BLOOD PRESSURE (HIGH AND LOW)

There are a number of easy, natural ways to keep down your blood pressure, aside from the obvious nutritional guidelines for avoiding high-cholesterol, fatty foods. Regular exercise and relaxation, along with adequate uninterrupted sleep will work wonders, as will eliminating tobacco, caffeine and sodium (salt). Try to increase the potassium in your diet (for details of potassium-rich foods, see page 123), and take garlic pearls, Vitamin E and calcium supplements. Cucumbers and celery also help to reduce high blood pressure. Try drinking passionflower tea, to alleviate the symptoms, and actually bring down your blood pressure.

Low blood pressure is far less dangerous, although a sudden drop in blood pressure may cause fainting or dizziness. Try not to take hot baths or stand for an extended period of time. Take kelp tablets (one to three daily), and ensure that you are getting enough natural sugars in your diet, in fruit and in healthy carbohydrates. See **Nutrition**, chapter six, for details. A well-balanced diet will keep your blood-sugar level steady, and through that, your blood pressure.

CANDIDA ALBICANS

Candida strikes more women than men. Problems arise when the yeast fungus present in the intestines is no longer controlled by body-friendly bacteria. Antibodies, the contraceptive Pill, steroids, and an excess of refined sugar can destroy that friendly bacteria, and our resistance to infection is lowered.

Symptoms of candida are wide-ranging, and can include severe menstrual cramping and irregularities, bladder infections, anxiety, nervousness, depression, headaches, lethargy, skin problems, bad circulation, overweight, cravings for sugars and carbohydrates, and more. Treatment includes: killing off the yeast fungus with nystatin, which can be used orally, topically, or directly into the vagina; altering the diet to deprive the body of food on which this yeast flourishes (white sugars, honey, fruits, cheeses, bread, beer, wine, mushrooms, soya sauce, tofu, vinegar, dried fruits, and some B-complex vitamin supplements); and, avoiding immuno-suppressive drugs and antibiotics.

The body's immune system must be strengthened through good nutrition. Try to eat a wide variety of whole, fresh foods. Aromatherapy will help with the depressive symptoms, and a clinical nutritionist, or medical herbalist will be able to advise on proper nutrition and herbal remedies. Vaginal douches of essential oils of rosemary will help encourage acidity of the vagina, which prevents the growth of candida. Colonic irrigation, with lactobacillus, will wash out the fungus and stimulate production of the flora. Garlic will help boost your natural immunities.

CIRCULATORY PROBLEMS

Sluggish circulation, caused by lack of exercise, emotional stress and nutrition, can lead to a whole host of problems, including coronary heart disorders, varicose veins, weakened capillaries, fatigue, lethargy, poor skin, hair and nails, and loss of short-term memory. A well-balanced diet, including a variety of fresh fruit, vegetables, lean white meats, wholefood carbohydrates and polyunsaturated fats will help your body to clear itself of toxins which slow down the circulation and clog the arteries. Plenty of water is a must, to make the kidneys' and liver's job of clearing the bloodstream easier.

Aromatherapy and massage can help stimulate circulation, and osteopathy and chiropractic will also work to ensure that the circulatory system is unblocked, with blood reaching every part of the body with ease. Lymphatic drainage (see page 173 for details) has also been known to improve circulation. Exercise, peace of mind and diet, however, remain the key methods of improving your circulation.

COLDS AND FLU

If you are suffering from a running nose and eyes, sore throat, tight chest, and possibly a temperature, avoid decongestants and over-the-counter medication, which will suppress the symptoms, not the cause.

Drink plenty of mineral water to flush out the system, and eat healthy soups and easy-to-digest fruits and vegetables, like broccoli, melon, bananas and fresh peas. Avoid dairy products, as the bacteria present can feed the viral bacteria of your flu or cold.

Buy some effervescent Vitamin C tablets, and take one gram (1000 mg) every two hours (if you are suffering from diarrhoea or stomach pain, you need to take less). Suck zinc gluconate for a sore throat, and you might try some of the herbal or vegetable cough linctuses available.

Place a large bowl of water near a radiator, and place a few drops of olbas oil in it, to keep your sinuses clear and put moisture into the atmosphere. Put fresh linen on the bed, and have a long, warm bath with essential oils, such as eucalyptus, pine or chamomile, which are excellent for easing colds.

Vicks Vapour Rub is very good. Place a little Vicks in each nostril before bed. The most important way to overcome a virus is sleep. Give your body a full forty-eight hours of complete rest, in which it can use all its energy to fight the virus. It is absolutely essential that your body be given time and rest in order to recover fully – people who do not take the time can seriously impair immune functions, making them vulnerable to all the viruses and bugs going round. Do not drink tea, coffee, alcohol or cola drinks, which deplete your body of minerals and vitamins necessary to fight off infection.

CONSTIPATION

Constipation is caused by a number of different things; but mainly, it is the result of improper eating habits and unhealthy bowels. In **Nutrition**, chapter six, we discuss the various causes and symptoms of constipation. You might also try full-body massage, with oils of rosemary and lavender to help stimulate bowel movement. Useful supplements include B-complex vitamins, magnesium, cod liver oil, Vitamins A and C, which will help the movement of waste products, the absorption and utilization of calcium, and the body's ability the break down proteins.

A natural general laxative, like dandelion root, may help, and the homoeopath would recommend silica, byronia or nux vomica. A diet high in fibre and fresh water will make stools easier to pass. Some people find colonic irrigation clears up the problem once and for all.

CRAMPS

Muscle cramps are often the result of vitamin and mineral deficiency, or a poor circulatory system. Vitamin B6 is essential to prevent night spasms, leg cramps, numbness in the extremities, and mild forms of neuritis. Biotin will also ease muscle pain, as will Vitamin B1 (thiamin), chlorine, sodium and Vitamin D.

Aromatherapy will certainly help to relieve painful cramps caused by nervous exhaustion, poor circulation and tension. Full-body massage or baths with essential oils of lavender, clary sage or rosemary are recommended. Shiatsu is particularly beneficial when cramp sets in, and the homoeopath suggests magnesium phosphate, one of the essential body salts, for relief. Virtually all of the complementary therapies will bring relief from cramp.

CYSTITIS

When you suffer from cystitis, you will feel a frequent urge to urinate, and may feel a burning sensation. You may also feel the sensation of not having emptied the bladder, and there may be blood in the urine, an unpleasant vaginal discharge, and aching in the kidneys. Cystitis can occur, or become worse, after sexual intercourse. It is the result of irritation, mechanical pressure and bacterial infection. Acidic foods, alcohol and poor nutrition can cause or worsen the condition.

You should drink plenty of plain water in order to prevent the urine becoming concentrated. Do not drink tea, coffee or orange juice if you are suffering an attack. Diluted bicarbonate of soda in water will counteract the acidity of the urine – mix a half teaspoon of bicarbonate of soda with one pint of lukewarm water. Drink a half pint of this solution every half hour until the symptoms have passed.

A new study indicates that drinking cranberry juice when symptoms first set in can virtually cure cystitis. It works by preventing the urine from sticking to the urinary tract.

Pay special attention to personal hygiene: wipe with a wet tissue from front to back after a bowel movement; do not use detergents, soaps or perfumed bath or body products; wash in a solution of vinegar and water (one half teaspoon to one pint, respectively) after passing water; and always cleanse the genital area immediately after intercourse.

Osteopaths are renowned for treating victims of cystitis, and aromatherapy, medical herbalism and clinical nutrition will all ease the symptoms – if not cure the initial causes. For more details, see **Nutrition**, chapter six.

DIARRHOEA

Diarrhoea is caused mainly by improper diet, irritable bowels, nervous tension or exhaustion, or increased acidity in the digestive system, caused by changes in water, diet or other external factors. Vitamin A is very helpful in reducing diarrhoea, as are walnuts, yellow dock, schizandra and bayberry root bark. Make sure you drink plenty of fresh water and eat lots of dietary fibre – this will prevent the stool from becoming too loose or acidic. If you are suffering from extreme diarrhoea, the cause may be viral. Do see your doctor immediately, as a great deal of your body's salts will be lost, causing dehydration and severe deficiency. Many doctors will prescribe an easy-to-drink electrolyte substance, which replaces lost minerals and body salts.

If your practitioner is caring and professional, he or she will want to become redundant as soon as possible. It is an important part of their job to set you on your way to feeling better, more knowledgeable and able to cope.

A number of the complementary therapies – particularly homoeopathy, medical herbalism and shiatsu – will help. For more details about bowels, their function and importance, see page 115.

ENDOMETRIOSIS

This disease of the pelvic organs occurs when endometrial cells (the lining of the womb) stray into the pelvic area. These cells tend to behave like the rest of the uterine lining, by bleeding and becoming stretched and swollen, and they enlarge when blood cannot escape. Endometriosis can cause painful periods, although the pain is not related to the extent of the disease.

If you feel pain deep in your pelvis during intercourse, if you suddenly suffer from painful periods, or if you are trying without success to conceive, do consult your doctor about the possibility of endometriosis.

Try drinking raspberry leaf tea, which will relax the uterus during painful periods. Or try acupuncture, which is excellent for providing pain relief during the menstrual cycle, or during intercourse. There are several homoeopathic remedies which will ease the discomfort, and there has been cause to believe that candida is one of the factors that cause endometriosis. If you suspect you might have the disease, consult your doctor immediately. Endometriosis can be cured, but over a long period of time the damage done can be irreversible.

FIBROIDS

About one in five women will develop fibroids by the time they reach forty-five. Fibroids are benign endometrial tumours, and they are treated according to their size. Small fibroids often provide no cause for concern, and they usually shrink after childbearing age. While there may be no overt symptoms, heavy menstrual bleeding, discomfort during intercourse, swelling and/or a feeling of heaviness in the abdomen, pressure on the bladder and bowel, or infertility may indicate the possibility of fibroids.

Heavy menstrual bleeding is a symptom of fibroids, so anaemia may ensue. Ensure that you are getting plenty of iron in your diet, and try cramp bark to help spasmodic pain, improve hormone balance and uterine function. Unchecked, fibroids can spread throughout the uterus and pelvis, causing infertility. If you suspect you could be suffering from fibroids, contact your doctor.

FLATULENCE

This is probably the most common digestive disorder. There are several causes, the chief one being that foods create an imbalance in the digestive juices, making the job of processing food in your gut very difficult. Eating too much of any one food, sugars, wheat, curries, beans, Chinese takeaways and junk food are common culprits.

Flatulence can be caused by constipation or diarrhoea, and can be painful. To relieve pain, lie on your stomach and breathe into the stomach, relax and allow the wind to release through the rectum.

Stress and anxiety can cause a large amount of gas in the intestinal tract, as the digestive system becomes overacidic. You must take time over your meals.

Try peppermint, fennel or limeflower teas, which aid digestion. Lemon balm or meadowsweet, taken internally, can ease the discomfort, and irritation of the intestine may be treated with Vitamin E supplements. Avoid coffee, chocolate, fatty foods, spices, fizzy drinks and alcohol when you are suffering from flatulence.

An osteopath or chiropractor may be able to help by relieving stress or pressure on the intestines, due to improper posture or spine alignment.

A bath in essential oil of peppermint, or rosemary, will relieve the cramping feeling that often accompanies flatulence. See pages 115–116 for further details of flatulence and other bowel disorders.

HAYFEVER

Hayfever occurs when the mucus membranes of the sinuses become inflamed due to an allergen, such as pollenating grasses or trees, causing heavy sneezing and watering of the nose and eyes. Sensitivities to foods, dust, certain material, animal fur or toxic substances may also trigger this type of reaction.

Pollen doesn't reach its highest level until six or seven p.m. in the country, or ten to midnight in the city, where the air takes longer to cool. Don't sleep with your windows open, even if it rains. Keep car windows shut and wear sunglasses when outside. Holidays and days out and about are best spent in mountain areas, where counts are lowest.

There are some excellent homoeopathic remedies for hayfever such as Overcetin.

Hayfever can be hereditary, but on the whole it develops out of the blue, sometimes due to the hormone changes in puberty and a spurt of growth leaving the organs a little debilitated and sensitive to pollens. Hayfever, it is believed by many, is the result of an overload on the immune system by the many pollutants we are exposed to today.

In the winter months, a hayfever sufferer will often be prone to tonsilitis, glandular fever, sore throats, cystitis and occasional migraines.

Orthodox treatment, in conjunction with the contraceptive Pill will often disrupt the body's natural chemistry, which can irritate the situation and leave that person reliant on drugs. This can lead to irritability, inherent weakness, lethargy and sometimes slovenliness.

Pay attention to your diet and check it includes fresh fruit and vegetables to strengthen your body's defences. Increase the fibre content of your diet, and cut down on dairy products to reduce mucus. Vitamins C, A, E and B-complex are all helpful. Shiatsu can relieve symptoms, and a homoeopath, or a medical herbalist, will be able to suggest numerous preventative and curative measures.

HEADACHES

Most of the time, when your head aches, you are suffering from tension, fatigue, vitamin or mineral deficiency, hormonal changes, poor posture, an excess of toxins in the blood, or viral infection. When you get a headache, lie back with closed eyes and relax. Light temple massage with oil of peppermint, rosemary, lavender or sandalwood may help, and drink plenty of lukewarm, fresh water, to help cleanse your system.

Under no circumstances should you drink alcohol or caffeine drinks, eat dairy produce, or smoke. Each of these vices will actually worsen the symptoms. Breathing and relaxation exercises (see pages 138 and 152) may help. If you are prone to chronic headaches, consult an osteopath or a chiropractor, as it may be due to postural or spinal difficulties. A balanced diet, containing plenty of fresh, unprocessed foods is a must. The less toxins your body has to deal with, the less stress you place on it – and therefore, headaches will become far less frequent, or obsolete. Take aspirin or paracetamol only as a last resort, but if your headaches persist, pay a visit to your practitioner. A daily feverfew tablet has been known to prevent headaches.

HYPERACTIVITY

This generally occurs when your body has been falsely stimulated – either by nicotine, caffeine, social drugs, alcohol, excess sugar and additives, or extreme allergic reaction. Hyperactivity is most common in children who exhibit extreme allergies to the additives and preservatives in food and drink.

Hyperactivity causes undue stress on the heart and circulatory system – and it has even been recognized to contribute to criminal behaviour. If you feel hyperactive after eating processed food, or drinking fizzy drinks or alcohol, you may have an allergy. A visit to a clinical nutritionist, or a medical herbalist, can set you straight. In the meantime, try a soothing aromatherapy bath. See page 174 for details.

IMPOTENCE

Impotence is the loss of being able to acquire and maintain an erection. This can be due to both psychological and physical factors. Stress, such as a poor relationship, being over-anxious and tired, or depression are all reasons for temporary failure.

Have a look at your weight and nutrition. Be really honest about how much you drink – alcohol often affects men's ability, and liver disease, due to alcohol, lowers the lever of testosterone, which is the major male sex hormone. High blood pressure and diabetes are common causes of impotency. If you are worried, see your doctor. He can test your blood pressure, and urine and hormone levels.

Cranial osteopathy can relieve stress-related problems, and aromatherapy can release tension (see page 175 for details of essential aromatherapy oils). Furthermore, deficiencies of zinc can cause severe impotence, as can selenium. Ensure that you are getting enough in your diet (see pages 123–124), or arrange for supplementation.

Ginseng has been used to cure impotence. Shiatsu and reflexology can also help.

INSOMNIA

When untreated, insomnia can become extremely dangerous – leaving your body no time to rejuvenate or regenerate cells. Common causes are tension, stress, a guilty conscience, an over-abundant intake of processed food or other toxins, indigestion, poor posture, anxiety or physical pain. One hour before going to bed, try drinking a cup of strong, steeped chamomile or limeflower tea. Avoid caffeine and alcohol. Contrary to rumour, alcohol will not help you sleep.

An aromatherapy bath in lavender or chamomile oils will soothe and relax you; make

The biggest problem we come across at Holistix is that it can take an enormous amount of energy to get most individuals to shift from doing nothing about their health or physical dissatisfaction, to actually doing something. The will to learn, to want to change any aspect of your life will eventually provide the momentum to change it all.

sure it is not too hot, as the heat will stimulate your circulation.

Try sprinkling a few drops of lavender oil on your pillow, which may help you to relax. Massage, shiatsu, chiropractic, osteopathy, Bach flower remedies, medical herbalism and clinical nutrition can all provide relief.

There are also some excellent homoeopathic remedies on the market, like nux vomica, or passiflor. Cranial osteopathy can release pain and tension that could be causing insomnia, and hypnotherapy can be an excellent option. If your insomnia persists, see your practitioner.

IRRITABLE BOWEL SYNDROME (IBS)

Throughout the text, we have talked about a number of psychological causes for irritable bowel syndrome. There are also various physical factors which can produce symptoms. This name is given to a common syndrome of abdominal pain, alternating bouts of constipation and diarrhoea, flatulence and distension of the abdomen. Typically, the stools are small and hard, and there may be four to six bowel movements daily.

Although its causes are still disputed, its symptoms respond dramatically to a change in nutrition. The inclusion of two spoonfuls of bran in your daily diet, or a switch to a diet containing wholemeal flour and a higher proportion of cereals, will double the volume of faeces passing through the colon (large intestine) reducing pain, spasm and acidity.

Controlling stress, regular exercise, eating at regular intervals, and drinking plenty of fresh water will ease IBS. A number of the complementary therapies will help; in particular, clinical nutrition, medical herbalism, Bach flower remedies, chiropractic, homoeopathy, osteopathy and aromatherapy. If symptoms persist, see your practitioner.

MENSTRUAL PROBLEMS

Menstruation can start from as early as the age of eight but it more often occurs from the age of ten or eleven, and continues to about forty-eight. The menstrual cycle is dependent on the individual, and usually lasts from twenty-four to twenty-eight days.

It is recognized that tampons are convenient, but it is wise to remember that they can dry up the natural secretions of the vagina if used to excess. This may cause irritation and discharge, and could lead to infection. It is important that they are changed frequently. The menstrual flow should be free to flow normally in the heavy bleeding period and at night, so use a sanitary towel. This may seem boring, but it is more healthy.

Changes in the colour of the blood during periods are normal. It is also quite normal for periods to be heavier from time to time (if you are not taking the contraceptive Pill). Periods can become heavier if you suffer from tension, stress, illness, or if you are on drugs. When changes occur in your lifestyle they can be reflected in your menstrual cycle.

Irregular periods: The causes can be a hormonal imbalance (consult your practitioner or gynaecologist); stress (ask for the help of your practitioner or counsellor if you need to deal with a difficult problem); an eating disorder, such as anorexia nervosa or bulimia; certain drugs, and exercise and sport, when done excessively or at competitive levels.

Painful periods: Known as dysmenorrhoea, there

are two main types. The first (primary dysmenorrhoea) is not linked to pelvic disease, and it affects teenagers and young women. The pain is due to hormone-like chemicals called prostaglandins which can cause the womb to cramp, resulting in lower back pain and abdominal pain.

The second type of painful period (secondary dysmenorrhoea) occurs in older women, and there is usually an underlying pelvic disorder, such as chronic pelvic inflammatory disease, or endometriosis, to blame. In a small number of women, the coil (IUD, or intra-uterine device) can cause very severe period pain.

Tension tends to make painful periods more so. Gentle exercise, such as yoga, and cranial osteopathy, are particularly helpful. Consult your doctor. Hot-water bottles, hot baths and resting in bed all help. Mint and chamomile teas are soothing. Acupuncture and shiatsu can relax the abdominal muscles and help your body produce natural analgesics.

Cramp bark, yarrow or lemon balm may also provide relief.

Heavy periods: These are not unusual in young girls, who haven't established a regular cycle, or in older women who are approaching the menopause. If you are distressed or worried about heavy bleeding, which continues for more than twenty-four hours, seek medical advice.

Cranial osteopathy and shiatsu will improve the muscle tone of your uterus, and raspberry leaf tea – a uterine tonic – will ease the cramping that often accompanies a heavy flow.

MORNING SICKNESS (NAUSEA)

It is still unclear exactly what causes morning sickness in pregnancy, but experts suspect that it has to do with the extreme hormonal changes undergone by the body, and the body's wish to rid itself of toxins that may have been present before conception, or throughout pregnancy. Low blood sugar, low blood pressure and food deficiencies have also been suggested as causes.

Before conception, take care to eat a healthy, balanced diet, with plenty of fresh, unprocessed foods. Drink as much water as is comfortable, and try to drink cleansing and restorative herbal teas like fennel, nettle, rosehip or peppermint. Dandelion root coffee is excellent, as it acts as a liver tonic. When pregnant, keep up the routine, avoiding all toxins like caffeine, alcohol, nicotine, additives and preservatives, and excess sugar and salt. If nausea persists, try ginger tablets, available on prescription from your doctor, or drinking fennel, peppermint and chamomile teas, which will aid digestion.

See **Essential Oils**, page 174, for details of aromatherapy treatments which can help. Try to rise slowly in the morning, sitting and sipping herbal tea before actually getting out of bed. Dry crackers can also relieve the nausea. Shiatsu can provide relief by applying pressure to the stomach meridian, and there are numerous homoeopathic remedies available for pregnant women.

If vomiting is persistent and painful, see your doctor. When you are pregnant, it is a good idea to advise your GP of any therapies you are considering. Natural pregnancy is the healthiest and most sensible way to lead one of the most important nine months of your life. Think natural – in everything you eat, drink and breathe.

OSTEOPOROSIS

This is an abnormal leeching of the mineral content of bone, leading to the bone becoming brittle and prone to fracture. It is commonest in women after the menopause and may lead to spontaneous fractures occurring in the vertebral column, the wrist and femur (hipbone).

This process can be limited by Hormone Replacement Therapy, which is especially useful in cases where early and total hysterectomy have been performed. Taking calcium supplements has shown no benefit in halting this condition, although strong, healthy bones are built from calcium, so in your younger years, calcium is extremely important (see page 123 for details). Keeping mobile and regular exercise has a beneficial effect on bone metabolism and is an important preventive measure. A certain amount of osteoporosis will occur naturally past menopause, with only a severe degree of osteoporosis being considered pathological.

Acupuncture or shiatsu with Chinese herbs

helps in many cases to stop the leeching of calcium, and to increase absorption of external substances needed to replace healthy bone.

If you already suffer from osteoporosis, you might try hypnotherapy for pain, and osteopathy or chiropractic to reduce postural damage and ease pain. Exercise will also help to relieve pain.

Hormone-like substances – for instance, sage and hops – may be of some benefit. Ensure you are getting sufficient Vitamins A, D and magnesium, to encourage calcium absorption.

PELVIC INFLAMMATORY DISEASE (PID)

This general term describes chronic inflammation of any of the organs in the pelvis (uterus, Fallopian tubes or ovaries). The sexually-transmitted disease gonorrhoea can be a cause of PID, but there are certainly other causes, including past history of fibroids, endometriosis and uterine cancer.

Abdominal pain, back pain, persistent cramps, pain during and after intercourse, flu-like symptoms and blood spotting, foul-smelling discharge and infertility are symptoms.

Acupuncture can help any inflammation or pain, and can even increase the production of white blood cells. A sluggish lymphatic system can cause a number of toxins to be present in the blood, some of which can increase the risk of PID. A lymphatic drain might ease the symptoms. Any detoxification programme – enemas, irrigation, herbs and dietary changes – can help remove these toxins from the blood.

Try an aromatherapy bath or massage with oils of rosewood, palmarosa, or any other anti-infection essential oils.

A healthy diet is essential to clear up the infection. Drink plenty of water, and relax.

Rest is essential and antibiotics might be necessary.

PRE-MENSTRUAL SYNDROME (PMS)

PMS, also known as PMT, is suffered by millions of women for anything from three to fourteen days before a period (and in some cases even longer). There are 150 symptoms associated with PMS and these are categorized into a number of groups.

The most common symptoms are anxiety, irritability, depression, fatigue, bloatedness, cravings for food, breast tenderness and tension.

Improving your nutritional status can greatly alleviate the symptoms. You should aim to:

○ Reduce consumption of refined carbohydrates – sugar, cakes and biscuits;
○ Limit intake of dairy products, which affect the absorption of magnesium, a mineral that PMS sufferers are frequently deficient of;
○ Reduce intake of coffee, tea and alcohol;
○ Cut right down on salt;
○ Eat plenty of leafy green vegetables and salads daily;
○ Eat wholefoods, including wholegrains (take care with wheat though, as it is a common allergen), fresh fish and poultry;
○ Use vegetable oils, such as sunflower and safflower, and eat edible linseeds, sunflower, sesame and pumpkin seeds for their linoleic oil content;
○ Exercise regularly – this helps prevent muscle cramps and spasms;
○ Cut down if you smoke (or cut it out!); and
○ Take supplements of Vitamin B6 (in a B-complex), magnesium and evening primrose oil.

Also, acupuncture, shiatsu, aromatherapy, Bach flower remedies, clinical nutrition, medical herbalism, reflexology, homoeopathy and osteopathy can help the symptoms of bloating, cravings, mood swings, lethargy, headaches, clumsiness and anxiety.

PMS is treatable, through diet and various complementary cures. Don't suffer in silence. *Beat PMT Through Diet* by Maryon Stewart (Ebury Press) is very useful.

THRUSH

This is a common problem, caused by the yeast fungus candida albicans, which results in inflammation of the vagina and produces redness, swelling, itching and discharge. Causes include: use of antibiotics (thrush may follow on from treatment of cystitis with antibiotics, for instance), use of vaginal deodorants (which are not recommended), pregnancy and the

The more time you spend trying to justify an addiction, vice, or unhealthy habit, the more you should realize your need to change it.

contraceptive Pill. Irritation during sex can trigger it off.

You should avoid washing with scented soaps and bubble baths, use a herbal body shampoo, wear loose-fitting cotton underwear, and avoid tights. Diet can help – avoid sugary and starchy foods (on which yeast thrives), and foods that are high in yeast (see information on candida albicans, page 82).

Try inserting live yoghurt into the vagina (it can be particularly useful for three days after menstruation), and wear a sanitary towel. The bacteria in the yoghurt will multiply and destroy the thrush. You can add mineral salts to your bath. Ensure that your partner uses a sheath to protect himself and to avoid the infection being passed back to you. If you suffer from recurrent thrush you should check to see if he is infected, too.

Medicated creams and pessaries such as Canestan can provide relief. It is best to stop having intercourse until the situation is normal and avoid tampons during periods as they will increase irritation.

Eating a wholesome diet, and eliminating acidic or sugary foods can help. Acupuncture can be used to stimulate the body's natural immune system. Try adding essential oils of fennel, or rosemary to your bath, or rosemary as a vaginal douche. Sitting in a bath of steeped tea is often soothing, and fennel and cleavers infusions (tea) can provide relief from infection.

URETHRITIS

Urethritis is inflammation of the urethra – the tube through which the bladder discharges urine. Urethritis can occur due to various known infectious organisms, or as a result of trauma; but when bacteriological investigations fail to yield positive results, the inflammation is said to be non-specific, the term used in the UK to imply 'non-venereal'.

The symptoms are pain and a burning sensation on passing urine, and urinary frequency. There is a urethral discharge, and the disease is confined to the sexually active. Non-specific urethritis is more common in males; but as the urethra is anatomically longer in the male it may be that it is under-diagnosed in females, and many cases of cystitis in women may be cases of non-specific urethritis.

It develops five to thirty days after sexual intercourse, and varies in the intensity of its symptoms. The condition may last for several weeks and its recurrence rate is high. The cause, as the name implies, is unknown.

Viruses, bacteria, funguses and other genital parasites, as well as allergies, have been blamed, but there is no proof of the actual cause.

Avoid acid or acid-producing food and drink with any bladder infection or problem. Acid foods include: alcohol, white sugar, junk food, strong tea, sweets and chocolate, rich creamy foods, fried foods, curries and 'takeaways'. Eat plenty of live yoghurt and drink herb teas. Comfrey and marshmallow tea help to neutralize the acid balance, and of course, drink water, water, water!

Some of the suggestions for the relief of vaginal thrush, page 89, or candida albicans, page 82, will be helpful for urethritis sufferers.

VAGINAL DISCHARGE

A clear discharge around the middle of your menstrual cycle is normal, as it is the time of ovulation. If you become sexually excited, secretion is perfectly normal, as is a slight wetness and colour, which may become heavier before your period.

A continuous heavy discharge needs attention. Some different types of discharge are: thick and cloudy; fairly thick, white and crumbly, with a smell; heavy, dark yellow or brown with fishy smell; yellow and with an unpleasant smell; white discharge with irritation (usually thrush).

Follow the instructions and suggestions for candida albicans, page 82; although they are not caused by the same bacteria, their treatment is similar. If you have pain passing water, or if none of the self-help techniques provide relief, contact your gynaecologist or practitioner.

Homoeopathy, medical herbalism, shiatsu, and acupuncture can successfully treat vaginal infection. Avoid acidic foods and drink plenty of water. Dandelion root coffee, a mild diuretic, and nettle tea will help cleanse your urinary tract.

VARICOSE VEINS

These occur in the veins that return blood to the heart. Much of the veinous network is assisted by the action of muscles, which help pump blood back to the heart. In the leg veins, there are valves which prevent this blood from flowing back. If these valves lose their tone and become less efficient, this will lead to enlargement of the veins in that area.

You can help to prevent varicose veins by increasing the efficiency of the muscle-pumping action of the legs. Factors which adversely affect this action are wearing high heels, crossing the legs when sitting, and poor circulation. Varicose veins can be eased by toning up the muscles, thereby improving circulation; avoiding, whenever possible, wearing heels; making it a rule not to cross your legs; and doing simple basic exercises to keep the feet, knees, hips, back and, indeed, the whole body well exercised. You should, if possible, avoid standing for long periods. Even using a rocking chair can be useful, as it actively exercises the calf muscles, which are important in circulation.

Aromatherapy, acupuncture, shiatsu, and particularly osteopathy can improve circulation, and try a stimulating bath or massage with aromatherapy essential oils like peppermint, juniper berry, rosemary or fennel. Herbs such as nettle and yarrow can help improve circulation.

Eat plenty of garlic, onions, and foods which include bioflavonoids (citrus fruits, apricots, blackberries, cherries and rosehips), to increase the elasticity of the veins, and strengthen the walls of the capillaries. Vitamin E (wheatgerm and broccoli are excellent natural sources) is recommended to repair and restore suppleness to broken capillaries and blood vessels.

Many people suffer from bloating, putting on or losing weight erratically, cravings, feeling lethargic and nauseous and having skin problems. Very often these people have tried all sorts of diets, doctors and alternative therapies that may have worked for a while but then the symptoms have returned. These symptoms are a sign that there is usually something deep-rooted within their system that may have stemmed from a virus of old. Viruses can stay around the body for many different reasons, particularly something like candida or glandular fever, or viruses that you pick up from abroad that you may know nothing about. That results in the body not being able to work properly in digestion, retaining nutrients, vitamins and minerals and, most of all, the natural flora of the bowel. It is *not* dangerous but you may feel that this rings a bell with you. If so you should talk to your chosen practitioner and ask them to check your internal deficiencies and, for the moment, design your nutrition around that factor, but with the sole aim of being able to feel, eat and sleep normally and fully.

Like me, you may find that you have to do a lot of searching and experimenting with different practitioners to get to the root of the problem

Joanne

Joanne came from a happy, stable environment. She was twenty-three and lived at home with a good job and steady boyfriend. She'd suffered recurring bouts of tonsilitis which were always treated with an antibiotic medication. As a result, she suffered from thrush, severely, and was being treated with yet more prescribed antibiotics. We suggested she try a different course. We checked her nutrition, made adjustments, advised her to douche with live yoghurt, and avoid tampons, tights and nylon underwear for a few months.

She needed to increase her intake of water. We also advised her to perhaps have her tonsils out and see an ENT specialist. We are happy to say that she followed our advice and both the thrush and the tonsilitis have now cleared up.

and knock it on the head. Don't give up, it's really worth it.

Ninety-nine percent of your ailments, diseases or discomforts are tied up together and they are equally and greatly affected by your:

○ emotional state;
○ nutrition;
○ level of physical fitness and self-image;
○ stress/relaxation factor;
○ breathing and posture;
○ general organization and hygiene; and
○ personal finances.

You will have to back up your treatment with good nutrition, exercise and breathing techniques, otherwise nothing will remain effective, as my own case history shows (see page 128).

If you suspect that you have a poor body image, bad posture and habits you should:

○ Do regular stretching to open up the body's energy meridians and joints;
○ Breathe fully and correctly (see chapter Seven, pages 141 and 138, for stretching and breathing exercises);
○ Sit with your legs, arms and feet in an open position, not crossed, your chest opened and lifted and your shoulders relaxed;
○ Get out in the fresh air every day – go for a walk; and
○ Take time to relax mentally and physically, especially in tense or frightening situations.

Think about it, you won't be able to counter-act poor circulation, joint or back problems, colds, flu or serious diseases until your body is running smoothly. Give yourself a chance to breathe; look at your health from all angles: mental, physical, emotional, and financial.

My message to you is simple. Follow the guidelines below, and really think about what you want to achieve. A good attitude makes it all possible.

1. Start to learn about your body.
2. Discover how your body *should* function.
3. Read up on those areas that are causing you discomfort; for instance, libido, PMS, cystitis, so that you develop an understanding of your body, and can intelligently question your practitioner or therapist.
4. Don't complain more than once about your symptoms to a friend or practitioner without actively doing something about it.
5. Don't give up if a treatment doesn't work immediately. Remember your symptoms have been around for a long time, plus the fact that most of us cheat and are inconsistent. So you have to monitor your behaviour as continuously and as thoroughly as you would monitor your work.
6. Make sure you are addressing your symptoms from all of the following points of view:
   a) emotions;
   b) stress from present problems;
   c) nutrition;
   d) exercise;
   e) relaxation; and
   f) pampering.
   Are you getting all you need?
7. Don't use the excuses that you have:
   a) too much to do;
   b) not enough time;
   c) other priorities and commitments; or
   d) too much socializing.
   You can add to this list.

Now is the time to take action. Make a list of your physical ailments and note down what you can deal with – for instance, by changing your eating, sleeping and breathing habits. Then pay a visit to your GP or an alternative therapist, who can offer advice on exercise, supplementation and alternative cures. Some of your problems could be based simply on a vitamin or mineral deficiency, or on stress, which is causing digestive and posture problems.

Today, there are cures for almost every common ailment, and by preparing your body to become entirely fit and healthy, most of these ailments can be prevented altogether. When you do get ill, your newly healthy body will be able to heal itself more quickly than you ever imagined. Prepare yourself *now* to fight ill health, fatigue and that general under-the-weather feeling. You can expect to see results within a few months.

SIX

Nutrition

NUTRITION PLAYS AN enormous role in your life. It affects the shape and feel of your body, your sexuality and your self-confidence. It can control your mental attitudes, and affect your relationships. And it is the major influence on your ability to excel at work, and on the energy you have to enjoy life – to be creative, to extend your horizons and outlook. Most of all, it governs every aspect of your health.

This chapter is not a diet or an eating plan. Instead, I have aimed to point you towards the foods with high nutritional value and to explain why other foods can be detrimental to your health. There are tips here on simple substitutes you can make for these 'no-go' foods, and shopping lists with recommended foods.

When changing your eating habits, the most vital piece of information – that I can't stress enough – is that there are masses and masses of foods and tastes that you can have. You don't have to be or feel deprived just because you realize you should not have certain foods.

By now you will be well accustomed to the many emotional and practical reasons that prevent the majority of us from sticking to a healthy eating plan; dealing with these reasons is vital if you are to improve your eating habits. The chances are that many of the following apply:

○ How often have you gone on a 'diet'?
○ How many times have you honestly followed a food regime from beginning to end without giving up or cheating?
○ How many regimes have you followed religiously, only to be disappointed with the results?
○ How many short cuts, like slimming pills and slimming aids, have you taken?
○ How many times do you resolve to follow a diet, start the next day, and then halfway through the following day, give up and say: 'I'll start tomorrow'?
○ When on a diet, do you set it up to be as easy as possible? That is, for instance, avoiding keeping tempting 'bad' foods in the home?
○ How often do you fast, lose the weight, then binge again almost immediately, only to regain the weight, or more?
○ Do you hide your body with your clothes?
○ How energetic and great do you feel when you're on a diet or a fast?
○ If and when you've lost the weight you wanted to, how good do you look? Do you tend to feel half the size, but badly in need of sleep, of toning up and of a less pallid complexion?
○ When you're on a diet, and you know you have lost a quarter or half of the weight you are targeting, do you think: 'Oh great, I've done it now and I look good', and then slowly begin to veer away from your plotted course and find yourself, two weeks later, at square one again saying: 'Well, that didn't work, so I'm not going to bother'?
○ How often do you use the excuses:
  'My work is social and I have to eat and drink such and such';
  'I travel a lot so there's no choice';
  'I am entertained at people's homes, both socially and for work. I can't tell them what I can and can't have';
  'I don't have enough time to organize things, I have other priorities';
  'I have to cook for my husband, children or boyfriend, and they would laugh or be annoyed if I ate what I was supposed to eat';
  'It's not socially acceptable not to have certain things'; or
  'I just don't have the will-power'?
○ How often do you eat or drink something, and then feel heavy around your stomach, or find your energy falls flat?

Using nervous energy has been likened to taking out an unrepayable mortgage on your body.

○ How often do you wake up feeling heavy-handed, tired, bilious and woolly-mouthed?

○ How often do you skip breakfast and then start bingeing mid-morning?

○ Do you find yourself drinking masses of tea or coffee in a furious attempt to get your energy up and remain concentrated, only to feel a wreck at the end of that day, and to begin the vicious circle all over again the next?

○ Do you have a breakfast consisting of supermarket cereals, toast, butter and jams, milk, tea or coffee? Then do you wonder why you have a sugar craving throughout the day?

○ How often do you replace lunch with a sandwich, a pot noodle, a cup-a-soup, or just a glass of wine with cheese and bread? Do you go back to the office and, come mid-afternoon, fight madly to stay awake, needing to go for a coffee or chocolate bar because you are bored, and lethargic?

○ How often do you eat or binge as a result of being:

      upset; scared; nervous; bored; or frustrated?

○ How often do you eat late at night? Are you a middle-of-the-night eater?

○ Do you ever associate excess weight with your general health?

○ Are you scared about what to eat so you pick around food and cease to enjoy it?

○ Do you have 'only one drink' every evening, 'just to relax'?

○ Do you believe you are doing everything you should when following a healthy diet, but find that nothing is happening in the weight-loss area?

○ Do you really understand how food can work *for* you and not against you, and how enjoyable and beneficial good food can be?

○ Do you visit alternative therapists or beauticians for 'slimming' treatments, but still drink alcohol, coffee, tea, or fizzy drinks, and eat the less-than-wonderful foods?

○ Be honest with this question: Do you expect diets to work overnight, and do you think that if you keep trying the fads of the month some of them will do it for you?

Perhaps in answering these questions, it will begin to dawn on you that someone somewhere has missed the point. That maybe diets and regimes are not the answer. That, perhaps, instead of making excuses for not doing what works for your health or weight, the priority should be your personal satisfaction?

Looking after your body thoroughly, having clear skin, perfectly-cared-for feet and nails, no unpleasant body odour, and knowing with confidence that you are constantly reviewing all these areas, will continually give you a huge source of satisfaction and delight. Nutrition, clear bowels and urine are, in other words, body maintenance which continually supports your mental state; the low times become less frequent, satisfaction becomes the norm, your body will be controlled, the areas you hate, like cellulite, will be improved, and all-round satisfaction will be maintained.

In order to look, feel and be one hundred per cent well, and to have a clear mind, it is essential to understand the blocks and negative thoughts that prevent you from doing what is necessary to create and maintain a feeling of wellbeing and fitness. Our emotions are constantly changing. In women, PMS can and does bring on depression and bingeing. Your self-esteem quickly dissolves when you put on weight and inches, when your skin and complexion are a mess, and your hair loses its gloss, your eyes their sparkle. Small wonder that you fall into depression!

BEFORE YOU PICK UP ANOTHER DIET BOOK

There are still many misconceptions about what comprises healthy eating. We are often misled – by food manufacturers who have jumped on the 'healthy eating' bandwagon – into thinking that buying tinned baked beans with a reduced sugar content equals healthy eating. In general, there is very little real understanding of nutrition – both in terms of what our bodies need, and the poisons which can cause them to dysfunction. And, when it comes to losing weight, the confusion is even more pronounced. Some people believe that nutritional advice is only required if you are under- or overweight. Worst of all, many so-called experts still talk about dieting rather than advising clients to change their eating habits for life.

In my experience diets do not work long term. Dieting is unrealistic, unhealthy, boring and traumatizing when you can't stick to it. Let me explain further.

When you and I think of diet, there are several things that turn us away from a simple understanding and enjoyment of healthy eating. We tend to think only about what we cannot have, and this drives us into resentment and depression. We inevitably give in to those temptations, and often end up eating double the quantity. Having fallen, we feel upset and sometimes angry. It's simply too easy to think: 'To hell with it, it probably doesn't work anyway'. Then it's back to our old habits – or maybe even worse. All this because nobody ever gave us the correct information to *understand* it all, or told us how great we could feel, physically, mentally and emotionally. The end result is that even if people are really strict with themselves when on *The Diet*, and do in fact lose weight, once off the diet, nine out of ten people find that within two weeks to two months they have put on weight and are back to square one.

I wonder why?

The answer is very simple: *dieting*.

Dieting is a completely artificial and unrealistic way of losing weight, for it starves the body and slows down the metabolism. Instead of burning up stored fat, as dieters hope, the body gets used to working on fewer calories and readjusts itself to that level. If a dieter then increases his/her calorie intake even slightly, the extra calories will join other fat stores (on hips and thighs, for example) because the body's slowed-down metabolism will no longer require them. It's a vicious circle.

THE GOLDEN RULES OF WEIGHT LOSS

If losing weight is included in the list of what you want to achieve, there are a few golden rules you have to make with yourself in order to succeed and maintain your new figure.

Be realistic about the amount of time it is going to take. Don't be fixated with the idea of losing weight quickly. Your body requires a decent period of time to heal and re-adjust to a new eating programme, let alone to lose weight. Your metabolism will have to sort itself out, and your internal systems will have to learn how to function again.

You should make a list of the excuses that you are likely to use, which will stop you getting any kind of long-term result, such as:

drawing attention to yourself; stress; travelling; fatigue; depression; failing at work; anger; jealousy; boredom; dissatisfaction and apathy in any area of your life; having to socialize a lot; not wanting to be rude; not having enough time; and partners and children who would disapprove.

These are only a few examples – you may have more to add.

You see, every time you cheat, or stop and start, your body's ability to heal itself, and to get into balance becomes weaker and weaker. It then takes that much longer to achieve its balance. It's a bit like being beaten up and never completely recovering before being beaten up again. Not very nice, is it?

So you have two choices:
1. To eat and drink whatever you want because it's more important for you to indulge yourself;

OR

2. To be satisfied, delighted and healthy in the way you feel and express yourself physically, and the way you look.

And that, simply, is what it comes down to.

This is the area that is hardest for me to persuade you to change, as I don't – and you wouldn't want me to – live in your pocket every minute of the day. I have no control over your actions when it comes to caring for yourself. It is very important for you to nurture your ability to define what you want, and to imagine what it would look and feel like.

Every day, we see between three and five new people who are starting the Holistix course. At least two-thirds say they want to lose weight

If you feel bloated or sick after a meal, drink a cup of hot water with celery leaves seeped in it. It is a wonderful cleanser.

or to improve their health. When going through their consultation we find that eating habits and attitudes to food are playing a big part in their health or weight problems. These are just a few of the problems:

1. Bowels not working properly;
2. If vegetarian, far too much cheese and dairy produce, an over-abundance of nuts, sweets, chocolates, sugary drinks, alcohol, and not enough roughage or protein are being consumed;
3. Lousy overall level of nutrition, which may or may not be self-evident;
4. They suffer from ME or candida, and their poor nutrition either partly causes these illnesses or slows the whole digestive system, and the ability to retain and produce the vitamins and minerals needed to remain normally healthy;
5. They have always been overweight for some reason or another – a life of low-level nutrition, with the bowels never working more than three or so days per week since childhood;
6. Suffering from constant minor illness; and
7. The biggest cause is usually on-going emotional stresses, including upset, anger and apathy/boredom in any of the following areas:
   - exams;
   - studying;
   - work;
   - personal relationships;
   - divorce;
   - finance;
   - death;
   - problem children;
   - difficult parents;
   - accommodation problems; or
   - getting old.

In many cases there is a combination of these reasons, and anyone who comes to 'get fit', 'lose weight', 'put on weight', 'become healthier' or whatever, usually opens up a personal spaghetti junction.

The good news is that each person feels a huge mental weight lifted at having everything out in the open, so there's no longer a mystery as to what's what and why.

It's up to each person to discover his or her individual problem, and then to decide how to deal with it. And that includes very ill people as well. In fact, it is the serious cases like those suffering from cancer and multiple sclerosis, who are often the least dramatic, sulky, self-righteous or indignant, taking full responsibility for getting on with changing their eating habits.

I do acknowledge that losing weight and then maintaining it, and overcoming problems such as obesity, anorexia or bulimia, to get back to a state of normal health and good energy, is extremely hard. When you consider how you have felt for a considerable time, and take into account the fact that perhaps nothing you've done to date has worked, it's easy to see that you can't expect instant results. It figures that you are going to have to really sit down and change your approach. You need to:

a) Think about what to do;
b) Decide the extent to which you are going to have to change your habits;
c) Make your lifestyle work for you, and not against you;
d) Become aware of which everyday, uncomfortable emotions and events lead you to abuse yourself by eating badly;
e) Ask for other people's help and understanding in your switch to good habits, and your elimination of the bad;
f) Make a list and a plan to see you through the time it will take for you to achieve your goal; and
g) Put into motion all of the above ideas and plans.

THE ALTERNATIVE TO QUICK-FIX DIETS

Before you do anything, sit down with a piece of paper and list what you can remember about the food you ate between the ages of five and twenty – in particular, tinned foods, semolina and other rice-puddings, sponges, tinned vegetables, supermarket cereals, pasta, fried breakfasts, chips, bread, red meat, salads and vegetables covered in salad cream or butter, salt on food, cakes and chocolate, rich foreign food on holiday, tinned spaghetti and baked beans, processed meats such as ham and salami, sugar, additives, preservatives, vinegar, wine vinegar, dairy products such as cheese, yoghurt and butter, pastry, fish fingers, frozen fish and other meals.

You may become aware that while you were growing up, most of your food was processed food or fast food, high in fats, salt and sugar, and generally low in nutritional value.

CLEANSING AND HEALING

In order for your body to heal itself and become strong again – for cravings to be reduced, your digestion to rebalance itself, and to extract the nutrients from the (hopefully) good foods you are going to eat – you need to have a six- to eight-week period of absolutely impeccable nutrition.

Fasting: Some people think that fasting or eating just fruit and water for two or three days will achieve a cleansed state, but I'm afraid you can't correct and heal the body in that period of time. In fact, before fasting, you should have had a very healthy and fairly long-standing record of good nutrition. Going from eating unhealthily, drinking alcohol, tea and coffee for long periods, straight into fasting (and then reverting quite quickly back to poor eating habits), puts extra strain on your system.

Once you have had at least six weeks of eating properly, and you feel strong and healthier as a result, you can do a vegetable and homemade soup fast once a week, if you like. This is more cleansing and gentler than a fruit fast – especially for those people who are sugar-sensitive.

One other point to remember is that you may be recommended by alternative or orthodox practitioners to fast for medical reasons. If that is the case, make sure that when you come off the

---

Barbara

B arbara's physical complaints were numerous: chronic constipation, bleeding from her rectum and she slept badly, having nightmares so that her energy was really low. Her periods were prolonged and heavy, and she was overweight by two stone.

On an emotional level, she was fairly out of control. She binged constantly on junk and fast food, and suffered depression and severe lack of confidence, to the point that it had taken her six months to get the courage to phone us.

As a result of all this, she slouched and was quite pathetic; her voice was low and whiney, with no energy or dynamism.

In her Consultation, we

established that her nutrition would need to shift enormously: from junk, processed, fried and fast food to fresh, wholesome food – regularly, three times a day.

We were able to get her to see that her use of food as a comfort and substitute for the affection and love of her parents was a need that she had now outgrown. Then we helped her to realize that she was in control of her own life, and that she really wanted to be able – and was, in fact, perfectly able – to let go of this pattern.

This whole idea was astounding and exciting to Barbara and we then took her through the practical stages of what she would need to do, in terms of shopping, cooking and nutrition, and explaining that she would need to get her house and kitchen in order.

Over the next few weeks, she really put these ideas into practice.

When she came unstuck, she would always give us a call, have a chat and get back on the right track again.

The results were extraordinary and immediate. She began to sleep properly, her energy increased dramatically, her bowels began to move daily, without pain or bleeding, her periods became less painful and prolonged, and she began to lose weight.

Through the exercise classes, her posture improved, so that she looked inches taller. And her shape became sleek and streamlined as she lost weight and toned muscles. She also developed style and grace, which she had never believed possible. Her confidence and self-esteem increased to the degree that she left her job, which she loathed, and decided to travel and explore the world.

fasts, you re-introduce yourself to eating with very light, easily digested foods, such as soups, soft fruit and fish. If you are fasting, make sure you are not in a period of excess stress, and that you can allocate more time to sleep and self-pampering, so that your energy for work etc is not greatly impaired.

It is essential that recurring physical conditions and certain illnesses are treated with special care, preferably in conjunction with a dietary therapist or nutritionist (not a dietician, who deals primarily with calorie content rather than with nutrition as a form of medicine). Remember, you are completely unique. Even if you and a friend have identical symptoms, the offending causes aren't necessarily the same.

Foods to avoid to cleanse your system: To really cleanse the body, and combat the weight and health problems, I would recommend that you start by cutting down and then out:

○ wheat;
○ yeast;
○ salt;
○ dairy produce (except a twice-weekly dish of live goat's milk yoghurt with acidophilus);
○ tea;
○ coffee;
○ alcohol; and
○ all additives and preservatives.

Go carefully with your fruit intake, too. Eat only soft fruits, such as pears, melons, nectarines and peaches, and limit them to two a day – on their own. Cut down on oranges, pineapple, grapefruit, tangerines, apples and grapes. These are all known to create cravings and to ferment in the body.

The reason why you must cut down and *then* out is so that your body doesn't go into shock, often having become addicted to these substances.

When buying foods be sure to *double-check labels*. You will be flabbergasted at how many foods contain the ingredients listed above (particularly wheat and sugar), plus additives and preservatives. You should also take care at friends' houses and in restaurants, because

yeast, salt and sugar are found in mustards, bottled sauces, vinegar, wine, mayonnaise and most gravies.

FOOD ALLERGIES

There are many conflicting views surrounding food allergies and food sensitivities: the way they are diagnosed and their relevance to weight and health problems.

There are several factors which affect the presence of allergies:

○ Age;
○ Sex;
○ Heredity;
○ Stress of all kinds;
○ Attitude;
○ Pollens; and
○ Environmental pollution.

The tests to determine allergies can be useful, but have been shown in some instances to be inaccurate. The only way you will know for sure which foods you are allergic to is to go on an exclusion diet. This is best done with a practitioner's overview. You stop eating the substances you have been told, or suspect, you are allergic to for a seven to fourteen day period (depending how deeply rooted the problem is), then re-introduce one food at a time, eating it at each meal over a three-day period. If, during that period, allergic symptoms appear – headaches, bloating, fatigue, lethargy and spots, in particular – then you should avoid that food altogether for six weeks, and test again.

You may, however, be advised by your practitioner to cut out that food for up to six months.

You must stick to the avoidance period before retesting it, as it only takes a tiny drop of the substance to which you are allergic to trigger off the reaction. Given you are allergic, or sensitive in the first place, your body will be acutely reactive, so don't think you can get away with it. There may be one or more substances that you may be told, or find, that you will always have to avoid.

Food sensitivity is extremely common. Without necessarily realizing it, people can

Jeffrey

Jeffrey's physical symptom was atrocious skin. It had always been that way, for as long as he could remember, and he had despaired of it ever changing. Doctors had put him on repeated antibiotics for years, to no avail. He had suffered numerous allergies during his early teens, which were then replaced by acne when he was about seventeen. As a person, he was very shy and nervy, slight in build and unassuming in demeanour.

During his Consultation we established that his diet consisted of a very high intake of dairy produce, fats, caffeine and, in particular, alcohol. His schedule workwise was erratic, and consequently his eating pattern followed suit.

Once Jeffrey could see the type of food he was putting into his body, it became easier for us to point out the likely correlation between his nutrition and his skin. We suggested that he went to see a homoeopath to be tested for allergies, as it seemed likely that some sort of foodstuff was aggravating the problem.

We strongly suggested he give up alcohol, and then, in terms of food, that he eat only fresh, unfatty, unprocessed foods for an initial two-month period, to see what kind of difference it made. We also spent quite some time in the Pamper, working out a skin-care routine, and experimenting with different products. Often, over the next few weeks, Jeffrey would come up with excuses and reasons as to why he couldn't make the changes. But each time he was doubtful and depressed, we would discuss it and he would regain excitement and incentive. He took our advice, saw a homoeopath and learned exactly what foods he was allergic to, and then completely avoided them over the next weeks.

I don't think anyone was more astonished by the results than Jeffrey himself. Within one Holistix course, his entire skin cleared. He actually looked like a completely different person. Then, instead of trying to make himself slight and insignificant because of his embarrassment around his face, suddenly he wanted to be noticed and get involved. And everything was affected – his work, his social life, his relationships, and so on. Previously, he had been content to disappear into the crowd. Now he wanted to stand up and be counted.

---

become sensitive at any time to anything. Sometimes you may have a rash for no particular reason, or you may feel a bit lethargic after certain foods. In alternative and nutritional medicine, food sensitivity is looked at in several different ways, depending on the philosophy of the practitioner.

Discovering your food sensitivities can be a short cut to solving your weight problem, and many other health problems. Remember, people with food allergies should *never* eat processed or junk foods, with too many ingredients and seasonings, or those with artificial colours and preservatives. Once those parts of your diet are cut out, a number of your sensitivities could cease – taking with them the headaches, apathy and lethargy which lead to overeating.

It's important to note that you must aim for *variety* in your daily food intake. Don't get stuck on eating, say, just chicken every day. Rotate your foods as much as possible, as sticking to one food constantly is one of the main reasons that people develop allergies.

When you cut out 'favourite' foods, you will get cravings at first, but slowly and surely they will disappear. It's a bit like a lost love: at first you feel desperate, upset and angry, and it feels like you will never get over it. However, in time, it becomes just a memory!

You have to ride that first hard part. This is extremely important because that hard part is going to come up between three and eight times during the cycle of losing weight and getting healthier. More importantly, getting through that 'tough stage' is the only way you will continue to achieve and maintain your results. Remember that you may have to contend with:

1. A lifetime of bad eating habits;
2. No nutritional education;
3. Your daily ups and downs and emotional problems – you can no longer use food to deal with these;
4. Addictions to tastes; and
5. Cravings due to deficiencies of certain nutrients.

The following is a list of common allergens, which your practitioner (GP or alternative) can test for. Some practitioners' lists may differ from this one, and their methods of testing you can vary, but the benefits of knowing your allergies and sensitivies is unquestionable. Don't hesitate to get a second opinion, if you're not sure about the results. And why not ask your practitioner to help guide you on your own elimination programme of testing food.

FOOD SUBSTANCES

Gluten	Cabbage	Gooseberries	Mushrooms
(wheat)	Tapioca	Strawberries	Barley
Seafood	Apples	Onions	Cocoa/
Dairy produce	Tea	Vanilla	chocolate
Yeast	Animal Fats	Rhubarb	Bananas
Eggs	Beetroot	Offal	Nuts
Alcohol	Tomato	Chicken	Raspberries
Corn (maize)	Coffee	Goat's milk	Plums
Oats	Lettuce	Pork	Grapes
Rice	Beer	Beef	Pineapple
Soya	Oranges	Lamb	Cucumbers
Oils	Peppers	Duck	Tap Water
Carrots	Celery	Potatoes	Condiments
Coconut	Rye	Runner Beans	Garlic
Pulses	Cheese		

TOXIC SUBSTANCES

Aluminium	Arsenic	Cadmium
Nickel	Mercury	Lead/Petrol fumes
Aerosols	Propane gas	Saccharin

OTHER SUBSTANCES

Animal dander	Silk	Aperitifs
Housedust	Pollens	Airborne scents
Vegetables	Grasses	Acids
Hops	Hay	Herbs
Wool	Curry	Spices
Nylon	Tobacco	Gelatin
Cotton	Wines	Carbon Dioxide
Plastics	Spirits	Exhaust fumes
The Pill	Liqueurs	Plants/Flora/Fauna

SUGARS/FERMENTS

White sugar (beet	Cane/demerara
or cane)	Honey
Molasses	Corn Sugar
Maple syrup	Malt
Fruit sugars	Dried fruits

WHEN TESTING FOR ALLERGIES, IT IS USEFUL TO TEST TO SEE IF YOU ARE DEFICIENT IN ANY OF THE FOLLOWING:

VITAMINS

Vitamin A (retinol, carotene)	B5 (pantothenic acid)
Vitamin B-complex	B12 (cobalamin, cynocobalamin)
B1 (thiamine)	B13 (orotic acid)
B2 (riboflavin)	B15 (pangamic acid)
B3 (niacin)	B17 (amygdalin)

Para-aminobenzoic acid (PABA)	Vitamin E (tocopherol)
Choline	Vitamin F (fatty acids)
Inositol	Vitamin H (biotin)
Lecithin	Vitamin K (menadione)
Vitamin C (ascorbic acid)	Vitamin M (folic acid)
Vitamin D (calciferol, viosterol)	Vitamin P (bioflavonoids)
	Vitamins T and U

MINERALS

Calcium	Nickel
Chlorine	Phosphorus
Chromium	Potassium
Cobalt	Selenium
Copper	Silica
Fluorine	Sodium
Iodine	Sulphur
Iron	Vanadium
Lithium	Zinc
Magnesium	Water
Molybdenum	

In some cases, the body reacts adversely to being deprived of things which it is used to having, so don't worry if you feel unwell for a few days. Whether or not you feel unwell, try to take life quietly and *do make certain that you replace the 'forbidden foods' by others*. Many people can feel unwell simply because they are hungry. The following list shows you how to replace forbidden foods with something you *are* allowed to eat – in some of your favourite, everyday recipes. Some of the foods – particularly the replacement for wheat flour – may seem strange to you, but they are available in healthshops, some supermarkets like Sainsburys or Waitrose, and shops catering to vegetarians, Indians and Orientals. Be adventurous with your cooking and, above all, do not go around feeling 'deprived'. Enjoy the new foods and perhaps let your friends try your experiments; you will find they will offer other suggestions or perhaps bring their own samples to try.

Make a mental note of your worst cravings and food habits, and consider things with which you can substitute them.

MAKING HEALTHY FOOD DELICIOUS

You can make many delicious sauces with the following ingredients: tamari, soya milk, onions, rice flour, soya flour, garlic, herbs, tomatoes, pulses and fruit.

Use your imagination and take some time to

concoct some interesting sauces, using the healthy-eating cookbooks mentioned in **Further Reading**, page 191.

Try these ideas, too:

○ Brown rice is great with chopped onions and garlic and can be mixed with baby sweet corn and carrots to make up a tasty dish.

○ You can buy fish, like tuna steaks and swordfish, cut it into cubes, and cook with garlic, lemon, onions, peppers and tomatoes.

○ Parsnips and fennel are brilliant sliced or diced, boiled or roasted.

○ Ratatouille is delicious as a starter or your main meal.

○ Chicken, turkey or game can be grilled, baked, or roasted with different seasonings and garnishes.

For more meal ideas – including starters, breakfast, lunch and dessert, turn to page 126.

FOOD ALTERNATIVES

FOODS THAT MAY HAVE TO BE AVOIDED	ALTERNATIVE
Milk or Cream	Goat's milk
	Soya milk
	Plamil (a form of soya milk which is thick enough to be used as a cream substitute)
	Delice cream (a soya product)
	Velactin or Prosobee
Butter and Margarine	Granose, Tomar or Vitaseig, or any margarine not containing whey
	Vitaquell (contains wheat)
	Olive oil can be used in most recipes
Cheese and Yoghurt	Soya cottage cheese
	Goat's milk live yoghurt
	Quark
Cornflour	Potato Flour, rice flour or buckwheat
Baking powder	Salfree
Chocolate	Carob
Sugar	Fructose (fruit sugar)
	coconut
Salt	Ruthmol
Tea	Herbal tea
	Rooibosch tea
Coffee	Dandelion root (contains lactose – milk sugar)
	Chicory

FOODS THAT MAY HAVE TO BE AVOIDED	ALTERNATIVE
Coffee (contd.)	Barley Cup or Swiss Cup (contains barley)
Eggs	Vinegar and water (recipes for egg-free sponges in most cookery books)
	Carageen
Yeast	Soda bread or scone mix
	Gluten-free bread
	Manna bread
Wheat flour	If you are not sensitive to other grains, replace with pure rye
Biscuits	Vessen oat cakes, rice cakes
Dressings	Try olive oil, lemon, garlic and pepper mixed together (shake well and it's delicious)
Jams/Spreads	'Whole Earth' range of no-added-sugar jams etc
	Diabetic ranges of jams and marmalades
Peanut butter	Tahini sesame spread
Nuts	Sunflower seeds, pumpkin seeds, pine kernels, almonds or cashews
Crisps	Organic corn chips/organic potato crisps
Drink	Still mineral water/Aqua Libra

A FEW ALTERNATIVES

1. A cream or milk to put on your breakfast cereal:
2 ripe bananas
1 egg white
Water
Liquidize to required consistency.

2. Instead of breadcrumbs for coating foods: try oats or ground rice, with some herbs or spices for flavour.

3. Crumble topping: use healthshop cornflakes or rice crispies instead of flour.

4. Biscuits: flapjacks and oatmeal cookies (macaroons).

5. Wheat-free cake and biscuit flour
2oz ground almonds
2oz rice flour
1oz soya flour
1½oz coconut
Mix together and use in the place of 4oz of wheat flour in any cake or biscuit recipe.

ACID AND ALKALINE FOODS

We eat a diet which is very often composed of eighty percent acid-forming foods, and this leads to many everyday ailments. We should tip the balance to eat eighty percent alkaline foods. I have included many foods that we don't particularly recommend in this list, so that you know which category they belong to.

ALKALINE	ACID
Fruits	*Fruits*
Apples	Citric preserves:
Apricots	jellies
Avocados	canned
Bananas (ripe)	sugared
Berries (all)	glazed fruits
Carob, pod only	Bananas, green
Cherries	Cranberries
Currants	Olives (pickled)
Dates	Plums
Figs	Prunes and juice
Grapes	*Vegetables*
Lemons and Limes	Beans, all dried
Mangoes	Brussel sprouts
Melons (all)	Chickpeas
Olives (fresh)	Lentils
Papayas	Onions
Peaches	Peanuts
Pears	Rhubarb
Raisins	Tomatoes
Vegetables	*Dairy products*
Beans, green, lima, string, sprouts	Butter
Beets and tops	Cheese, all
Broccoli	Cottage cheese
Cabbage (red and white)	Cream, ice cream
Carrots	Custards (ices)
Cauliflower	Milk (boiled, cooked, pasteurized, dried, canned)
Celery	*Flesh foods*
Chard	All meat, fowl, fish
Chicory	Gelatin
Chives	Gravies
Collards	*Cereals*
Cucumber	All flour products
Dandelion greens	Barley
Dill	Breads, all kinds
Dulse, sea lettuce	Buckwheat
Eggplant	Cakes
Endive	Corn, cornmeal, flakes, starch
Garlic	Crackers, all
Kale	Doughnuts
Lettuces	Dumplings
Mushrooms (most)	Macaroni, spaghetti
Parsley	Noodles
Parsnips	Oatmeal
Peppers (green and red)	Pies, and pastry
Potatoes, all	Rice
Pumpkin	Rye-Crisp
Radish	*Nuts*
Sorrel	All nuts (more so, if roasted)
Soybeans	Coconut, dried

ALKALINE	ACID
Spinach	Peanuts
Squash	*Miscellaneous*
Swede	All alcohol
Turnips and tops	Candy
Watercress	Chocolate
Dairy products	Coca-Cola
Acidophilus	Cocoa
Buttermilk	Coffee
Goatsmilk yoghurt	Condiments
Milk (raw)	Corn Starch
Whey	Dressings
Flesh foods	Drugs, aspirin
None	Eggs, especially the whites
Cereals	Flavourings
Corn, green (first 24 hours)	Ginger, preserved
Millet	Jams, Jellies
Miscellaneous	Marmalades
Agar	Preservatives
Alfalfa produces	Soda Water
Coffee substitutes	Tobacco
Ginger, dried	Vinegar
Honey	*Acid-forming behaviour*
Kelp	Lack of Sleep
Tisanes – mint, clover, alfalfa, mate, sage	Overwork
Yeast cakes	Worry
Nuts	Tension
Almonds	Anger
Chestnuts, roasted	Jealousy
Coconut, fresh	Resentment

Apple Cider Vinegar

Neutral
Oils, olive, corn
Cotton seed, soy, sesame, etc
Fat

PROTEINS

Proteins should make up fifteen per cent of your diet (that adds up to about four to six ounces per day). Some of the foods which contain the most and highest-quality protein are:

Fish
Free-range chicken
Organic Scotch beef
Goat's milk yoghurt
Free-range eggs
Tofu and tofu products*
Soya milk
Sunflower seeds, pumpkin seeds, sesame seeds, pine kernels and almonds
Pulses (i.e. lentils, kidney beans and black-eyed beans

    Protein is an essential element of the diet, and without an adequate protein intake, you will see very rapid adverse effects on health, such as losing body tissue, which is a form of starvation.

These must be taken in moderation, as they are known to initiate a number of mucus-based problems.

The amount that is required depends on the individual, their sex and age. Proteins act in two ways. There are those that are important for body structure, to build muscle, internal organs, nerves and skin. And there are 'functional' proteins, which are involved in metabolism, and include hormones, antibodies and enzymes. Proteins make up the next largest constituent of the body to water.

Proteins are composed of carbon, hydrogen, oxygen, nitrogen, sulphur and phosphorous. Protein molecules are made up of amino acids, of which there are twenty different ones. All must be present when a protein is synthesized. If one amino acid is missing, that protein cannot be made.

When we ingest animal or plant protein, it is broken down by enzymes into peptides, and then amino acids, before rebuilding into new proteins, which our bodies can actually use.

Proteins are classified in two groups: complete and incomplete. The complete proteins are those which contain all the amino acids necessary to the body for growth and maintenance. These are generally from animal sources, such as meat, fish, poultry, eggs, milk and cheese. Incomplete proteins contain many amino acids, but not all the essential ones in sufficient amounts. These are found in cereals, legumes, some nuts and seeds. This type of protein is important in the diet, as it decreases the amount of animal protein you need to take in (and hence the amount of saturated fat). If you are a vegetarian, you must balance your foods carefully to ensure you obtain all the nutrients that you need. For example, always mix a grain with a legume to balance your amino acids. Or mix millet and beans with sesame seeds.

It is recommended that thirty per cent of our protein intake should be in the form of complete proteins. For children, because they are growing, the levels should be nearer to fifty or sixty per cent.

CARBOHYDRATES

Carbohydrate foods include starches, grains, vegetables and fruits, and range from the simplest sugars to highly complex compounds (such as fibre).

Good carbohydrate sources which are low in fat are:
Organic short-grain rice, Millet, Couscous, Bulgar wheat, Buckwheat, Groats, Rye bran, Barley, Potatoes, Bread (preferably gluten free), Oats (porridge), Carrots, Parsnips, Swedes, Turnip

The main role of carboyhdrates is to provide energy; some sixty to seventy per cent of the total energy requirements of our bodies comes from carbohydrates. When carbohydrates are not available to the body, it will mobilize its store of glycogen (the body's way of storing glucose) and eventually tissue fat, to derive the energy that it needs. The more complex types of carbohydrate, such as starches, should make up about fifty per cent of the total carbohydrate intake. More simple carbohydrates, sugars such as glucose and sucrose, should make up another thirty per cent, and milk sugar (lactose) should make up

If you don't empty your bowels daily, you'll experience: heartburn, bad breath, burping, possible bleeding gums, mouth ulcers and cold sores. Your skin will be cloudy, spotty, dull and puffy, and your hair may look dull and lifeless. You may experience a thick and heavy feeling, sometimes with appalling headaches and migraines. The brain chemistry can alter and leave you feeling anxious, depressed, frustrated, angry and moody. Sex becomes a turn-off. Got the picture?

about another ten per cent. There are other, less important sugars that make up the balance.

Our ancestors consumed far greater quantities of complex carbohydrates in their diet than we do today. It is only since the middle of the last century that refined sugars have become such an increasing part of the diet, and more widely available.

The digestion of carbohydrates begins with the saliva, and continues through to the small bowel. Carbohydrate breakdown is controlled by hormones that function to keep the blood sugar level constant. If there is excessive glucose in the diet, it is converted to glycogen and stored in the liver for emergency use.

Even though glucose is vital for the production of energy, it is not an essential nutrient in the diet, as more complex carbohydrates are readily broken down in the body to form the glucose that is required.

Sugars are simple carbohydrates, and when eaten in food like sweets, chocolate, sweet drinks or cakes, etc, they will cause a sudden rise in blood sugar levels. The body reacts by producing insulin from the pancreas, to lower the blood sugar level. If this process is repeated several times a day (as is common in Western diets), the pancreas loses efficiency; and every time any sugar is eaten, it reacts by producing too much insulin, causing hypoglycaemia. Symptoms range from weakness, headaches and tiredness to irritability. Alleviating the symptoms with more sugars, coffee, tea, nicotine, etc, only leads to the pancreas eventually failing to produce insulin at all. This can result in diabetes.

Looking at the modern-day diet, which contains eighty per cent sugar, it's not surprising that people feel down and unhealthy! It is imperative that all sugars, including white, brown and honey, are cut right down in our diets in order to rebalance our bodies' natural functions.

Complex carbohydrates are either digestible or indigestible. The digestible variety, such as starch, can easily be broken down to more readily usable forms. Indigestible carbohydrates (fibre, the most complex form) are not broken down in the digestive system, but provide the bulk of the faeces, combined with water (they can also bind with toxins and some drugs). The intake of these indigestible carbohydrates can help to speed up the clearance of the bowel, and is important in the diet, as they give a feeling of fullness. However, because they are indigestible, they add little in the way of calorie value to the diet and can therefore be a good friend to the dieter!

FIBRE

The recommended intake of fibre is about thirty grams per day, and some sources of fibre are also important in terms of other nutrients; for example, green leafy vegetables are a good source of fibre (and an excellent source of vitamins and minerals).

Even though increasing fibre in the diet is important, simply adding bran to an already inadequate diet is not the answer. If your diet is bad, it is likely that you are already depleted in certain substances, so adding bran just increases the clearance rate of your bowel. A number of minerals and vitamins bind to fibre, so in an unhealthy person, what little good is there can be lost through the body's cleansing process. Deficiencies will be made worse. The best way to increase the fibre content of your diet is to reduce your refined carbohydrate intake and to include more fresh fruit, vegetables, whole grains, beans and lentils. The best form of fibre is vegetables, and you can eat as many as you like. Try to have a balance of root and leaf vegetables, and don't overdo the following as they are from the deadly night-shade group: tomatoes, peppers, aubergines, and red peppers. They all contain varying degrees of a poison called solonine, a nerve toxin.

Vegetables must be served raw or steamed to ensure that the nutrients are not boiled away. I find that the nicest way to cook them is to place them in a pan of cold water, slowly bring to the boil, boil for one minute, then drain and toss in Vitasieg margarine and lemon.

FATS

We tend to associate fats with ill health (heart attacks, atherosclerosis, for example); however, fat in some forms is essential to the diet and the metabolism. The most important function of fat is that it acts as a carrier of the fat-soluble vitamins (A, D, E and K), and without fat we could not absorb these vitamins at all.

If it is not immediately needed, fat is stored in the body for use in an emergency. Fat helps to regulate body temperature, as fat under the skin acts as an insulator and prevents excessive heat loss or gain, and cushions internal organs, protecting the body from mechanical injury and giving your body its individual shape. It is also an important ingredient in the structure of our cell walls, and therefore vitally important throughout the body.

There are two families of essential fatty acids (EFAs): Omega-6, derived from linoleic acid (vegetable oils and linseed), and Omega-3, from alpha-linoleic acid (fish oils). Both play essential roles in membrane structure, and are precursors of prostaglandins (hormone-like substances, which help with the immune system, fight infection, lower blood pressure, and inhibit the production of excess cholesterol and blood clotting).

It is very important to have the right balance of these essential fatty acids, for they are necessary to clear the arteries of excess saturated fat, cholesterol, alcohol, and chemical carcinogens, etc. Too much clotting and clogging could cause thrombosis and heart disease.

More and more is being discovered about the subject of fats. For instance, margarine versus butter. When a margarine is hydrogenated, hydrogen has been passed through the oil to make it a spreadable solid. Not only does this process turn the fatty acid into a form which our bodies cannot break down, but it also makes it a saturated fat. And it's called high in polyunsaturates? Always look for unhydrogenated, polyunsaturated margarines.

Much is publicized about polyunsaturated and saturated fats. Saturated fats are the hard fats, such as lard and the fat in meat, and they tend to increase the body's cholesterol levels (high levels of this are linked to heart disease). Basically, they constitute the animal fats.

Polyunsaturated fats tend to lower the cholesterol levels in the blood, and these fats are generally liquid at room temperature, and include the vegetable oils. Fish, such as salmon, mackerel and herring also contain polyunsaturated fats. Olive oil is a mono-unsaturated fat, and this group has a beneficial effect on cholesterol levels. It is estimated that if only about twenty per cent of the calories eaten are in the form of fat, this will help control cholesterol levels.

VITAMINS

This is a group of organic substances, required by the body in small amounts for normal metabolic function. They are essential to many of the biochemical reactions in the body. It is impossible to sustain life without all of the essential vitamins. Vitamins are either fat or water soluble, and, therefore, each can play a different role in different areas of our bodies.

MINERALS

These are important in the body in two ways. Substances such as calcium, phosphorous, magnesium, sodium, potassium and chlorine are not only important, as they help in some metabolic reactions, but they are also involved in building up structure, for example bones and cells. *Vitamins cannot be assimilated without minerals*, and although the body can synthesize some vitamins (for instance, Vitamin D), it cannot produce minerals. Without minerals we would also not survive; in a sense, minerals are the spark plugs in the chemistry of life.

TRACE ELEMENTS

These substances are required in very small amounts. Their function is in metabolism, again playing an important role in biochemical reactions. For instance, zinc has about 130 dependent enzyme reactions; no other trace element is needed in so many body functions and systems.

TOXINS

A toxin is essentially a poison that is harmful to another living organism. It is a term that is often used today in association with the normal waste products of metabolism. Toxins are substances which cannot be (or are difficult to be) removed. They range from alcohol, lead, heavy metals, pollutions, drugs, and our own metabolic waste from stress, bowel bacteria and our cells (see page 101 for a list of common toxins).

CHOLESTEROL

Cholesterol is a fat-like substance, commonly found in animal fats and oils. The body manufactures its own cholesterol in the liver, and some is absorbed from the diet. It is important to manufacture bile salts and some of the body's steroid hormones. Bile is important in digestion, as it helps to emulsify and break down fats.

HORMONES

A hormone is a chemical substance that is produced in endocrine organs and has a regulatory effect on certain cells, other organs, and moods. Hormones are very much the carriers of messages from the brain. For instance, in a woman's monthly cycle, hormones are sent round the body to prepare the womb for possible receipt of a fertilized egg, to the ovaries to release an egg, to the follicles in the Fallopian tubes to move that egg along, and to the uterus to expel its lining if conception fails to occur. Virtually every bodily function is controlled by hormones.

THE FOODS TO LIMIT

The main reasons for avoiding the following foods are that there are substances in these foods that contain unhealthy fluids and toxins – literally poisons.

These build up in all areas of the body over a period of time, sometimes provoking an allergic reaction, usually attacking the central nervous system and the bowels, creating tiredness, poor circulation, cellulite and many other unwanted conditions and health problems.

The following are some of the ailments which can be caused or made worse by toxins in the body:

Cellulite	Spots
Arthritis	Bad breath
Congested bowels	Bleeding gums

In order for your body to heal itself and to become strong again – for craving to be reduced, your digestion to rebalance itself, and to extract the nutrition from the good foods you are going to eat – you need to have a six- to eight-week period of absolutely impeccable nutrition.

Low energy	Cystitis and bladder
Thrush	problems
Candida	Period pains
ME (Myalgic	PMS
Encephalomyelitis	Stomach disorders
Irritation and	Bad circulation
depression	Discoloured skin
Headaches	Body odour
Allergies	Yellowing eye-whites
Sleeplessness	Excess weight
Ulcers	Back problems
Indigestion	Nervousness
Tension	Skin disorders

Sugar: White sugar and supermarket brown sugar have no fibre content. White sugar is particularly bad. It is a refined carbohydrate and the chemical processes involved in turning a natural brown substance into a snow-white powder entail the use of bleaches and other agents, which have a deleterious effect on our system, throughout the intestinal tract right to the colon. As a result, it is damaging to intestinal bacteria and mineral status. This affects the blood content, which in turn affects the brain and causes reactions throughout the body. It exhausts the pancreas and the adrenal glands, causing reactive hypoglycaemia. For example, much hyperactivity and destructive behaviour in children is thought to result from excess sugar intake; similar mental effects, causing altered behaviour and thought patterns, can be observed in adults. The following conditions can be strongly associated with significant sugar consumption:

○ Obesity
○ Diabetes Mellitus (adult type)
○ Gastrointestinal disease (indigestion, inflammatory bowel diseases, irritable bowel syndrome, diarrhoea)
○ Gallstones
○ Tooth decay
○ Kidney stones
○ Skin disorders

Remember that in many forms sugar is toxic. Watch out for its presence in the food and drink you buy.

The following is a list of the main foods containing sugar, which should be avoided, or cut down to once a week:

Bananas	Dates	Grapes
Raisins	Malt	Glucose
Honey	Mustard	Cakes and pies
Vinegar	Tinned foods	Molasses
Biscuits	Most breads	Most alcohol
Ketchup	Bottled sauces	Packaged
Maple syrup	Mayonnaise	muesli
Figs	Dried Fruits	

Just about every pre-prepared, bottled or packaged food contains sugar. And beware of some tropical fruits, which are toxic to those with sugar allergies.

White flour: White flour is another refined carbohydrate. It has no nutritional value, as it has been bleached and had all the fibre removed, and been pumped full of additives and preservatives (which many of us are allergic to).

Tea, coffee and chocolate: The caffeine and other stimulants contained in tea, coffee and chocolate affect the central nervous system directly and can cause insomnia, depression, the shakes, headaches and migraines, increased tension and stress. These products also give an artificial high, much like alcohol, and a false and short-lived feeling of energy. They can also cause high blood pressure, restless legs at night, and high blood cholesterol. The caffeine stimulates the adrenal glands and results in reactive hypoglycaemia (sudden and dangerous swings from high blood sugar levels through to low).

Apart from these discomforts, consumption of tea or coffee at mealtimes can reduce the amount of iron absorbed from vegetables by one-third, and so you may run the risk of becoming iron deficient. Tea and coffee also inhibit zinc and calcium absorption. Spots, acne, dark circles under the eyes and poor skin colour are some of the complications which can ensue from the excessive consumption of these drinks and chocolate. They are addictive and build up toxins in the body. Cut them out and you will soon notice how different you feel at the end of the day – far less nervous and tense, more able to cope with life. As the caffeine content in your body depletes, the calmness you feel will extend to your sleep. You can replace tea by herb teas, coffee by dandelion root coffee, and chocolate/cocoa by carob products, all of which are caffeine-free. You may experience withdrawal symptoms of headaches, fatigue and moodiness for up to seven days; however, after that you will feel remarkably different.

Alcohol: Alcohol goes straight into the bloodstream, where it remains for an extended period of time, so the sugar contained in the alcohol is extremely difficult to eliminate. The results are a sluggish mind and body, and a great tendency to cellulite and broken capillaries. Until your body is fully cleansed, and has had a chance to heal itself, you must be prepared for these things to happen. Some people think that alcohol is a stimulant, whereas it is, in fact, a brain depressant. So too much alcohol has adverse effects on the body's metabolism and nutritional state. Obesity is common among drinkers, especially in younger beer drinkers. Even an occasional drink can have a profound negative effect. For example, missing lunch and having a couple of drinks instead can result in low blood sugar and, through that, low energy levels in the afternoon, leading to poor concentration.

Drinking alcohol may give us a false sense of self-confidence and the ability to communicate, but the reality is quite the opposite. Just remember how you feel the morning after, with aching head, coated tongue and embarrassing half-remembered words and behaviour from the night before. Although people will take alcohol to

*P*eople with food allergies should never eat processed or junk foods, or too many ingredients and seasonings, or foods with artificial colours and preservatives. Once those parts of your diet are cut out, a number of your sensitivities should cease – taking with them the headaches, apathy and lethargy which lead to overeating.

'drown their sorrows', the real effect is that it depresses the function of the brain and its ability to deal with trauma. Women metabolize alcohol faster than men and so feel the effects sooner; those women who drink excessively are also more at risk from cirrhosis of the liver.

Sweet wine and champagne have a high sugar content, and are therefore acidic. Red wine is particularly acidic; beer, lager and cider all have a high sugar content *and* high acidity. If you are going to drink, have a glass of dry white wine, with or after a meal, and drink plenty of water with it, to flush it out of the system.

Salt: Sodium chloride (salt) is essential for life, maintaining an equilibrium between the fluids in our body. Salt regulates the acid balance, works with potassium for muscle contractions, nerve transmissions and carbon dioxide transportation. Unfortunately, we have tipped the scales with processed foods, the use of monosodium glutamate in meats, stock cubes, etc. Primitive man consumed large amounts of vegetable potassium, which kept sodium levels in balance. Today, we consume twenty per cent more sodium, and much less potassium.

The overabundance of salt causes the body to retain water and toxic fluids, which also creates cellulite. It decreases the body's ability to digest food, to retain vital minerals, such as calcium, increases cholesterol and can cause weight gain. Too much salt gives you a craving for sugar.

Salt is also one of the causes of high blood pressure. You get plenty of salt naturally from food, so if you are trying to cut down on salt, use a low sodium salt, ie Ruthmol (found in healthfood shops).

Dairy produce: There is only one thing about milk that is good, and that is its calcium content. Mothers, babies and infants have a particular need for calcium, but it must be remembered that calcium can be garnered from a number of other, healthier sources. Babies should be drinking their mother's milk, which is far different from dairy milk as we know it. Mothers' milk contains antibodies and hundreds of nutrients, which dairy milk cannot provide.

Dairy produce is the first thing to cut out – or to a minimum – especially if you are suffering from excess mucus, catarrh, asthma, eczema, and even migraines. Milk is high in fat, difficult to digest (due to neutralizing stomach acids), and it affects the mineral balance in our bodies.

When milk is pasteurized, the good bacteria is destroyed, and the proteins become more difficult to digest (which can lead to allergies). When eaten with wheat, milk can make a gooey, sticky substance, which clings to the walls of the intestines, hardening them, and preventing the nutrients from being absorbed. It also creates ideal conditions for the development and growth of putrefying bacteria, leading to problems like candida, constipation, thrush, etc.

Milk also encourages the growth of bacteria in the intestinal tract and makes absorption of nutrients and digestion of other foods more difficult.

In addition to the well-publicized weight problems caused by dairy products, their high fat content is also a common cause of lethargy. Drink soya milk, goat's milk or skimmed milk if advised and stick to the many types of goat's milk cheeses available today (though no more than twice a week). Your best source of calcium from foods other than dairy products are: salmon, green leafy vegetables, tofu and broccoli.

Meat: Almost all commercially reared animals in

As a substitute for coffee, try dandelion root coffee, a delicious, rich-tasting alternative. Dandelion root coffee is a natural diuretic as well as a liver tonic.

this country have a certain amount of steroids (for artificial increased growth) and antibiotics mixed into the feed. The majority of us are allergic to these additives in the short term, and nobody quite knows what they are doing to us in the long term. Red meat places a burden on the system, since it takes a great deal of energy to break it down and convert it to amino acids. Also, if the kidneys find it difficult to excrete all of the toxins red meat produces, they may accumulate in the tissues and joints, crystallize, and cause enormous health problems.

Red meat also tends to be high in fat. For instance, a slice of ham is twenty-five per cent protein and seventy-five per cent fat, while a plate of beans is thirty-six per cent protein and six per cent fat.

Large quantities of protein overwhelm the system, which can lead to partly digested peptide molecules; because they are left undigested in the colon, toxins form and putrefaction develops, causing allergic reaction. Spread proteins throughout the day.

So, in addition to cutting down on cow's milk and cheese, avoid red meat. If you are going to eat meat once a week, stick to small portions of lamb, which is invariably free range. Avoid pork at all costs, as it is the most polluted of meats. It's time the meat production industry cleaned up its act.

Processed foods: Avoid them. The preservatives, colourants, salt, sugar, cheap fats, and cheap ingredients used in processed and fast foods have no nutritional value and are, in fact, bad for us. Just imagine the amount of chemicals that are added to these foods to maintain their appearance from the time they leave the factory until they arrive on your plate.

Fried foods are particularly bad. The oil used for·frying is generally of a poor quality, and, at high temperatures the oxygen damages it, turning it into a toxin which is harmful to the body and could lead to cancer. Fried foods line the digestive tract causing indigestion, bowel congestion, a bad taste in the mouth, and bad breath – quite apart from the fact that the food itself has little nutritional value.

Wheat: The manner in which wheat is grown these days, and the way in it is usually processed to produce modern foods, is very different from the processes of past centuries when wheat could be considered the clean and nutritious mainstay of our diet. Many individuals develop an intolerance to wheat and its products. This has been known to cause irritable bowel syndrome, although this condition also has many other causes. The kind of wheat eaten by most people today has a very high gluten content, which literally sticks to the sides of the intestines, hardens, and prevents nutrients from being absorbed. It also becomes a breeding ground for germs. Wheat-based foods include the following: Bread, Sorrel, Nut roasts, Pastry, Bottled sauces, Cakes, Biscuits, Batter, Soy and tamari sauces, Crispbreads, Muesli, Ryvita, Taramasalata, Tofu burgers.

Yeast: Yeast should be avoided because as soon as it comes into contact with other foods containing sugar, it begins to ferment and create gases in the stomach. It also causes thrush, candida, ME and various allergies. In general, yeast will interfere with the bowel flora in the colon, setting up excellent conditions for the healthy bacteria to be overcome by undesirable bacteria. Bowel flora is designed to complete the digestive process and control infection from harmful bacteria viruses, fungus and yeast-eating worms.

Due to a diet or processed, unnatural foods lacking in fibre, meats contaminated with hormones and antibiotics, and vegetables contaminated by fertilizers and pesticides, conditions for organisms living on putrefaction are increased. The antibiotics tend to wipe out the bad bacteria, as well as the good (for instance, lactobacillus). And candida albicans, normally kept in check by good bacteria, changes into a mass of filaments like fungus, and spreads – affecting the mucus membranes and leading to thrush, respiratory illness, stomach and intestinal irritation and, through that, allergies and a weakened immune system.

Foods containing yeast are:

Alcohol	Bread	Soy Sauce
Vinegar	Marmite	Bouillon
Pâtés	Stock cubes	Yeast extract
Biscuits	Nut roasts	Vegetable pâtés
Savoury spreads		

Tomatoes and citrus fruit: These fruits can adversely affect people who suffer from arthritis and related complaints. If you are in this group, try avoiding tomatoes and citrus fruit for a month to six weeks, to see if your condition improves. If it does, cut out tomatoes and citrus fruit from your diet altogether. In any case, do take plenty of exercise, carefully watch what you eat, and drink plenty of water.

The caffeine and other stimulants in coffee, tea and chocolate affect the central nervous system directly, and can cause insomnia, depression, the shakes, headaches and migraines, and increased tension and stress. These products also give an artificial high, much like alcohol, and a false and short-lived feeling of energy. Taken in large doses over an extended period of time, these products can kill your energy completely.

Cigarettes Smoking robs the body of Vitamin C, and it may take several hundred milligrams of Vitamin C a day to correct this deficiency. It also depletes the body of zinc and calcium.

Smoking also has a negative affect on the body's absorption of B vitamins. Cigarettes contain a cocktail of toxic chemicals. Nicotine, in particular, is addictive and has high levels of cadmium. Lung cancer and heart disease are just two of the conditions brought on or aggravated by smoking. If you smoke you will be affected, in one way or another, so start to cut down now and then cut it out altogether. You will soon begin to notice the difference in your breathing, your energy, your eyes and your skin – yes, smoking ages the skin, and is the major cause of cellulite for some sufferers. You will also become aware of the smell that clings to people who smoke, and to offices and rooms where smokers have been, including your own home. Give it up and you will see that the changes to your body, your skin and everything to do with you are dramatic and beneficial.

Vitamins A and E, and selenium are anti-oxidants, which will help improve health for smokers until they are able to give up. Vitamin C, which is robbed from the body by nicotine, should also be taken: up to 2 grams (2000mg) per day. Vitamin E should be taken at 400 IU daily, Vitamin A, (betacaroeine formula) at 10,000 units daily, and 50mcg of selenium. Quantities like these can probably not be found sufficiently in food for daily use. Now you know what smoking does to your body.

Curries and highly spiced food: Mild spices are generally accepted by the digestive system and the body. However, high-voltage curries and highly spiced food are not. If you consider how you normally feel after a very hot curry, with flushed face and perspiring body, you will get an idea of what is going on inside. Your digestive system is in violent uproar, trying to cope with the onslaught. If you must eat curry and hot spices, drink plenty of water to help the body cope and flush away the toxins.

Eggs: Eggs are commonly known to have a negative effect on childhood disorders, including childhood eczema, hyperactivity, sleep disturbances and behavioural disorders. Egg yolks are high in cholesterol, and should therefore not be consumed in excess, but they are a useful source of protein. Eggs suffer the indignities of commercial production as much as chickens (antibiotics, chemical feed and hormones). Some people may be sensitive to the yolk, but not the white of the egg, although the yolk is rich in vitamins and minerals. Also, eggs cooked in food – a cake, for example – may not produce an allergic reaction in an egg-sensitive person. So, buy free-range eggs and eat no more than two a week. Look for eggs that are tested and proven to be salmonella-free.

VEGETARIAN DIETS

One of the questions most often asked is: How do I get my protein? Always make sure that you mix a grain with a legume (pulses), as what is nutritionally lacking in the grain will be made up in the legume. Sprinkling seeds and nuts out of the shell, or a few almonds on most dishes will also ensure a healthy supply of protein.

Beware of overdoing cheese and dairy products to compensate for losing meat. Many vegetarian recipes use cheese, so try to stick to goat's cheese and soya products where possible.

Another question is: Where do I get my calcium, if I'm not taking dairy produce? The best non-dairy source of calcium is sesame seeds, in such things as Tahini, and dark green, leafy vegetables, for instance broccoli. Almonds are another good source, and unlike most nuts easily digestible – grind them and add water to make almond 'milk'.

Experiment with soya mince (for instance, provomix, which you can use to make sausages, pies, and a number of other traditional meat-based dishes, if you really are missing the meat) and tofu, which you can use in things like curries and stews.

Bran and wholegrain wheat can block the absorption of minerals, particularly calcium, magnesium, iron and zinc, so take care not to overeat these foods. It is worth bearing in mind, too, that the consumption of tea and coffee inhibits the absorption of iron and that iron

If you give in to impulsive eating, you will get cravings all of the time. Tell yourself directly that giving up junk and unhealthy food is all part of the package of changing a lifetime's habits. Once the gunge is out of your system, this will cease to be the case.

deficiency can be a problem for vegetarians. You should not consume tea or any caffeine-based drink with meals. Stick to herbal teas; for instance, fennel and peppermint teas aid digestion, and nettle tea is a rich source of iron itself.

Cod liver oil capsules, or, if you are vegan, a B12 vitamin supplement, or evening primrose oil, are an invaluable supplement in a vegetarian regime. Vegetarian diets are low in Vitamin B12 and it can be found in small quantities in dairy produce, brewer's yeast and eggs. Complete deficiency is rare, however.

Organically grown fruit and vegetables: Buy them whenever you can. Most healthfood shops and many supermarkets now stock good ranges of organically grown foods. Don't let the prices, which are almost invariably higher than for chemically grown foods, put you off. Because more of the nutrients in the food are available to your digestive system, you should find you need to eat less to be satisfied.

If you have to use chemically grown fruit and vegetables, wash and scrub them thoroughly. Non-organic fruit or vegetables should be peeled whenever possible to avoid pesticides or chemicals.

EATING LATE

Your digestive system, after having worked well for you all day, likes to knock off by eight in the evening, at the latest. If you cannot eat before then, choose something light upon which to dine. People often feel tired in the morning because the body cannot rest properly if it is having to digest food from late-night eating. If you are going to a concert, the theatre or any other late-evening activity, eat something before you go, so that a little light food afterwards is all that you will need. Respect your digestive system. Upsetting it will cause digestive gases to form with a resultant bloated stomach.

BREAKFAST

The old wives' tales are true: breakfast is the most important meal of the day, giving you natural energy instead of nervous energy upon which to work. Using nervous energy has been likened to taking out an unrepayable mortgage on your body. Muesli is particularly good for you if you have a history of constipation. See also, **Breakfast suggestions**, page 126. A healthy, light breakfast, with some fresh fruit or vegetables balances the blood sugar, which is usually low in the morning, and it is this that produces the natural energy. How much better to start the day enjoying this natural energy than trying to kick-start yourself with a cigarette, a cup of black coffee, and most likely to follow, a thumping headache and a foul temper.

THREE SQUARE MEALS A DAY

Lunch and dinner are as important as breakfast in keeping up a healthy and well-balanced diet. The benefit of eating three regular meals each day is that your body balance is kept in perfect order. You will be one hundred per cent energetic, and experience no sinking of energy when called upon to perform extra tasks or make important decisions. You will be creative and satisfied with your output. Miss a meal and you may miss an opportunity or an important point at a meeting. Skipping lunch and compensating by eating a huge dinner is particularly self-defeating, as the digestive system cannot cope. It takes approximately four to eight hours to digest a meal, and since it has to work harder when you are sleeping, there is little time left for the body to renew itself.

Colin

*C*olin looked like a typical, jovial overweight businessman, pink-cheeked with podgy hands and bulging stomach. Most people found him funny and popular.

The truth was, however, that he was grossly uncomfortable in his body, low in real energy, lacking in self-confidence, had never had a girlfriend, and quite expected to feel like that for the rest of his life.

With Colin, the main objective was to be weight loss, because most of his other problems stemmed from his physical appearance.

So we asked him about his lifestyle and nutrition. In terms of his job, he was under quite a lot of pressure and had to work hard, which meant that most days he skipped breakfast, grabbed a sandwich, crisps and a Mars bar for lunch, stimulated himself with coffee all day and usually ended the day with a Chinese or Indian takeaway and a few beers, late at night. It was obvious that there was a certain amount of room for improvement!

We told him that the first stage was going to be getting himself organized. Obviously his working schedule precluded him spending time cooking and shopping, but his income allowed him to employ someone to do it for him. We suggested that they cook enough food for a few days, and ensure that the fridge and cupboards were always well-stocked with all the right foods.

He could then prepack his lunch, and maybe a light snack for the evening, and take them to work. We explained how he must eat three meals a day, not skipping breakfast, and avoid large meals late at night. Colin was suddenly excited and optimistic about the possibility of changing, and mainly relieved to have back-up and support because he knew he would often be tempted back into old habits.

We spent a long time with Colin over the next few weeks, offering suggestions for foods, recipes, substitutes and so on. He liked to snack. So we suggested some nutritious nibbles.

A few months on, Colin now wonders why he ever put up with his weight and appearance for so long. Apart from the obvious pleasure in losing two stone in weight, feeling more comfortable and relaxed with people, feeling less inhibited and, as a result, not always having to play the fool to hide his discomfort, the biggest surprise was how much he enjoyed eating this way. He loved the tastes and textures of really good food, and I don't think he'd eat a Mars bar now if you paid him.

EATING OUT IN RESTAURANTS

Choose the right restaurants and this could be a real bonus, not just because you may be the guest! There is now a huge choice of restaurants serving the sort of food you can and should eat: fresh grilled fish and occasional seafoods, melons, light soups, an immense variety of fresh vegetables and salads, sugar-free sorbets and other good and delicious food. The chic thing to drink with your meal is mineral water with ice and lemon. Make the most of the opportunity to have all the good things you enjoy, without the effort of having to shop for them, cook and wash up. However, be aware that a lot of restaurant dishes contain hidden ingredients such as vinegar, wine, mustard, malt extract, yeast extract and flour. Make a little laminated list of 'no's and put down what you can have so you can give it to the waiter. If you have a problem with social drinking, simply say that you are allergic to alcohol, which, in fact, is more often than not true.

THINGS TO EAT WHEN THE GOING GETS ROUGH

There are lots of energy-giving foods you can eat when you haven't enough time to eat properly, or you are tempted to binge, which are really good for you: pumpkin and sunflower seeds, all raw vegetables, carob instead of chocolate cookies, a muesli bar, fresh fruit, almonds, organic cornchips, Japanese rice crackers without sugar or yeast, low-fat yoghurt. There are many health drinks that are fine: have a really good look around your local healthfood shop, read the labels carefully and make your own choice.

DRINKS

Almost all herb teas – and there is a vast range – are healthy. Check the label says 'caffeine-free'. Try them out and see which ones taste good to you. Herbal teas also have a number of health-giving properties. For instance, chamomile tea is soothing and helps your body digest food. Nettle tea, which is a great source of iron, is also a blood purifier and a kidney tonic. Fennel, peppermint and slippery elm teas all aid the digestive system and calm the stomach. Red raspberry leaf tea is tremendous in pregnancy or throughout bouts of PMS; it acts as an uterine toner, and can relieve menstrual cramps.

As a substitute to coffee, try dandelion root coffee, a delicious, rich-tasting alternative. Dandelion root coffee is a natural diuretic, as well as being a liver tonic.

Give your body a hand in clearing out the toxins; the alternatives to regular coffee and tea are not only delicious, but enormously beneficial to your health.

Vecon, a natural vegetable extract, obtainable in all healthfood shops, makes a good hot drink, like a light clear soup. All clear soups are good; for instance, chicken and vegetable. Hot water and lemon is very cleansing, and very weak tea with lemon is also acceptable.

It is essential to drink two to four pints (around one to two litres) of water every day. Drink still mineral water rather than carbonated water, which can make you feel bloated and can lead to flatulence. Spread your water intake throughout the day.

Don't drink water with a meal, as it will dilute the digestive juices and make digestion more protracted. Instead, drink thirty minutes before a meal or forty to sixty minutes after a meal. This will help to counteract bloating and to aid digestion. If you are thirsty just sip water, don't gulp.

If you feel bloated or sick after a meal, drink a cup of hot water with celery leaves seeped in it. It is a wonderful cleanser.

Drink freshly squeezed fruit juices in moderation (avoid concentrated juices), and mix half and half with water. One glass mid-morning will give you a lift. Hot water with lemon is purifying. Drink this in the office instead of tea and coffee. Use filtered water if possible. Remember that alcohol, regular tea and coffee, and fizzy drinks do not count as clean fluid intake. Try to cut down on or avoid alcohol; it plays havoc with your blood sugar levels, de-mineralizes the body, dehydrates the body fluids and damages brain cells beyond repair.

SEASONINGS AND DRESSINGS

Dressings must be low fat. Make them with live goat's milk yoghurt, lemon juice or a very few drops of extra virgin olive oil. A little pepper is fine and garlic, onions and all herbs are delicious. There are a number of fresh, oil-free dressings on the market, available both at healthfood shops and now, more than ever, your local supermarket.

SOUP AND STOCK

The most delicious ingredient of any soup or casserole is stock made from chicken and chicken bones. Make a good amount of stock and freeze it in small blocks so that you always have a quantity available when you need it. Do not use stock cubes which are high in salt. To get the most nutritional value from your stock, boil the bones in a small amount of water with one teaspoon of vinegar. The vinegar leeches the calcium from the bones, and makes your stock an excellent non-dairy source of the mineral.

WHY A DAILY BOWEL MOVEMENT IS
ESSENTIAL

When the bowels are not emptied daily, the faeces in the bowel cause toxic fluid and gas to invade the intestinal tract, digestive system, central nervous system, glandular structure, skin and breath.

If you don't empty the bowels daily, you'll experience heartburn, revolting bad breath, burping, possibly bleeding gums, mouth ulcers and cold sores. The skin will be cloudy, spotty, dull and puffy. The hair may look dull, be greasy and lifeless. The eyes are often dull and red, like a road map. Your head may be thick and heavy feeling, sometimes with appalling headaches and migraine. The brain chemistry can alter and leave you feeling anxious, depressed, frustrated, angry and moody. Sex becomes a turn-off – you feel uncomfortable with a full bowel, wind and gas. Irregular bowel movements can be a big contributing factor to any weight problem.

So please take stock of your digestive system and bowels. Make sure you get plenty of fibre-rich, whole foods, and as much water as you can drink. There is simply no alternative but to have a clean, clear bowel. Not convinced? Well equate the faeces in your bowel with some meat left on

a dish in the kitchen – left for twenty-four or forty-eight hours. How will it look and smell? Disgusting. And that is just how the faeces in your bowel would be.

The 'Perfect Stool': The 'perfect stool' should leave the body comfortably and fully, be fairly bulky and very light in weight; it should float in the toilet water! Adjust your fibre intake accordingly, more if the stool is hard, less if the stool is loose.

Other stools which can indicate trouble are as follows:

○ Pebbly stools show that your intestinal tract is not working freely. Check your nutrition and water intake.

○ Whitish stools can indicate signs of anaemia. Check with your doctor.

○ Slimey stools could indicate infection. Again, check with your doctor.

○ Blood in the stools *must* be checked with a doctor.

Constipation, which we went into in more detail in Chapter Five, is the result of a poor digestive system and improper nutrition. There are, however, several other reasons:

Embarrassment: Holistix has had many patients who have become constipated after marriage, or with a new lover, because they are embarrassed about making a smell in the bathroom or suffering flatulence in front of their partner. Fine to be sensitive – but not to be constipated. There are plenty of handbag-sized air fresheners around. Keep a disinfectant to throw into the loo. Remember, everyone is human and no different to you.

Travelling: Sitting for hours on a plane or in a car is a common cause of constipation. The pressure on the plane, a change of climate, food and time difference can cause the bowel to block. Don't forget to drink fresh mineral water, even more than usual, lay off alcohol and eat plenty of cooked fibre.

Taking Normacol at bedtime on the first night after any flight can be a good idea for any sufferers. Two teaspoons of Normacol will soften the contents of the bowel, which will then be easier to pass.

When having a bowel movement, squeeze

your buttocks together on the loo, as you start to feel the movement on its way out. This will mould the faeces into a more comfortable shape to expel.

The alternative to Normacol is muesli – eat muesli with yoghurt and fruit for breakfast, and for dessert after dinner. Pears and kiwi fruit are also excellent.

Hospitals: After surgery it is important to move your bowels. Two difficulties arise: one, the tender tummy, and two, constipation from lying in bed. I believe you have to take responsibility for this as too often in hospital the matter is ignored. Ask for Normacol at night, as soon as you are able to drink and eat light food after surgery. In the morning ask for a glycerine suppository to ease and speed the process.

Whilst cleaning out your system, you may find that your body reacts in some interesting and unusual ways to the new foods, but only for a limited period of time. Your bowel movements may become a mixture of diarrhoea and constipation, you may suffer flatulence, your skin may be a little problematic, and your energy levels will be erratic. This is completely normal. Your body's attempt to rid itself of toxins (the residue of unhealthy eating) will often manifest itself in digestive or skin problems. Think of it as a complete purge.

To help you on to the bedpan, use your elbows, hands and heels to lift the body into a comfortable position. Try to relax! Breathe in and out deeply, and relax the anus. If you are able to sit on a loo, squeeze the buttocks together, take your time and only push gently. Make sure you're drinking plenty of water.

Pregnancy: At this time, you should be even more aware of keeping your bowels clear, of drinking water and having enough fibre. As you advance in pregnancy, the baby drops lower in the uterus, squeezing the intestines, and constipation can occur. Take extra fibre in your diet rather than laxatives. You don't want to endanger the baby by a sudden, harsh pushing bowel movement. If there are any problems at all with this, cranial osteopathy is very effective.

Stress: Stress and worry can cause the body to tense, the system to become distended, the muscles to tighten around the anus, and the bowel to become blocked. This can become habitual and very uncomfortable. Plenty of exercise, fresh air and healthy food will help, plus time for relaxation. Make a decision to make the effort not to suffer with constipation.

Anxiety: Anxiety plays havoc with the bowels, and can cause huge amounts of flatulence (wind) that can be excruciatingly painful. The best way to deal with the pain is to lie on your tummy and breathe deeply into the stomach. The muscles will unknot and the wind should gradually move down and be expelled through the anus.

Fear: When there has been a long history of constipation it is important to recognize the underlying cause. Abuse in childhood leaves conscious or subconscious fear in the mind; and the victim needs counselling. Once fear is expressed, the problem can be solved.

Children are often nagged endlessly by an overanxious and demanding parent, made to sit on the potty or loo too long, threatened or told scary stories. This will remain in the child's mind and affect the behaviour of the bowel, sometimes for years or even a lifetime. Children are also punished for soiling a bed or not being able to control themselves at some time. Taken to extremes, these admonishments can leave lasting scars and lead to fear.

Louise

A young girl of twenty-four came to see us. Her bowels had started to block at thirteen years of age, and she was constipated still, her bowels moving twice a week. The movements were hard and painful. She assured me it was hereditary. Since her mother had the same problem, it must be fine! On further investigation, we found her mother was dominating and the girl had been painfully shy most of her life. More important, she had never experienced enough love or had enough attention as a child.

Her constipation ensured she received attention from her mother. It was a cry for help and love. Having been to a good Catholic school, sex was frightening and 'wrong' to her, so her relationships were poor, and the sex indifferent. Her skin was spotty, her breath was fetid, and she was allergic to fish.

She sorted out her nutrition and added cod liver oil to her diet. We put her on a short course of Normacol and glycerine suppositories. Within four to six weeks, her symptoms had disappeared. Her personality and her current relationship improved.

Her comment was: 'It's really good to have someone tell me what to do. Thank you.'

Constipation can cause haemorrhoids. Having to push and force a stool from the anus forces the blood into the mucous membranes and veins, causing swelling of the veins. A haemorrhoid is exactly the same as a varicose vein, but in the anal opening.

Haemorrhoids can lie inside and outside the anus. At times, they are very painful and extremely itchy and can bleed. We have not come across any treatment that has worked one hundred per cent, but they can be operated on or injected. You can bathe them in warm salt water, use comforting ointments and suppositories, which will help. Maintaining a free, clean bowel will be the best way to avoid them.

A 'fissure' is a tiny wound like an open cut or sore on the edge of the skin around the anus, painful in the extreme. With luck, a fissure can heal with immaculate hygiene and a healing cream. Often they need operating on, and cutting out. Not a pleasant job, but well worth doing to be rid of the awful discomfort. Stress and constipation are the main cause.

If none of the above reasons for constipation apply to you, or if you have dealt with one of the above and still have constipation, seek the advice of a medical and alternative practitioner as soon as possible.

Diarrhoea is also a frightening and debilitating experience. There are numerous causes of the condition, including the ingestion of a bacterial toxin, or sudden change in eating habits. But a sudden case of diarrhoea, with voluminous, watery stools in a previously healthy person, is nearly always due to infection.

The prevention of acute diarrhoea, by strict hygiene, is more effective than its treatment. One effective homoeopathic treatment is nux vomica. Antibiotics are of value *only* in prolonged illnesses, such as typhoid. It is important to keep up fluid intake in order to prevent dehydration.

Hygiene and bowels: You can never be too clean or too fussy. The anus, being the only point where solid excrement is rid from the body, must always be kept immaculately, spotlessly clean. Wash dirty hands before and after a bowel movement. Always wipe thoroughly from front to back. Wash with liquid gel in a bidet, or wipe until clear with 'Wet Ones', or use damp cotton wool. Dry well and wash your hands. Change pants or knickers at least daily; cotton are better than nylon. Make sure you wash the whole of the genital area at least twice daily.

Sweating and bowel problems: Inefficient bowels can cause profuse sweating, because of the build-up of toxic waste pushing back from the bowels into the body. Sweating normally during hot weather or physical exertion is healthy.

Sweating because of unclear bowels is not healthy: the smell is bad, the body is uncomfortable, and often the victim will feel unhappy and irritable.

A daily bowel movement *is* essential. If your excrement habits are unusual, or you are worried about them, try altering your diet, and drinking more water. Make a time for yourself each day when you'll have your daily bowel movement.

Never rush it: that's where fissures and tears come in. On the other hand, try not to read too much on the toilet, or sit around too long. Your intestinal muscles will become lazy, and possibly inactive.

Your whole body will reflect the benefits of healthy bowel movements – with its toxins released daily, the body can get on with keeping fit, fighting disease and the good things in life.

WATER

Water flushes the kidneys and washes the bladder, cleaning away acidity and infection. Medically, the water literally washes away the contingent impurities, regulating the concentration of salts and the acid balance of the blood, excreting all the *waste* products. Lack of water causes the kidneys *stress*. They must have a constant supply of water to wash away the wastes, infections, germs and acid deposits, in order to keep the bladder clean, fresh and comfortable.

Drinking: One to two litres of still mineral water or filtered water a day is *essential*. Still and filtered water is pure, and free of salt and impurities. Gassy water has too much sodium (salt), and tap water, apart from tasting foul, is recycled ten times in England (although not in Scotland). Carbonated water can create burping and flatulence.

How the bladder works: The bladder is the reservoir for urine. It is the kidneys that excrete the urine, and the ureter conveys the urine from the kidney to the bladder. The urethra is a canal passing from the neck of the bladder to the external opening.

Passing urine: There are many reasons for frequency, which are listed here so you can recognize the cause of your discomfort and learn how to prevent it.

○ *Stress and tension*: Frequency is often linked to the sympathetic nervous system. Stress, tension, anger, upset, depression and fear all tend to increase the urge to empty the bladder. The impulses are sent from the brain and trigger off the muscles. The source of the tension needs to be addressed.

○ *Overweight*: A large, heavy body and bulging stomach, sitting heavily on a weak pelvis and bladder creates huge pressure on the bladder. To lose weight, see page 96.

○ *Pregnancy*: The more advanced, and heavy the baby is, the more pressure is placed on the bladder, creating a constant need to pee. Urinate frequently, whenever you feel the need. It's totally natural.

○ *Post natal*: After a Caesarean section or protracted birth, weakened muscles can mean a frequent need to pass water. Time and care are needed to restore the muscles and exercise will do this. See **Pelvic exercises**, page 148.

○ *Periods and Tampons*: Heavy periods and the use of tampons can place pressure on the bladder. We recommend not using tampons at night, or when bleeding is heavy.

○ *Sex*: Sex puts pressure on the bladder, too. It is useful to remember to pee before the fun begins.

○ *Constipation*: Constipation and blocked bowels are another cause. See **Why a daily bowel movement is essential**, page 115.

Leaking: All the above reasons also cause leaking. There are several other reasons, too. When the bladder is weak, it will leak when running, jumping, laughing, coughing, sneezing and crying. Some of the most common reasons for leaking are as follows:

○ *Surgery*: After most surgery to the stomach, the bladder is weak. Make sure your pelvic floor muscles are strong *before* you enter surgery, and practise control while in hospital – starting and stopping the flow with your muscles while urinating.

○ *Old age*: Older men and women have less control over their urination habits. Continue to exercise pelvic floor muscles, and avoid wearing tight clothes which would apply pressure to the bladder area.

Smell and colour: Beetroot, asparagus, alcohol and coffee, some medication, multi-vitamins, lack of water, poor nutrition or disease can account for strong-smelling urine. If, after increasing the quantity of water you drink, your urine is still bright yellow or strong-smelling, contact your doctor.

THE BASIS OF A HEALTHY EATING PLAN

Food: Quality Versus Quantity: As a general rule, aim to up the quality of the food in your diet, and reduce the quantity. But be sensible. Intake requirement varies with each individual. Look at what your scales tell you and make up your mind what is necessary and unnecessary for you. If your weight problem is really bad, cut out pasta, rice, bread, bananas and avocados, which, although nutritious for the normal person, cause problems for the overweight. Canned and fizzy drinks are full of gas, sugar and preservatives, which again build up toxins in the body. They are also notorious vitamin and mineral robbers.

Drink plenty of water – two litres a day is what you should aim for. Still mineral water maintains a natural alkaline balance in the body, by continuously flushing out the system, thereby preventing a build-up of toxins. In our view, this flushing-out process with pure water and proper breathing are two of the most important and, at the same time, simplest elements of healthy living. Except in Scotland, avoid drinking tap water.

ALCOHOL ADDICTION, ANOREXIA AND BULIMIA NERVOSA AND DEPRESSION

On the surface, there may not seem to be much of a connection between these conditions. The one thing they have in common is that sufferers tend to feel isolated and alone. If you fall into this category, the first thing you need to do is be honest with yourself, acknowledge that you have a problem and then ask for help. Do not be ashamed to share your problems – trying to handle it on your own does not work. There are many people in the same situation as you and they can learn from you just as much as you can from them. Obviously it is not that simple. If you suspect you have an eating disorder, or if you just want to talk, please see a counsellor. It cannot be stressed often enough how damaging

these illnesses can be. The destruction caused can affect your body function forever. There are numerous cases of anorexia victims never regaining their menstrual cycles, thereby precluding children. Bulimia victims have suffered from prematurely rotting teeth, from stomach acid, and if laxatives were abused, chronic diarrhoea – for life.

Think about what you want from life. If any of it requires good health – or even just health in general, get smart and talk to someone about your habits.

It's frightening, but oh, so much less frightening than death.

GOOD FOODS TO EAT

Vegetables (root, stem, leaf and sprouted): Try to ensure that thirty per cent of your total diet is made up of vegetables. Eat half of them raw, the other half cooked. Steamed vegetables are best (but don't boil them). Add interest to salads with low-cal dressings, and by sprinkling them with seeds, such as sunflower and pumpkin. Spend an hour or two getting to grips with some new vegetable recipes or salad combinations. Omit the ones you have found you are sensitive or allergic to.

Vegetables to eat regularly in unlimited amounts: Carrots, Parsnips, Turnips, Swede, Beetroot, Red and white cabbage, Brussels sprouts, Broccoli, Radishes, Cauliflower, Kale, Celery, Lettuce, Onions, Leeks, Garlic, Cress, Chicory, Fennel, Watercress, Sprouted seeds, French beans, Runner beans, Marrow, Courgettes, Cucumber

Vegetables to be eaten in moderation (these are acidic): Aubergines, Peppers, Potatoes (contain toxins – do not eat in large quantities), Tomatoes, Spinach, Rhubarb, Swiss chard (high oxalic-acid content), Mushrooms

Brown Rice or Millet: You can consume a minimum of two ounces of rice or millet daily. The weight given is the weight of the grain before cooking. These grains are essential for elimination. Always use organic, short-grain rice. These complex carbohydrates contain fibre, give a sustained energy release and act like blotting paper, absorbing toxins from your body.

If you are a person who thinks that losing weight means skipping meals, you are very very, dare I say it, wrong! *Your body hates it: it throws cravings at you, has to live on all the worst toxins to survive, makes you ratty, and you usually end up looking and feeling depleted. And what for? The sake of a few lost pounds that re-appear later? People have found that if they drink a large amount of water, spread evenly throughout the day, and eat very simple non-fattening food they will lose as much – and usually more – weight because the body has got something in it to work on. It can hoover up and chuck out the rubbish.*

Meat and Poultry: Don't be tempted to cut the protein content of your diet. Protein is necessary in order for the body to produce hormones, and build tissue. Meat is a very good source of protein, but so are nuts, pulses and dairy products. Try adding nuts to rice and vegetable dishes, or sesame seeds for a rich taste and interesting texture.

If you do eat meat, you should, however, exclude: Beef, Pork, All processed meats, such as sausages, Salami, Burgers, Pâté.

You may eat: Lamb, Liver (organic, once a week only), Free-range chicken, turkey and guinea fowl.

Try to buy organic meat; non-organic meats contain steroids, hormones and antibiotics. And look at the scare that 'Mad Cow Disease' gave us!

Fish and Seafood: Eat fish regularly. Not only is fish high in protein, but it is a rich source of Omega oils, which are essential to a healthy diet. Delicious choices are: Monkfish, Dover sole, Calamare (squid), Brill, Halibut

Try to eat fish broiled or steamed, as it ensures that vitamins, minerals and proteins are not leeched out in the cooking process. Try fish and seafood with garlic and lemon sauces.

If possible, use only fresh fish. Avoid fish that has been salted, cured or smoked, such as smoked salmon or mackerel. Particularly good to try, as they are particularly high in Omega-3 and linoleic oils, are: Fresh or frozen herring, Eel, Mackerel, Salmon, Sardines, Tuna, Cod roe.

Other fish you may include: Plaice, Haddock, Cod.

Note: Watch your seafood intake. Seafood is one of the most common food allergies, and can be particularly dangerous to allergy-prone people.

Fruits: Fruit is a powerful toxin eliminator. It is best digested when eaten between meals. You can also eat it at the beginning of a meal. Don't mix fruits, just eat one at a time. This way the fruits don't react against each other.

Some important tips to remember:
○ Fruit takes only fifteen minutes to digest. But when mixed with either protein or carbohydrates, which take up to four hours to digest, the fruit becomes trapped in the stomach and begins to putrify and ferment.
○ Avoid mixing citrus fruits and solids, or berries with other fruits, or bananas with other fruits.
○ Fruits are okay to eat with salads or vegetables, and we recommend soft fruit.
○ Always peel fruit before eating; the skins are full of bacteria and sprays, etc.

Cereals: The following may be included: Oats, Barley, Buckwheat, Corn on the cob, Sweetcorn.

Pulses: Try these pulses because they are easier to cook, and sprout best. Soak the beans overnight. Beans should always be included in a diet as they are the easiest protein to digest, and are enormously high in vitamins and minerals. Lentils, Chick peas, Mung beans, Dried peas, Black beans.

Seeds: The following seeds are excellent choices. Not only do they contain protein, but they are rich in 'healthy' fats, which act to rid the body of excess cholesterol. These seeds are best soaked overnight to protect from rancidity, and for easier digestion. Make sure nuts and seeds are well chewed, as otherwise they can pass through the system undigested. Try: Pumpkin seeds, Sunflower seeds, Sesame seeds, Pine kernels.

Soya Bean Milk: This may be used in moderation; for example, on porridge or muesli, or in drinks, in place of ordinary milk. Provamel, in the red carton, is one of the best-tasting soya milks. All good healthfood shops stock it. Do not buy soya milk containing salt or sugar.

Yoghurts: Live goat's and sheep's milk yoghurt may be included in the diet, as they are lighter on the system than cow's milk products. It is necessary to consume some dairy produce, as lactobacillus, which helps replenish bowel flora, can only be obtained in this manner. But do avoid dairy products produced from cow's milk.

SUPPLEMENTS

As vitamin and mineral supplements are not necesarily absorbed by the body, we do not advocate taking them without a trained nutritionist's or practitioner's advice. I can't stress enough that improving the quality of the food you eat is by far the best way of providing your body with what it needs. If you do have to take vitamins, you shouldn't have to take them for more than four to six weeks (unless, of course, you take antibiotics, or drink alcohol or smoke, which unnaturally and consistently drains the body). Never think that the more you take, the better.

Natural supplements which *are* useful include:
○ Evening primrose oil, particularly if you are on a low-fat diet or suffer from PMS;
○ Cod liver oil and other fish oils, which help to prevent heart disease and are good for adding protein to skin, nails, and hair;
○ Acidophilus and bifidus, which counteract the effects of antibiotics and re-establish the presence of beneficial flora in the intestinal tract;
○ Spirulina, an algae plankton which is rich in Vitamin B12, Vitamin E, betacarotene, Vitamin C, organic iron, chlorophyll and protein. Excellent for vegetarians, or anyone who feels they need extra supplementation;
○ Aloe vera juice is good for cleansing, healing and helping digestive troubles. It can be used externally as well.
○ Linseeds are rich in Omega-3 oil and a good bulking agent, instead of bran, to help bowel movements.

There are some excellent books available on vitamins and other supplements, which give plenty of information on the foods that are rich in different substances, and in what quantities they are recommended. If you are in any doubt it is always better to consult a qualified practitioner in the field.

TIPS FOR HEALTHY EATING

In order to change your nutritional habits, you have to take things day by day. You are changing and breaking habits of a lifetime, and trying to avoid using food and drink as comfort, as you might have done in the past. Here are some tips which will help to foster your will-power:
○ Never go shopping on an empty stomach, or when you feel cravings coming on.
○ Try to shop in places other than supermarkets; for instance, healthfood shops, greengrocers and fish mongers instead. This will help you to avoid the temptations that a supermarket offers.
○ When cutting down on foods to avoid, do it slowly, not cutting out everything at once. Doing it too quickly can put pressure on the body, and on your emotions.

○ Do splash out occasionally and have what you want. Just try to get back on the straight and narrow immediately afterwards.

○ Mono diets and fasts should not be undertaken without guidance from your doctor or a practitioner in the nutrition field. Never fast unless you have preceded the event with three weeks of perfect nutrition.

○ When having a healing crisis (for example, eliminating spots, catarrh, headaches, aches and pains), make sure you drink plenty of water, herb teas and eat only a bowl of plain boiled brown rice, with nothing added. You will feel much better when it has passed.

○ Try to have a little fat with your meals; this stops cravings and feelings of hunger as fat takes longer to break down. Good fats to consume are olive oil, seeds and nuts, avocados and bananas.

○ Enjoy your own cooking. Think about the benefits on both a physical and vanity level. If you are creative with nourishing food, you will be inspired to carry on.

○ When giving up tea and coffee, headaches are part of the withdrawal symptoms. The level of toxins in your body is probably still high, and your body will have to work to rid itself of them. Drink plenty of water to help your body in its struggle, and crush a piece of ginger with lemon and honey in lots of water. This will help.

○ Don't go into a meeting, confrontation or heavy personal communication with an overloaded stomach. The energy it takes to digest the food leaves your body and brain depleted and your thinking will be dulled. Stick to something light and eat at least one hour before the situation.

○ One of the most common causes of skin and weight problems is lack of sleep and daily trauma. In these situations the body tends to blow up and get very windy. Make sure you eat cooked vegetables, not raw, and you try to keep acid food, like fruit, to a minimum.

THE STARTER SHOPPING LIST

Pressed organic olive oil/Sainsbury's light olive oil/grapeseed oil

Tamari Sauce with blue label (wheat- and sugar-free); Miso (for making gravy)

Short-grain, organic brown rice (large bag)

Provamel soya milk

Organic porridge oats

Vegetarian cheeses

Free-range eggs

Pumpkin seeds

Sunflower seeds

Pine kernels

Sesame seeds

Chick peas

Millet

Herbal teas/dandelion root coffee

Sourdough bread

Vitaseig margarine

Organic corn chips

Organic rice cakes/rye cakes/sesame cakes/barley cakes

Live goat's milk yoghurt

Humous

Organic meats (Scotch beef, calves liver, lamb)

Free-range chicken (preferably organic)

Fish

Vegetables (fresh)

Fruit (fresh)

Two boxes of mineral water

Berritos corn chips

Yeast- and wheat-free Japanese rice crackers

Lemons

Onions

All seasonings except heavy spices and salt

Ingredients for homemade wheat- and sugar-free muesli:

Soya flakes, Barley flakes, Millet flakes, Rye flakes, Rice flakes, Sunflower seeds, Pumpkin seeds, Edible linseeds, Organic oats, Oat groats (a whole form of oats, like rice), Organic corn chips, Organic rice crispies

RICH SOURCES OF VITAMINS AND MINERALS IN HERBS AND FOOD

VITAMINS, MINERALS AND THEIR ROLES	HERBS	FOOD
Bromine		Watermelon, celery, melons
Calcium (Protects and builds bones and teeth, aids blood clotting and buffers acid in the stomach)	Comfrey, marestail, oatstraw, marshmallow, licorice, red clover, hawthorn berries	Sesame seeds, seaweeds, kale, turnips, almonds, soybeans, dandelion leaves, hazelnuts, horseradish, honey, lemons, mushrooms, lettuce, oatmeal, olives, onions, oranges, salmon, spinach, grapes, tomatoes whole wheat
Chlorine (Works to utilize fats and cholesterol, aids memory, aids in sending nerve impulses; helps liver)	Kelp	Tomatoes, celery, lettuce, spinach, sorrel, asparagus, beetroots, prunes, coconut, dill, cabbage, kale, parsnips, rhubarb, onions, celery, whey
Fluorine (Reduces tooth decay, anti-ageing to bones, curbs osteoporosis)		Barley, beetroots, brown rice, Brussels sprouts, cauliflower, egg yolk, garlic, goat's milk, leeks, oatmeal, red cabbage, rye, sauerkraut, spinach, watercress
Copper (Converts iron to haemoglobin, staves off anaemia)	Ephaedra	Peaches, turnips
Iodine (Gives energy, helps control body's metabolism, improves memory and alertness, essential for healthy hair, skin and teeth)	Black walnuts, Irish moss, bladderwrack, Iceland moss, kelp, dulse	Turnips, shellfish, onions, potatoes, dark berries, carrots, cabbage, dulse, endives, garlic, mushrooms, green kidney beans, egg yolk, celery
Iron (Aids growth, promotes immune system, prevents fatigue, essential for metabolism of B vitamins, reproduction of haemoglobin)	Red raspberries, yellow dock, kelp, nettle, dandelion, gentian	Wheat and rice (bran and germ), Brazil nuts, all greens, apples, raisins, grapes, walnuts, dill, dandelion leaves, chives, pumpkin, squash, plums, pineapple, sesame seeds
Manganese (Needed for normal bone structure, important for thyroid gland's hormone production, important for digestion and muscle reflexes, reduces tension and improves memory)	Comfrey, cramp bark, uva ursi, gravel root, oatstraw	Apples, peaches, rye, turnips
Magnesium (Essential for nerve and muscle functioning, known as anti-stress mineral, improves cardio-vascular system)	Valerian, kelp, dandelion	Wheat (bran and germ), whole oats, walnuts, almonds, rice, sorrel, rye, cashews, cabbage, okra, oats, dill, aubergine, pecans, oranges, celery
Potassium (Regulates body's water balance, regulates nerve and muscle function, helps dispose of body waste, aids in allergy treatment)	Kelp, dulse, Irish moss	Soybeans, bananas, cayenne pepper, artichokes, asparagus, cauliflower, cucumber, kale, grapefruit, radishes, sorrel, tomatoes, watercress, beans, peas
Selenium (anti-oxidant, preventing or slowing down ageing, important for prostate glands in males, prevents skin conditions, neutralizes carcinogens)		Wheatgerm, bran, tuna, onions, broccoli, tomatoes, shellfish
Silica (Needed for strong tissues, such as arteries, tendons, skin, eyes and cartilage)	Marestail, oatstraw	Lettuce, parsnips, asparagus, beetroots, horseradish, oats, rice, radishes, sunflower seeds, most cereals, all fruits, dandelion, greens
Sodium (Essential for normal growth, aids in preventing sunstroke, helps nerves and muscles function)	Kelp, seaweed, marigold, bladderwrack, Irish moss	Olives, cayenne pepper, dulse, apricots, barley, currants, figs, dates, eggs, horseradish, lentils, oats, red cabbage, strawberries, turnips

VITAMINS, MINERALS AND THEIR ROLES	HERBS	FOOD
Sulphur (Tones up skin and hair, helps fight bacterial infection, aids liver, part of tissue-building amino acids)	Garlic, kelp, black cohosh, dandelion	Onion, watercress, asparagus, Brussels sprouts, carrots, coconut, cucumber, garlic, figs, egg yolk, greens, kale, okra, parsnips, potatoes, spinach, strawberries, turnips
Phosphorous (Formation of bones and teeth, present in every body cell, assimilates niacin, needed for nerve impulse transfer, essential for kidney function)	Kelp	Rice and wheat (bran and germ), pumpkin seeds, squash seeds, sunflower seeds, sesame seeds, brazil nuts, blueberries, fish, kale, mustard seed, radishes, aubergine, leek bulbs, rhubarb, cauliflower, prunes, seafood, spinach, walnuts, watercress
Zinc (Accelerates healing, prevents infertility, helps prevent prostate problems, promotes growth and mental alertness, decreases cholesterol deposits, helps in formation of insulin, maintains cells and enzymes, important to protein synthesis)	Red raspberry, eyebright, alfalfa, uva ursi, slippery elm, hydrangea, cramp bark, echinacea, yellow dock	Apricots, peaches, nectarines, oysters, wheatgerm, cocoa, mustard seeds, pumpkin seeds, brewer's yeast, eggs
Vitamin A (Counteracts night blindness, builds resistance to respiratory infections, promotes growth of teeth, bones, hair and gums, removes age spots, aids immune system)	Alfalfa, oatstraw, dock	Carrots, mustard greens, asparagus, cayenne pepper, dandelion greens, sorrel, carrots, kale, spinach, cress, sweet potatoes, parsley, apples, garlic, ginger, papaya, rye, high-coloured fruits and vegetables
Vitamin B1 (Thiamine) (Promotes growth, aids digestion, improves mental attitude, helps nervous system, helps prevent stress)	Oatstraw, red clover, alfalfa	Rice bran, wheatgerm, sunflower seed, sesame seed, apples, garlic, ginger, papaya, turnips, rye, peanuts, oatmeal
Vitamin B2 (Riboflavin) (Aids in growth and reproduction, promotes hair, skin and nail growth, helps eyesight, helps prevent stress)	Alfalfa, oatstraw, red clover	Hot red peppers, almonds, wheatgerm, millet, apples, garlic, ginger, rye, leafy green vegetables, fish, eggs, yeast, cheese, liver, kidney
Vitamin B3 (Niacin) (Essential for sex hormones, increases energy, aids nervous system, helps digestion, prevents migraines, reduces cholesterol and bad breath)	Alfalfa, red clover	Apples, garlic, ginger, onions, papaya, parsley, rye, turnips, watercress, wheat
Vitamin B5 (Pantothenic Acid) (Aids in healing wounds, fights infection, strengthens immune system, increases energy, important for conversion of fat and sugar to energy, builds cells, necessary for adrenal glands)	Barberry	Rye, turnips, garlic, papayas, parsley
Choline (Assimilates cholesterol, aids nervous system, increases memory, helps liver)	Dandelion	Parsley, turnips, leafy green vegetables, liver, brain, heart, egg yolks, wheatgerm
Vitamin B12 (Cobalamin) (Forms and regenerates red blood cells, increases energy, improves concentration, maintains nervous system)	Alfalfa, comfrey, red clover	Rye, sprouted seeds, legumes, eggs, kidney, liver, milk
Vitamin B17 (Amygdalin) (Purported to control cancer)		Apricots, peach seeds, apples, cherries, plums and nectarines
NB: Brewer's yeast and other yeast cultures contain all B vitamins, as do spirulina, and molasses.		

VITAMINS, MINERALS AND THEIR ROLES	HERBS	FOOD
Vitamin C (Ascorbic Acid) (Helps body absorb calcium, helps form collagen, heals wounds, decreases cholesterol, prevents blood clots, prevents scurvy and gum disease, reduces effects of allergens, aids immune system)	Alfalfa, barberry, hawthorn berry, marigold, rosehip	Oranges, apples, watercress, garlic, onions, turnips, cayenne, sweet red pepper, blackcurrants, parsley, walnuts, lemons, green leafy vegetables, tomatoes, cauliflower, potatoes, sweet potatoes
Vitamin D (Prevents rickets, essential for calcium and phosphorous utilization, assimilates Vitamin A, necessary for strong teeth and bones, can help prevent colds)	Alfalfa, fenugreek	Apples, watercress, fish liver oils, tuna, milk, salmon, herring, sardines
Vitamin E (Anti-oxidant, anti-coagulant, anti-ageing, energy-giving, prevents and dissolves blood clots, alleviates fatigue, aids in prevention of miscarriage, protects lungs)	Alfalfa, flaxseed, marigold, peppermint, rosehip	Apples, parsley, rye, wheatgerm, watercress, whole wheat, soyabeans, broccoli, Brussels sprouts, spinach, vegetable oils, eggs, leafy greens
Vitamin F (Promotes healthy skin, hair, aids in preventing cholesterol deposits, combats heart disease, prevents skin disease)	Red clover, evening primrose, borage	Garlic, vegetable oils, wheatgerm, linseed, sunflower, safflower, soya beans, walnuts, peanuts, avocados
Vitamin K (Prevents internal bleeding, promotes blood clotting)	Alfalfa, oatstraw, kelp	Apricots, garlic, yoghurt, fish liver oils, leafy green vegetables, soya beans
Vitamin P (Strengthens capillary walls, helps immune system, aids in preventing bleeding gums, increases effectiveness of Vitamin C)	Oatstraw, rosehip	Buckwheat, the white skin on citrus fruit, apricots, blackberries, cherries

The snack pack: If you're a nibbler and are used to biscuits or chocolates, here is an idea for a box of nibbles which you should probably have with you at work:

- Pumpkin seeds, sunflower seeds and pine kernels (high in calories);
- Chopped carrots, celery, courgettes, cucumber and radishes;
- Rice cakes, oat cakes, rye cakes and sesame cakes;
- Japanese rice crackers (with no yeast, wheat or salt); and
- Berritos (organic corn chips with no added salt).

The going away pack: If you're going away for a few days, then you should try to take a few basics with you. The snack pack is a must, but you may want to add the following:

Organic porridge oats, Soya milk, Manna bread, Lemon and garlic dressing, Vitaseig margarine, Herbal tea

This way you can have exactly what you would want for breakfast and you've got plenty on which to nibble throughout the day. If you're eating out a lot for lunch and dinner, and you let the waiter know your requirements, you shouldn't have any problems eating well.

That is about everything for you to start with. The important thing is to play with the foods, experiment with tastes, make up sauces, try different ways of cooking vegetables, and don't always have chicken – eat fish as well. Also, you must get yourself organized with the food – planning, preparing, and easy packaging will make it a lot easier for you to stick to. If you can afford to, you may like to think about getting someone in once a week to cook some food for you, or, alternatively, set aside some time at the weekend to really get into cooking.

Whatever you do, it's important that you make this work for you. Eating should always be a pleasure as well as a necessity, so it may be that you need to buy some nice tableware – or a decent tray, if you're someone who never uses the table – some new saucepans, knives or utensils, or just an apron and the cookbooks.

The basics on the shopping list will provide you with a wide variety of ideas, tastes and textures, and don't be afraid to experiment. As long as you are careful to read ingredient labels, you should be able to discover all kinds of foods that are tasty and nutritional. And if you come across any real goodies, let me know!

BREAKFAST SUGGESTIONS

- Muesli (wheat free) and soya milk with chopped melon or pear.
- Oat porridge with water and soya milk.
- Eggs – scrambled, poached or boiled with gluten-free bread, or salt-free rice cakes.
- Fresh pears, melons and/or nectarines.
- Live goat's milk yoghurt sprinkled with sesame seeds, or a selection of nuts and dried fruit.
- Scottish oat cakes with organic peanut butter.
- Grilled tomatoes with basil on toasted gluten-free bread
- Grilled grapefruit halves, soaked in fresh cherry or raspberry juice, and topped with toasted walnuts.
- Steamed vegetables with cashews and rice cakes.
- An action-packed breakfast could consist of half an avocado, sliced, with a banana and almonds.

STARTER SUGGESTIONS

- Homemade soups, based on vegetable or chicken stock.
- Clear consommé.
- Melon, topped with toasted sesame seeds.
- Fresh raspberries on ice.
- Puréed mackerel, with garlic, green onions and a dash of plain live yoghurt, served with oat cakes.
- Organic corn chips, topped with chopped tomatoes, basil, green pepper and grated goat's milk cheese.
- Humous with oatcakes or organic rice cakes.

- A light, brown rice and crisp vegetable salad.
- Asparagus, puréed with one chopped tomato, one crushed clove of garlic, ½ teaspoon of chili powder, ½ cup of plain live yoghurt, one small chopped onion and a low fat soft vegetarian cheese. Instant, low-cal and healthy guacamole! Serve with organic corn chips.

Vegetarian: A mixture of vegetables which can be steamed, boiled slightly, baked, casseroled, or eaten raw, is always a satisfying meal. Or try some of the following.

- Baby sweetcorn with carrots, marrow, green beans and cauliflower, lightly tossed in vitaseig margarine and black pepper, with parsley sprinkled on top.
- Mashed swede, turnip, celeriac and vitaseig margarine with lemon.
- Lightly sauté finely chopped onion or celery in olive oil, and add to any vegetable dish to really add flavour.
- Season prepared vegetables with ruthmol and black pepper. Sauté an onion until golden, add a handful of celery, yellow or green pepper, and sauté until slightly soft. Then add to the other vegetables and cook slowly by either baking or steaming.
- Make creamed potatoes using vitaseig margarine and soya milk. Season with herbs and black pepper.
- Try roasting turnips, parsnips and large carrots instead of potatoes.
- Grill tomatoes, and season with a sprinkling of goat's milk cheese, toasted pine kernels and oregano.
- Stuff green peppers with a mixture of goat's milk cheese, sunflower seeds, celery, tomatoes, onions and organic rice. Grill and top with a mixture of toasted sunflower seeds and thyme.
- Bake leeks, tomatoes, courgettes, aubergines, mushrooms and pepper in freshly squeezed tomato juice. Season with oregano, basil and thyme, and top with grated goat's milk cheese.
- Mix pumpkin seeds, tomatoes, sunflower seeds, hazelnuts, onions, peppers and

If you are a craver of fats or sugars, especially when your energy is low, or for women around menstruation, split your big main meals into five or six small meals. This way you don't end up picking or gorging yourself on all the worst foods. Make sure you pick the tastes you want and you should find this satisfies any blood-sugar lows and cravings that might crop up.

sesame seeds with one egg, a teaspoon of vitaseig margarine and one cup of gluten-free bread crumbs. Season to taste with black pepper, garlic, and herbs. Bake for 45 minutes in a moderately hot oven, for a delicious nut roast.

Rice dishes: Rice is an important part of any diet. Not only is it low in calories, but brown rice is a rich source of iron, phosphorus and Vitamin B. Make sure you always wash rice first.

- ○ Boil garlic and olive oil quickly, and then add rice and boil. Try adding celery for extra flavour and fibre.
- ○ Always keep a large bowl of rice on hand, you never known when you'll need a fibre-fix! Rice is delicious hot or cold.
- ○ Try using cauliflower to flavour rice.
- ○ Fresh chillis add colour and spice to any rice dish.
- ○ Add raisins, seeds and tartari to rice.

Non-vegetarian: when eating chicken or fish, make sure you don't eat the skin. Remember that the white parts of poultry and fish are always the least fattening.

- ○ Marinate chicken with garlic, onions and herbs, and grill or barbecue.
- ○ Try some Chinese recipes for chicken; the Chinese are renowned for their inventive use of vegetables and chicken.
- ○ Chicken, hot or cold, combines well with any fruit. Try a cold chicken salad garnished with grapes and kiwi fruit.
- ○ Slowly cook chicken with vegetables and stock for a delicious chicken casserole.
- ○ Grill chicken, pour over yoghurt and let cool. A delicious alternative to chicken salad. Try adding fruit for flavour.
- ○ Make a sauce of tomatoes, basil and garlic, and pour over grilled chicken. Grill again for a few minutes and serve with rice and vegetables.
- ○ Marinate fish in fresh herbs and lemon juice, then grill.
- ○ Try substituting fish for chicken in any of the above dishes.
- ○ Steam fish with a cup of white wine – the toxins, alcohol and calories evaporate, leaving a light, subtle flavour.
- ○ Cook cod or any white fish in freshly squeezed orange juice. Delicious!

DESSERT SUGGESTIONS

- ○ Low-fat fruit yoghurt, sprinkled with toasted almonds.
- ○ Fresh fruit, marinaded in raspberry juice and fresh angelica.
- ○ Grilled Scotch oatcakes topped by a tiny amount of vitasieg margarine and cinammon.
- ○ Try freezing any fresh fruit juice, and serve as an ice lollie.
- ○ Beat an egg white until frothy, and fold in a container of low-fat fresh fruit yoghurt. Add finely chopped fresh fruit, and violà, a creamy mousse.
- ○ Fresh strawberries, served with a sprinkling of carob and live strawberry yoghurt.
- ○ Live goat's milk yoghurt, whipped with a beaten egg white, three tablespoons of dandelion root coffee mixed with one tablespoon of hot water, ½ teaspoon of vanilla essence and grated carob. A delicious café au lait treat.

Carole Caplin

When I was a child, I was very fussy about food. I hated vegetables, fruit and fish; all I liked was chocolate, red and white meat, junk food and spaghetti bolognese.

When I went away to school, I got into toast, dairy products, fatty foods and chocolate in a big way. I can't ever remember being taught anything about food or nutrition. All I can remember are those horrible school dinners.

When I came back to London, I would skip breakfast at home, and have a doughnut and an iced bun instead on the way to school. This started at the age of thirteen and was to set a precedent for the next ten years. Between the ages of thirteen and seventeen my lunch consisted of cheese rolls with piccallili sauce, crisps, chips with vinegar, sausages, or sausage rolls and sweets.

I did enjoy home-cooked food, but mainly things like potatoes and meat. This went on until the age of seventeen, and when I was on the road dancing and modelling, many meals were in greasy spoons or motorway restaurants. So far, so good – I never put on weight and I never suffered from spots. The trouble started when I was in my twenties; I was in selling and marketing, and dabbling in the recording side of the music business. During my early twenties, breakfast consisted of toast and jam, bacon, sausage rolls, crunchy nut cornflakes, a pint of milk, and chocolate bars.

Mid-morning would see the beginning of my eating approximately forty chocolate digestive biscuits a day, another couple of pints of milk, several chocolate bars, interspersed with cheese and onion crisps, and Big Macs with chips and chocolate milkshakes. I would finish the day with a Vietnamese or Chinese meal.

Sunday mornings with my newspaper, I would order a Dime bar, a Flake, a Crunchie and two packs of cheese and onion crisps to be delivered. Needless to say, I was completely addicted not only to less than nutritious food, but also to an extraordinary amount of chocolate. At the age of twenty-three, my body had gone to pot. I put on two and a half stone, I was riddled from my calves up to my buttocks in cellulite, I suffered from one minor illness after another, my skin erupted in teenage-like spots, the roots of my hair were constantly greasy and it stopped growing, and I contracted a bad case of candida albicans.

I was constantly tired, bloated, bad-tempered and spotty. I went to doctors and gynaecologists who gave me antibiotics, which made my condition worse.

Vanity was getting the better of me – my real bugbear was my weight – so I cheated and took high-dosage slimming drugs. I lost some weight, still felt lousy, and put it back on again. I didn't bother trying any diets because by this time, I was addicted to sugar in all forms and to heavy fats. I eventually started on the route of alternative medicine, learning bits and pieces here and there, attaining some success with homoeopathic medicine. But, of course, I didn't address my nutrition, and so everything would come back again.

Eventually, I was tested for various allergies, and when I found out what they were, I did make an effort to give up the problem foods. Until it came to chocolate and dairy products. I was given a talking to about the future consequences of continuing to eat those things, so I stopped; but by then the damage had gone too far. I still didn't address my nutrition, I still didn't bother to find out what I had actually done to my body, so I continued to have months of good spells, which meant being less spotty and a bit more energetic. But nothing really changed. Then I would have other periods where I would crash right down again. I kept travelling the alternative route, trying to find short-cuts and tricks to bypass the food issue.

After four years of trying various practitioners, I visited a nutritionist by the name of Denise Sedar. By this time, I had found out everything about allergies and was worried enough to avoid eating any allergens. Denise taught me a lot about food, and picked up on my complete lack of knowledge, laziness and fear around the whole issue.

Amongst the many things that I learned from her – along with certain conclusions I have come to myself – was that I had treated my body so badly that my whole digestive system was unable to cope, my body's ability to break down foods was on a very low par, and my organs were weak.

I had developed such a weakness in all these areas that for six months I had to go on a very strict rota of foods that I could and could not have. Through that, I did a complete about-face. I investigated every alternative form of food that was safe for me, and others like me, to have. I did an enormous amount of research into what was available organically, where all the substitutes were available from, tried hundreds of recipes, discovered seeds and pulses, how to make sauces, and how to make food taste absolutely delicious.

Without exaggerating, from that day on I ate twice as much as I did when I was on junk food. And I went right down to my lowest 'natural' weight, got rid of the spots and cellulite, and now look a lot better than I have done for fifteen years.

I didn't find any of these changes easy. My main consideration was that I couldn't bear to have food that I disliked or that had no taste, so I asked some friends, Pete and Nancy, who always cooked wonderful dinners, with every ingredient healthy and nutritious, to show me what to do.

From there it's been fun, and I've never felt better in my life.

CONCLUSION

In **Staying Healthy** you will have been given ideas that will help define what health problems you really need to tackle. I have said that diets don't work, but there are certain different food philosophies that will appeal to each one of you. There is some marvellous information in the marketplace and I have recommended some books at the end of this book (see page 191). You can further experiment and understand about what works for you. However, what is common with a lot of these books is, of course, that they don't know you personally, so they may recommend that you eat and drink certain substances that actually don't agree with you. Make sure you adopt a regime to suit your body. The idea is that ultimately you reach a point where you can eat *anything* in moderation, but taking care to cut out the nasties to which your body reacts.

Whether or not this information is new or useful to you, you will find that you still have to contend with the incredible lethargy that follows your initial excitement at the thought of finding a miracle solution somewhere in this chapter.

No amount of cajoling, persuading or logic will change your outlook. You have to have a bigger purpose for losing or putting on weight, or becoming healthier than just looking or feeling better.

Your purpose for bothering to eat healthily has to encompass your whole life and what is particularly important to you. You also have to design your purpose to fuel all the different aspects of your life, love life, career, emotional wellbeing, relaxation, confidence, standards, children, friends, the whole lot. If you honed in on just one trigger point that could keep you in line, you may just change a personal pattern of a lifetime.

At the end of the day, the best way of eating is to have a cross-section of all the foods that are good for you. The key to nutrition is thinking carefully about what you eat, planning a day's meals so that all of the nutrients you require are covered, changing the habits of a lifetime, and genuinely wanting to make changes in the way you look, feel, act and see things.

Good nutrition is not always easy – to begin with. Once you get the ball rolling it becomes easier and easier, and much more fun! And when the compliments about your appearance and your cooking start pouring in, and when your skin, hair, teeth and nails become stronger and healthier, and when your health problems – headaches, thrush, candida, lethargy and stress – start fading away, there'll be no stopping you.

Good luck. Grab your shopping list and get started!

Whether we are overweight or not, most of us have an internal and external imbalance, symptomized by such things as bad breath, headaches, indigestion, irregular bowel movements, menstrual problems, bags under the eyes, flatulence, a weak bladder, back pain, physical and mental tension, skin problems, a body shape we are unhappy with, sagging skin, foot, teeth and gum problems, dull reflexes, bodily immobility, nervous tension, and so on. So a weight problem is just one symptom of this imbalance. The way to redress the balance in any of these areas is to maintain a way of eating throughout your life that will become the foundation for everything you want to achieve physically.

SEVEN

Exercise

THIS, WE ARE told, is the era of health and fitness boom. Yet, there are still a large majority of people who are either not exercising at all, or who are not satisfied with the results they are getting – whether they're from the exercise classes, the books or the videos they are using. And many of those who *are* exercising are not – as far as I am concerned – fit.

How fit, I wonder, are you? Take a look at the following questions. If you are doing vigorous, aerobic forms of exercise, they particularly apply to you:

○ Are you bulky and swollen-looking around your face, neck, stomach, pelvis, arms and legs?

○ Are you straight, lithe, graceful and strong, or are you bull-like, round-shouldered and heavy-footed?

○ How many of you can really stretch freely, straightening your legs without bending at the knee, at the same time as bending your body to your leg with a flat back and stomach, aligning yourself so that your body and leg are parallel, with both parts touching?

○ If you mirrored a simple choreographed dance, could you follow fluidly, not jerkily?

○ Are you losing the inches or the weight you want to lose?

○ For those of you who do very slow, methodical exercise, are you working enough on your stamina and strength?

○ Do you feel invigorated and alive? Are you learning how to increase your energy? Or are you laid-back and slow? Are your reflexes and responses quick?

○ Is your shape changing? Are you losing inches and unwanted flesh?

From time to time it is important to stop and consider whether the type of exercise you are doing is giving you the results you want. Grace, flexibility, excellent posture, a trim figure, stamina, strength and a sleek body, with no swelling or puffiness are the results of a sensible and successful exercise plan. If you do not have each and every one of these qualities, your exercise programme is insufficient or simply wrong for you.

EXERCISE: WHY BOTHER?

There are many people who ask me this question, and there are very many very good reasons why we should bother. But I do know how difficult it is to become disciplined enough to exercise regularly (I only started when a back injury left me no choice). First, you have to be committed to looking after yourself and your body. Second, you have to get yourself into your exercise gear and just start, no matter how lazy or uninterested you feel. Here are the reasons why.

We expect a lot from our bodies:

1. Our bodies are our form of self-expression. However, we often feel very uncomfortable on a physical level and, over time, move less and less, leaving very little space for self-expression.

2. We rely on them to give us the energy to get through life, to be successful, and to pull us through in a crisis.

3. We expect and like our bodies to sleep, to be able to relax and to let go of tension. Often, they are unable to do so.

4. We expect our bodies to function without question.

5. We draw on our bodies for sexual activity.

Yet, too often, we experience a feeling of clumsiness or fatigue.

EXERCISE: WHY WE SHOULD BOTHER!

Here are some of the numerous benefits you will notice when you exercise.

YOUR HEALTH

You will increase:
- ○ your circulation;
- ○ your stamina (and the capacity of your heart and lungs);
- ○ your flexibility; and
- ○ your energy levels.

You will become:
- ○ stronger (and help prevent the onset of osteoporosis – brittleness of the bones in later life);
- ○ more graceful;
- ○ better co-ordinated; and
- ○ better able to concentrate.

You will decrease:
- ○ depression;
- ○ tension (thereby experiencing fewer headaches, bad moods and fears); and
- ○ weakness (and no longer feel sloppy or awkward).

YOUR SHAPE

By standing correctly – as opposed to slouched and tensed with a hunched back, sticking-out bum and droopy bust – your shape will change immediately. Add to this, correct breathing and stretching to open out all the areas in the correct position, and you will find that your body pulls up like a zip.

It is vital to exercise when you are aiming to lose weight, in order to develop a firm new shape and to help shift nightmare nasties such as cellulite, and those affectionately-named 'love handles', the drooping flesh on the waist and hips.

YOUR EMOTIONAL WELLBEING

When you exercise regularly, you will find that you become better and better at being able to relax, by expending trapped energy (often trapped when you are holding in anger, fear and grief). By simply increasing your circulation, and breathing out tension, you will feel more in control of your emotions and better balanced. Your sleep will be deeper and more refreshing – something that all exercisers notice. And your face will lose its pinched look and its dull pallor. You would be surprised just how noticeable the expression on your face is to everyone but yourself!

YOUR CHILDREN'S HEALTH

When you develop an understanding of your own body, you will find that you are able to understand your children physically, and will be better able to spot when an ache or pain needs attention. You will be able to encourage them to exercise in a way that they can respond to.

I think there's enough here to find *something* worthwhile for you to be bothered enough to exercise! If not, please think again. Personally, the *thought* of exercise usually bores me silly. Yet when I do get on with it, I feel great afterwards, and I hold on to that memory in order to keep it up!

BODY EASE – AND UNEASE

If you don't feel comfortable with your body, take heart – millions of people don't. This feeling starts in childhood. At school there are two categories of people: those who are good at sport, and those who hate it because they feel they are not talented or co-ordinated enough, or simply because they can't be bothered.

Instead of being taught in school how to understand your body and the benefits of good posture and breathing, you are instructed to do certain sports at certain times of the year. There are no lessons to help those who are over-weight, less confident or unco-ordinated. There are many of us who leave school with a fear or revulsion of anything physical.

Unease with our bodies often takes hold during this period. Children are teased and called 'fatty' or 'skinny'. They are influenced by the opinions of other children as to what is 'unattractive' or 'abnormal'. So we begin to be self-conscious, and to adopt habits such as hanging our head to one side, hunching our backs or never really looking directly at someone when in conversation.

Some of us deal with our discomfort by adopting brash body language. I will never forget when I became aware of feeling very awkward. I was thirteen and walking down a street, when I noticed a whole lot of builders catcalling to some women further down the road. I became very self-conscious and nervous, and as I rushed by as quickly as I could, I tripped over the pavement, creating great laughter and comments of 'Have a nice trip!' After that, I imagined that all passing cars and pedestrians were staring at me, and always put on a bold front.

Our parents probably had little understanding of these problems; because their education was no different to ours many parents are not tuned into their children's weight or injury problems. I have worked with many people who have experienced.a back injury when younger, whether they knew it or not, which was not treated, or treated incorrectly. When exercising in later years, these people found that the complaint had worsened, and triggered a chain reaction, slowing down circulation in the area, which affected their muscles, blocked the flow of energy and, consequently, affected movement throughout their bodies.

Many people's attitudes to, and lack of understanding of, their bodies is astounding. I have been completely amazed at the high percentage of fifteen- to thirty-year-old men and women who are ravaged by cellulite, stretchmarks, rigid muscles, raised hips, twisted pelvises, weak knees and feet, poor stamina and inflexibility. There are very many thirty to sixty year olds who hold the firm belief that they are 'past it' because of the ageing process! I have seen countless people conquer their arthritis, aches, pains and moaning complaints of being too fragile, too fat, too old, too tired or too depressed to know that being 'past it' is a load of rubbish. Besides, 'past it' is too close to 'passing on' – and you're not dead yet!

If some of this starts you thinking, or takes you to the point where you can see that you are being plain lazy or stubborn, that's wonderful. If you are happy to deteriorate with each passing day, I will leave you to come up with excuses why you are right and I am wrong – and how I just don't understand your predicament. If this is your case, I will leave you with two last comments to ponder on.

Wouldn't it be great if you put the amount of energy it takes to argue about your limitations into actually doing something that is beneficial? It's up to you if you want to be 'right' about not being able to exercise. But remember, you really do have the option to give your body and your wellbeing the chance to heal and grow – and to discover a new lease of life. Still crossing your arms tightly, with a scowl on your face? Well, all I can say is that you are the one who is missing out.

Exercising is about making choices and getting on with it.

WHAT IS THE RIGHT KIND OF EXERCISE?

Before I started Holistix, I attended many different classes to see what was and what wasn't, being done. Not only was I appalled at the lack of checking for injuries or corrections to exercises, but frequently there were no safety checks for the overweight (and no letter from doctors giving the OK), and there were no explanations of the difficulties that people experience when performing particular movements. There were also no clues as to how to overcome those difficulties.

Personally, I felt embarrassed and uncomfortable, because no one welcomed me, and there always seemed to be a clique with the teacher at the front of the class, and I could not see properly or keep up. When the class had finished, I would skulk out with the rest of the skulkers, losing all enthusiasm for attending that class again. I am sure a lot of you have felt this way, but I want you to know that exercise can be different.

In exercise, thoroughness is the name of the game. The teacher must have the ability to spot physical difficulties, tension and fear. Exercises must be presented in such a way that someone who has difficulty performing a movement can be shown other ways of approaching the exercise in order to do it safely.

The right kind of exercise is exercise that has been developed for you, with your strengths and weaknesses in mind. Anonymity in a class, pain, discomfort, fear and confusion are *not* part of any successful exercise programme. In fact, I wouldn't call that exercise at all – torture would be a better word for it.

In the end, decisions about your health can only be yours. And we very often fail to see the significance of our decisions. Will you regret yours? Think about your long-term health, think about your future when you decide whether or not to exercise.

HOLISTIX EXERCISE

Holistix exercise is safe, thorough and effective. The exercises in this book, which are just some of the many we use in class, are all explained in depth, and can be adopted to suit your individual needs. They use postural and breathing techniques to ensure you get full benefit from each movement.

You won't be flinging your body around. We see clients who have tight muscles and blocked energy, as a result of pounding their bodies ruthlessly with fast and messy forms of exercise. That form of exercise is like trying to open a tin can without a tin opener. We believe that you can build your stamina and improve the capacity of your heart and lungs with breathing, stretching and toning exercises - combined with doing your favourite sports such as cycling, gentle jogging or swimming. I am not opposed to any form of exercise. I am opposed to someone being taught incorrectly and being accepted into any kind of strenuous exercise before they are ready. I believe it is essential to do a mixture of activities.

Holistix works to balance, strengthen and reshape the body. The exercises do require effort, but they are never exhausting if you do only what you can, and slowly build up. Instead of feeling tired or weak afterwards, you will feel invigorated and refreshed. Most importantly, however, you will notice the benefits after just a couple of sessions.

REVIEW YOUR BODY IMAGE

First, make a list of what you like about your body – and don't you dare be coy! Women, in particular, are very good at criticizing their

People are funny about exercise – we worry if we don't feel something, but when we do, we worry that there's something wrong.

bodies, but are not good at recognizing their assets. Then write a separate list of your dislikes: the areas you would like to work on, and whether you feel you need to improve your stamina, your co-ordination, flexibility and strength.

If you know one or more people you can trust to give you truthful feedback, ask for their opinions. This may provide some shocks – they may point out things they really like about you, which you have completely overlooked. Or they may mention something that you hadn't realized you did – like slouching, or hanging your head low.

If you really want to take it the distance, ask somebody to video you walking around a room wearing whatever you feel most comfortable in. Then sit down, take a deep breath, freeze-frame the picture on the television, and make your observations. Just the process of confronting your body image and your feelings of discomfort will help you to feel more relaxed with your body. However, do not become overcritical or focus just on the negative aspects.

NOTES ON KNEES AND BACKS

The knees are directly linked to the hips, and if your knees are stiff, you will overuse your hips to compensate. Eventually, your hips will then stiffen up, and this is what leads to immobility, and aches and pains in the lower back.

When bending and stretching out the knee in Holistix exercises, we lie on the floor, making sure our backs stay flat on the floor. We always ensure that our backs are not allowed to arch, and we encourage people to contract their spines, pulling their pelvises up off the floor, if necessary.

Bending and stretching the knee in this position really works on the hamstrings, which thereby works over the hips and knees. Their prime function is to move both the hips and knee joints. Basically, by stretching out any inherent tension in the hamstring, you increase flexibility and mobility in your knees and hips, thus relieving stress, and increasing movement in the lower back.

If you have had back or knee troubles in the

B reathing properly strengthens determination and helps you to face trying situations. Your nervous system will untie some knots – knots that give you headaches, spots, tension, and stomach aches.

past, pay especially close attention to your movements. Watch yourself in the mirror, notice what looks and feels right and wrong. Most importantly, however, *do not strain*. And as we discussed earlier, see your GP before beginning any exercise programme.

POINTERS BEFORE STARTING HOLISTIX EXERCISE

Check through the following to see if any of the categories apply to you:

- ○ You haven't exercised for a while, and you are feeling very stiff or immobile in areas such as the back or the knees;
- ○ You have been training with weights, Nautilus equipment, aerobics, or running;
- ○ You have a history of injury, whether it has or hasn't bothered you since it happened;
- ○ You suffer from a lot of tension in your shoulders, head and neck; or
- ○ You have regular or recurring aches and pains, trouble with breathing, or digestive problems.

If one or more of these apply to you, I would suggest you find a highly recommended, reputable osteopath. That doesn't mean someone who is the most expensive or well known in the area, it means someone who doesn't crack the same joint, time and time again, and who doesn't see you for a long stretch of time without giving you more than just relief between visits.

CONSULTING YOUR GP

After consulting an osteopath, check your weight and any minor, recurrent medical problems with your practitioner, before undertaking any exercise programme. Then you are free to carry out exercise with a clean bill of health. These checks are important, as they will build up your confidence in exercising effectively and safely.

PREPARING YOURSELF

If you don't bother to follow the above advice before or in the first week or two of exercising, you make the process ten times slower, with a chance of possible injuries. By not understanding the changes taking place, there is a greater chance of your becoming bored and giving up. That, to me, is just too demoralizing – you are worth more than that.

When you begin to exercise in a way that stretches and opens you up, you may come across certain sensations and difficulties. It is important that you know about these beforehand, so that they don't impede your enthusiasm, commitment and progress.

As with losing weight, everybody has different difficulties, and when it comes to exercise, sometimes you will feel that you are getting nowhere. You may even go as far as thinking you are getting worse. This is usually a sign of progress, because the muscles in the body are starting to realign and correct themselves, which also affects the surrounding ligaments and tendons. So your body will be in the process of healing and changing shape. Your circulation and metabolism will also begin to speed up, and become more fluid.

If you think of all the toxic substances that you regularly have been putting into your body over the years; of the exercise – in terms of using every muscle in your body – that you have not done in the past few years; of the antibiotics you have taken and the illnesses you have suffered; of the tension and pressures at work and at home that you have had; and, of all the other things that have not been working perfectly in your life, you may begin to understand that exercising is not going to be a piece of cake and that long-term results cannot occur overnight.

I am telling you this because we are our own worst critics and, because of that, tend to turn a blind eye to understanding certain factors, like the need for patience, consistency and keeping an eye open for all the possibilities that there are. Sometimes you are going to feel great. Sometimes you are not. The most important thing is to acknowledge the benefits you see and feel from working on yourself in this way. OK so far? Good. Now on to the nitty gritty.

WHAT TO WEAR

To be able to see your posture and body properly, you should wear a leotard that doesn't restrict movement and breathing, so avoid belts unless they are of loose elastic. Secondly, tights: if you are going to have bare feet, rather than wear shoes, wear stirruped or footless tights so you don't slip. Choose shoes in which your feet can move just as well as they do when they're bare. The most popular footwear is jazz shoes. They're like a ballet shoe with laces, and cover the front of the foot. Please don't wear heavy, cumbersome shoes like trainers. Leg warmers are also useful to keep the ankles and feet warm, which helps prevent cramping.

Please keep on hand some warm tracksuit bottoms and a top, to keep warm before and after exercising.

Men should wear a T-shirt and tracksuit bottoms or unrestricting shorts. No shoes.

IN THE CLASS

Firstly, looking at yourself in the mirror often is not an easy thing. It is really important to get used to doing this, so that you can keep an eye on whether you are in the correct position or not, and whether you are performing an exercise to the best of your ability. If you are in a class, it is important to check yourself against the teacher: this is known as mirroring. Scan his or her body while checking yours in between glances. Make sure you do this with the mirror and *not* by looking at the back of the teacher and then glancing down at your body.

When I ask people to stand in front of the mirror, I notice that very few look directly at the mirror, with a straight head. Often the head is tilted sideways or drooped downwards. So focus on keeping your head straight and keep checking it's still and straight, unless the exercise requires specific movement.

Secondly, whether or not you have worked on your breathing aerobically or with another form of exercise, you may, with correct breathing, feel dizzy or slightly sick. This is quite normal and occurs because your body is not used to receiving its full capacity of oxygen.

When participants start to breathe properly, followed by stretching and opening up the whole frame of the body, they have often noticed that they feel various emotions. Some people feel tearful or angry. This is perfectly normal. On a daily basis you build up tension and stress, at work and at home, without being aware of your body's capacity to store the impact (unless you are someone who gets things off your chest immediately, but even then a portion can remain inside). Breathing and exercising can sometimes bring it to the surface. Don't stop or run out of the room, should this happen, but give yourself permission to quietly go through the emotion and carry on. Whatever the emotion, if you do this it will pass quite quickly and you will actually feel surprisingly relieved and refreshed.

When you start exercising, there is one sensation that is experienced by the majority of people in the class. Whether you're working on your chest, shoulders or stomach areas, or just stretching your legs, you will notice that when you are new to an exercise, you will feel tension in your neck, head and shoulders every time.

There are a number of reasons for this:
1. Firstly, most people store their tension here;
2. Incorrect breathing adds more tension to that area (this will be explained in **Breathing**, on page 138); and
3. In general, you use your shoulders, neck and head more than any other area of the body, when exercising, especially when working on weaker areas, such as the stomach.

As we go through the exercises, I will talk you through the various tension points – how to recognize them, and how to release them.

There are hundreds of exercises that I could give you; however, I would need a separate book for that, so I am going to cover enough to give you a solid foundation to take you into exercise classes, other sports and the gym.

THE HOLISTIX EXERCISES

If you are consistent in doing the exercises and are taking the correct nutrition to back this up, your body will improve at its own natural pace. You have to work to get over beliefs like: 'I'll never be able to do this because I've never been able to before', and don't give yourself an unrealistic time limit, by when you believe you should be brilliant at performing each exercise.

Happily, your body will improve a lot quicker than your mind will ever give it credit for. You must pay special attention to having your feet, pelvis, back, shoulders, and head in the correct positions.

Last, but not least, what you *really* need is a good sense of humour and patience.

POSTURE

If you are in a class that does not correct your posture throughout, forget it! The risk of injury and of exercising incorrectly is just too great. By standing, and lying, in the correct position you are, in fact, using, pulling up and opening your muscles all the time.

Breathing and posture are the two most important elements in order to utilize the exercises properly. Because of incorrect posture and breathing, or for some people injuries, most of our bodies are out of alignment and stiff. So, the correct posture is a central point in making the exercises work for you in terms of your shape, while eliminating the risk of injury.

Here is an exercise to ensure better posture:

1. Make sure you have access to a full-length mirror.
2. Stand sideways to the mirror, feet and legs completely straight at the knee, about one and half feet apart. Bend your knees slightly. Put the back of one hand on the base of your spine and the other just

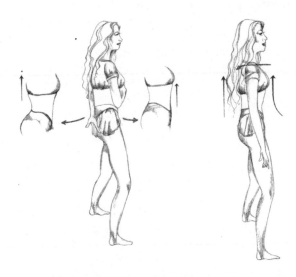

under your rib cage, on your pelvis.
3. Stick your bottom out and push your shoulders right back, creating an arch in your spine (make sure your knees are not bending inwards).
4. Gently push your pelvis forward using your hands to guide your upper body. Flatten out the arch in your back as much as you can, by pulling the ribcage backwards as your pelvis comes forward. Squeeze your buttocks tight as you push your pelvis forward.
5. Push your pelvis and bottom back again, sticking your bottom out, arching your back, and pushing your shoulders back and down.
6. And again, tighten your bottom and push your pelvis forward. Now stay in that position and drop your arms by your side.
7. Concentrating on the top part of your body, pull up through the body – first through the stomach then the rib cage and the chest.
8. Open the chest wide, allow your shoulders to pull back (not up) and drop them down towards the back of the room and floor. Now straighten your knees without elongating your neck, sticking your bottom out.
9. Your head should face forward, and your chin should be pulled comfortably closer to the neck. Look in the mirror. Clock the position, and truthfully let the whole lot fall back into your normal position (usually resembling a slouch!).
10. Now do the whole process again.

Hopefully, you will notice the difference in postures. Remember what it felt and looked like when you were standing erect. Concentrate on that feeling, and try the exercise whenever you feel yourself slouching.

Things to avoid: There are a number of natural, unconscious reactions your body might have. Check the following list to ensure you aren't slipping into these bad habits.

1. *Don't hold your breath – breathe normally.*
2. *Don't pull your stomach in – lifting it up, through standing correctly, will be enough.*
3. *Watch for your feet turning out. I want you to get used to your feet being absolutely straight, so they remain in line with your pelvic floor, especially at the toe, so that I can begin to help you straighten your upper legs and thigh muscles.*
4. *Check you don't overemphasize the pelvis forward. You'll know if you are doing this if the rest of your body is leaning backwards, as if someone had pushed you.*

BREATHING

Without proper breathing, exercise will have a limited effect. By consciously monitoring the way you breathe – at all times – your body will relax enough to open up, and allow exercise to do its job.

Go through the following exercise to test your breathing habits:

1. *Face the mirror, standing about a foot away. Stand in your natural position.*
2. *Take a deep breath in, and release. What do you notice?*
3. *Try it again, and this time watch your shoulders, chest and stomach. You may notice that your shoulders and chest rose upwards and that your stomach pulled in.*

Why is this not correct?

If you do this again, you will see that you are not filling your body fully with oxygen; you are actually drawing out the breath and creating more tension in the shoulders and neck by the lifting movement you are doing.

Little wonder that when we get nervous, upset or angry our tension gets worse, and we actually breathe less. Next time you're in a situation when you feel like this, notice how much you actually hold your breath (shoulders and chest raised) without releasing the air completely. This plays havoc with your digestion and circulation, often causing headaches and flatulence, and leading to lack of energy, constipation or diarrhoea. This wrong type of breathing, like bad posture, often stems from childhood when we learned to hold our breath against physical discomfort. It is related to being frightened, nervous, or in a stressful situation. Remember when you were told off about something? What was your reaction? In contrast to this, if you observe someone in bed when they're asleep, you'll notice that they breathe through the stomach. By breathing in this way your body will get the full amount of oxygen it needs. So, what we are doing is re-training ourselves to breathe properly, which in turn will help us to remain more relaxed. Now continue with the exercise:

4. *Face the mirror again, and check your posture. When you breathe in this time, make sure you breathe in through your nose and let the air out through your mouth.*

Secondly, put one hand at the top of your stomach, just under your solar plexus (the diaphragm area). This time, when you breathe in, aim to keep your shoulders and chest absolutely still and breathe the air into your stomach, causing your hand to move with the force of the air filling your stomach area.

5. *OK. Give it a go. Breathe in slowly, hold it and release slowly, pulling in the stomach. Usually the amount of movement when breathing in will be very small at first, but it will expand quite quickly with practice. Remember when breathing out to always release every last bit of air. We hold our breath often without knowing and this creates tension or flatulence.*

6. *Let's try it lying on the floor. Relax your body. Close your eyes, and repeat the process in exactly the same way as you did when standing. Do this for a good five minutes. It may take a while to get into the swing of it.*

Once you start practising this exercise, your body will click into the rhythm, and first time round you will probably notice that at the end of the session the room will brighten considerably. You may also start to yawn quite a bit. Don't worry, it's normal as you are feeding your body with increased oxygen. Practise at home or at the office and you'll find you will begin breathing correctly without even thinking about it.

WHY BREATHING IN THIS WAY IS SO IMPORTANT

1. Earlier, I mentioned that you tend to use your neck and shoulders to compensate for weakness in other areas. By breathing in the correct way, you can begin to eliminate this slowly but surely, enabling you to use the correct muscles in every exercise.

2. Breathing fully into your body alleviates tension throughout, and allows the circulation to flow better. This affects the results you can get from each exercise, and makes a huge difference in the speed at which you build your strength, stamina and flexibility in each and every exercise.

3. Breathing, especially breathing out in strenuous stamina and stretching exercises, helps to release pain. For example, if you bend over, taking your hands to the right ankle, bending your knee and relaxing your body onto your leg, breathing in, then stretching your leg straight, while *slowly* releasing the breath, you will ease the pain and stop the tension going into your neck and shoulders. Try it without breathing properly and you will find it is agony. This type of pain makes you resist an exercise, which makes the muscles rigid, and can lead to torn ligaments.

4. I'll let you into another secret: if done with the correct mixture of exercise, this type of breathing does just the same, if not more, for your heart and lungs as all that jumping around and screeching that is quite common in some aerobic classes. And you can avoid looking like a demented silly git doing it this way!

5. Breathing this way can calm nerves, upset and anger, and can help you to think straight, allowing your feelings and thoughts to come to the surface without sending you into a panic. Use this breathing exercise whenever you feel tense, angry or panicky.

6. Breathing properly strengthens determination and helps you face trying situations. Your nervous system will untie some knots – knots that give you headaches, spots, tension, stomach aches and so on

You must experiment with what's comfortable for you. Sometimes it will mean breathing deeply and slowly, in and out. Other times you will want to breathe normally – that's fine, just make sure you still breathe into your stomach and release the air fully. And holding the correct posture helps you do this with ease.

One last point to cover on breathing is that when you are confused about when to breathe in and when to breathe out in an exercise, you can work this out by executing the exercise slowly to see the point at which you personally feel the most strain or tension. At that point you must make sure you are expelling the air from the body. *Breathe in on the easiest part of the exercise and breathe out on the hardest part.*

A final note about posture and breathing: When you breathe, your upper ribs should move last. Your lower ribs should start the movement with the diaphragm. So, the diaphragm should contract, pushing down on the abdomen, which allows the tummy to push out. This gives you a bit of slack, then the lower ribs move. And the very last to move – if you're really breathing heavily – is the upper ribs.

But, of course, we are taught in reverse. Most women, especially of our generation, are taught to hold their tummies in, their bottoms in, and breathe from there. Men hold it in the chest, top of the arms and neck.

Think about the logistics of our posture, and the way a deep, proper breath feels. It makes sense, doesn't it? Aside from a natural, well-shaped abdomen, a fit and toned tummy will *not* stick way out when you breathe.

A NOTE ABOUT THE EXERCISES

You will work on specific areas. It is important to note, however, that every part of your body is being worked in each exercise, with special emphasis on a certain part.

Always ensure when standing that the backs of your knees are as straight as they can be, and that your shoulders are always dropping back and down. The hardest part is to get rid of the arch in your back.

CONTRACT AND EXPAND EXERCISE FOR THE RIBS, BACK, CHEST AND PELVIS

This exercise consolidates the work you have done on posture and breathing.

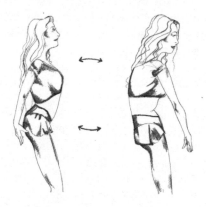

Standing correctly, breathe out. Bend your knees, arch your back, pull your shoulders back as much as possible, push your bum back, pull your arms back and contract, pushing your pelvis forward and contracting your shoulders forward and down, away from the ears. Really bend the back, and open and contract, relaxing the arms.

Repeat: *8 times. Do not make this movement with your elbows, just let your hands lead your body and do the movements fluidly and slowly. Don't jerk. Return to standing and shake your arms and legs.*

CHEST AND DIAPHRAGM EXERCISES

The first area we are going to work on concentrates both on improving posture and breathing, and opening up the ribcage, chest and bust, toning and lifting the torso.

When doing the following exercise, make sure that you use the bending action of your back, and the stretching/lifting action of your

ribcage, to make the best use of these parts of your body. When you do your stretch, remember to keep the pelvis tucked forward, as it can move out of position.

WARM UP (A)

Feet straight and wide apart, hands on shoulders, pelvis forward, pull stomach in to your back. Chin up, and breathe in, pulling the elbows right back, lifting and opening the ribcage, as far back as you can go. Elbows right up to the ceiling, lift your chin up, keep your bottom tight, and release the elbows forward and then down. Breathe out.

Repeat in the opposite direction. This time pull your elbows forward, bend the top of your back and pull the elbows up to the ceiling, stretching your torso even more (breathing in). Release the elbows back and down, breathing out.

Repeat: *8 times.*

WARM UP (B)

Same as above but with arms straight, stretch your fingertips. Pelvis should be forward, bottom tight, knees and feet straight. Keep the elbows straight, right the way through this exercise, and pull the arms up to the ceiling, breathing in, opening the chest, and lifting the chin. Pull your arms right the way back, keeping the elbows straight, and release your arms down, breathing out.

Repeat: *2 sets of 8 repetitions.*

Now do the same in the opposite direction, concentrating on opening the neck, chest and torso even more.

PUMP BREATHING

Clench your fists, rounding the backs of your hands. Bend the elbows, slightly. Open the arms back, punching two imaginary people with the backs of your fists, breathing out on each hit, and let the arms spring back (as though they are on pieces of elastic) across the chest.

Repeat: *5 sets of 8 repetitions.*

Keep the same bend all the way through. Don't straighten arms or have slack wrists. Also, don't hit back with the elbows, but use the fists and tops of the arms, taking the arms and elbows as far away from the side of your body as possible. Don't push your head forward in order to fling back your arms as far as they will go. Keep it straight.

SIDE STRETCHES (A)

Feet straight, press the pelvis forward. Open the chest, left arm behind your back, chin up and drop your head to the right, face slightly up to the ceiling. Your knees should be straight. Gently release over.

Hold your leg with the other hand, if necessary, pull the left shoulder back, and push, over to the side, relaxing your head and neck. Check that your pelvis is facing straight on and push gently. Pull up and over the other side.

Repeat: *2 sets of 8 repetitions, on each side.*

SIDE STRETCHES (B)

Pelvis forward, raise one arm up to the ceiling, your other arm on your leg. Knees straight, release over to the side and push for 8 counts, pushing through the hand. Pull up and repeat on the other side.

Repeat: *5 sets of 8 repetitions.*

OPENING OF THE ARMS, CHEST AND BACK

Feet straight, and about two feet apart, clasp your hands behind your back, checking that your fingers are entwined in the same way as mine.

Bend your knees, keeping them firmly pushed outwards, and arch your back evenly from your shoulders to your buttocks, so that you are not leaning too far forward with your upper body.

Now extend forward, tummy almost resting on the front of your thighs. Slowly drop your head and neck to the floor and let the base of your spine and bottom lift up high so that

you create a slide effect from the base of the spine to the head.

Without straightening your knees, pause, then – as your head drops closer to the ground, let your arms drop over your head and bounce from the hip, taking your hands closer to the floor.

Repeat: *bounce 8 times.*

Note: *I found this exercise impossible for ages. Just make sure you relax your neck – no tensing. Let the weight of your torso build the momentum for bouncing, and slowly you will open up, allowing you full flexibility.*

Now straighten your legs. Tighten your bum and slowly roll up, bringing your head up last.

If you have a bad back, relax, or do the next part very carefully and only go back a tiny bit; if not, push pelvis forward and gently pull shoulders down and back, tighten knees and slowly release back – only as far as you can. Gently come up and repeat the exercise again.

While repeating this exercise, those of you who want to can do the bouncing with straight legs. Advanced people: straighten out the back and torso as you do this exercise.

Repeat: *2 sets of 8 repetitions.*

COOL DOWN

Shake your arms and legs, and just relax. Notice how your body feels now that the chest and ribcage are more open; your breathing will be more regular too.

Depending on how relaxed or stressed you are, your body will always respond differently – sometimes your body will feel tighter than at other times.

BARRE EXERCISES

You can use a strong basin, banister, sturdy armchair or radiator for your barre – just as long as it will take your weight. I am going to concentrate on encouraging you to use your posture and breathing to open, stretch and strengthen your feet, calves, thighs, groin and lower back.

Then, to finish off you are going to stretch out the whole of your back, diaphragm and legs, concentrating on

beginning to restore mobility and flexibility to these areas.

Please do these exercises slowly, and start to notice when you are tensing your upper body, or if you are uncomfortable in any of the positions. Keep checking your position with mine, and follow the instructions carefully.

RISES FOR CALVES, THIGHS AND BUTTOCKS

Using a barre, wall, banister or radiator for support, bring your feet together, heels touching. Pelvis forward, tighten buttocks, pull up through your torso and chest. Shoulders should be back and down, relaxed, knees straight.

Keep head and chin facing straight, elongate your neck and pull up on to half point. Rise up and down without your heels touching the ground as shown below left.

Repeat: *2 times in this position.*

Repeat: *2 times, with feet turned out.*

Repeat: *2 times, with feet parallel.*

Repeat: *2 times again, with feet turned out and apart.*

Make sure you tighten bum, and relax your shoulders all the time.

You will really feel this, and have to watch you don't lift up through your shoulders. You will feel this in your calves at first, but eventually you will feel this deep in your bottom.

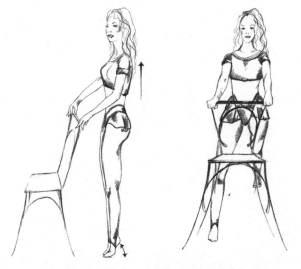

CALF STRETCH FACING BARRE OR WALL

Shake your legs and face the barre again. Body straight, hands on the barre, right foot forwards and left foot back slightly to the left of the right foot.

Both feet should be completely straight, body upright, head up, as shown above right.

Now bend the front knee and push from the pelvis forward. Keep back leg straight and back heel flat on the floor.

Push your left hip forward so that your pelvis is straight, and keep pushing, releasing tension in the back of the calf.

Bea

*A*lthough there was nothing wrong with Bea physically, she just felt that she wanted to do some exercise and get fit. She was a pretty frumpy, overweight lady, approaching her fifties and looking her age. Work had taken its toll on her – long hours and too much stress.

Her nutrition was OK, but there was definitely room for improvement. She ate a great deal of rare red meat and drank a couple of glasses of wine almost every day.

Mentally, she was very stable, fairly confident and enjoying her life. She was simply being a very normal, average middle-aged woman.

In her Consultation, we explained to her that being average wasn't the only option available. She had all the potential to be a beautiful, graceful, slim, elegant woman – if she wanted to – and that it would simply need her to take a good long look at herself and address certain areas.

When she came to class, she was quite convinced that she would never be able to do the exercises. (After all old women can't – can they?) But over the next few weeks she improved no end, constantly surprising herself.

Having seen a difference in this area, and the effect that the exercises were having on her body, she decided to go the whole way. She cut right down on her alcohol, cut out red meat, began eating fresh fruit and vegetables, and cut out the sweet, sugary desserts. Oh, and she replaced the strong coffee, which she practically used to mainline on, with herbal teas.

Most importantly, however, she was consistent both on her nutrition, and in her performance and attendance at class.

One and a half stone lighter, and one year older, she now looks ten years younger. Because her body and figure had changed, she bought new clothes. She opted for the more sophisticated look, as opposed to the matron-aunt look, changed the way she did her make-up, and finally emerged a new woman after a trip to the hairdresser. Her overall improvement was so inspiring I used her as one of the people in my exercise video.

Basically, if I look like her when I reach her age, I'll be delighted.

In time, extend the gap between your feet, as and when your body is ready.

Repeat: *1 set of 8 repetitions. Now change legs, and do another set of 8 repetitions.*

People with weak or damaged knees must be very careful in the next 3 exercises. Do only what you can, possibly only doing the second exercise to begin with, and remember to use your breathing. If you are worried in any way about strain you should consult an osteopath.

THIGH BENDS, INSTEP STRETCHES

This exercise strengthens posture at the base of the spine and pelvis. Do this exercise slowly, holding the barre with both hands, stopping when you want to.

Only do this sideways on, with one hand, when you feel absolutely confident about keeping your whole body in the correct position, particularly the pelvis and base of the spine.

Those with injured knees only bend an inch or so, building up slowly over a period of weeks.

Elbows relaxed, feet together, tighten your legs, buttocks tight, pelvis forward.

Pull stomach into the back, breathe slowly and continuously.

Lift rib cage and chest, shoulders pulled back and down, chin up and arms gently rounded out to the side.

Pull up on to half point and breathe in.

Slowly breathe out as you bend, keeping your pelvis forward and knees together, lift your heels as high as possible. Flatten out arch in your back as soon as you begin bending.

Check that your pelvis is forward, shoulders and chest relaxed and open, and breathe deeply into your stomach, gently pulling up through your pelvis, and breathing out at the same time.

Heels down, and again pull up and bend. Pelvis forward, breathe out and heels down.

Repeat: 4 on either side, and release.

Shake your arms and legs. That's a hard one, isn't it? It gets easier over time.

DEEP PLIÉS

This exercise strengthens the front of the thighs and stretches the inner thigh muscles.

Face the barre, body touching the barre, and feet wide apart and comfortably turned out. Pelvis forward, and breathe in to your stomach, relaxing your shoulders.

Bend your knees, breathing out as your body releases towards the floor. Keep your arms straight so that your shoulders and the top of your back are in a direct line with the base of your spine. Keep breathing in and out of your stomach slowly and deeply and stay there. Relax your shoulders.

You are now working on your groin and hips, so pull your knees back, and check you are not rolling your feet inwards. Keep opening your chest by lifting your torso and rib cage, and relax your shoulders completely back and down. Head up, stretch neck.

Now, breathe in and pull up, breathing out. Ease the hips out by moving your buttocks from side to side.

Repeat: 2 or 3 times more, bouncing gently and moving the pelvis carefully forward and back, and from side to side.

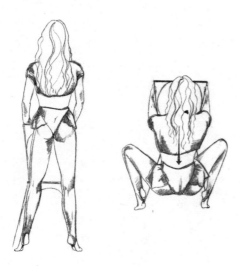

PLIÉS RAISED ON HALF POINT

Take the same position, except come away from the barre about 2 inches, and bring feet slightly closer together. Beginners: feet really close together.

Come up on to half point. Relax shoulders, and pull right up through the body. Breathe into your stomach, not your shoulders, breathe out.

Now breathe in again, and release down, keeping your pelvis tucked forwards, and the heels lifted high. Keep breathing and concentrate on relaxing your shoulders.

If your legs are shaking, do one of three things: bring feet closer together; relax position by letting heels drop; or, lift the

heels until they lock, then release, then lift, and so on.

Breathe in, pelvis forward and pull up, breathing out. Stay on half point, don't collapse! Focus on your breathing, release the tension in your neck and shoulders, tighten your bum and breathe in and release down, breathing out.

Don't overemphasize the pelvis forward in these two positions. Check your body against my position by checking it sideways into a mirror. If your pelvis is too far forward, push the base of the spine back, open the chest and slide your feet forward. Ensure your back is symmetrical from top to bottom, and your feet and knees are comfortable.

Repeat: 2 times. Shake your arms and legs.

BACK AND LEG EXERCISES

Now we are going to stretch all of that out and begin work on your spine, and the backs of your legs and knees.

Face the barre, legs 2 feet apart, feet straight. Now extend onto your barre (make sure it is not too high), arms and back completely straight, hands wide on the barre, stretching the shoulder blades and chest.

Keep your face parallel to the floor, but don't drop your

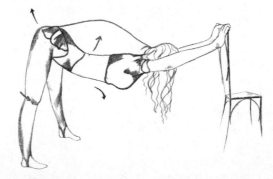

head. Make sure your feet are directly under your hips, not forward under your body.

Round your back, dropping your head, and now stretch through, arching your back by pushing your buttocks to the ceiling, and your chest to the floor.

Bend your knees and allow your back to open up even more. And round the back, hold it, and stretch.

Now straighten legs and move your bum from side to side.

Choose your own mixture of these movements, and add movements that you feel will release tension.

Repeat: 4 sets of repetitions.

Because of a curvature of the spine, and one leg being shorter than the other, I could not do this exercise at first and found it incredibly difficult. This did, however, do more to straighten my back than any other exercise.

Drop to the floor; if you have a mirror, turn around so that you can see the back of your bum and legs in the mirror.

Relax your knees, and let your weight go towards your toes, relaxing head and neck completely. Look at your buttocks and make sure they stay firmly in the middle.

As you progress, the base of your spine and your buttocks should be lifted as high as possible to the ceiling, and your chest should be dropped as low as possible toward the floor, creating a slide effect.

Straighten both legs, and now bend your right knee, body lying close to the inside of your thigh, as shown below left.

Take your hand to your right leg and hold your leg at the knee, calf or ankle, depending on how stiff you are.

Your body and head should now be on the inside of your leg, not lying on the outside of that leg.

Check your buttocks are evenly placed and in the middle, and keep checking this throughout the exercise.

Breathe in and stretch, breathing out, straightening the back of the knee as much as you can. Release, bending the knee. Repeat: 6 to 8 times each side, ending with a set of 8 continuous pushes on each leg, with knees straight.

Really use your breathing. Beginners: relax your back and chest. Just concentrate on the backs of your knees straightening as much as possible. Relax your head and neck as you progress. Concentrate on opening your chest and rib cage, and push from there with as flat a back as possible – or alternate between the two.

Now take your body to the middle of your legs, and bend your knees, your bottom to the ceiling, and your head and chest to the floor as in the second picture below left.

Grab hold of your knees, calves or ankles through the inside of your leg and hook your hands around the back of your leg in a comfortable position and relax the back and breathe in. Stretch, breathing out, and bend. Breathe in, relax and stretch.

Repeat: Hold it, release and repeat this 4 more times slowly and gently.

Now stretch again. Move bum from side to side and bend knees again, to release tension.

Stretch and push for the count of 8, with straight legs now.

Walk forward on the floor with your hands until most of your weight is resting on your hands, straighten your back and legs as much as possible.

Lift your heels off the floor, if this is really hard. Keep hands wide, and push your chest into the floor, and bum to the ceiling, keeping your back and elbows straight.

Repeat: Push for 2 sets of 8 repetitions.

Slowly walk back, bend your knees slightly and gently roll up, head last. Shake your arms and legs.

Don't worry if you stopped and started throughout,

that's perfectly normal. Remember to keep concentrating on straightening the back of your knees, while remaining in the correct positions.

Note: While doing any barre exercises, remember not to jerk the body. Stretch through, feeling all the muscles slowly opening up.

Well done on that one. It's a marathon exercise. No matter how hunched or bent you are you will get better in time. Remember there is no competition. The degree to which your body can move and stretch will improve all the time, only you might not register it as much as you register the difficulties and stiffness.

STRENGTHENING THE LUMBAR REGION (LOWER SPINE) AND PELVIS

The next set of exercises is to start the process of strengthening and toning your lower spine (the lumbar region) and pelvis, while concentrating on tightening your buttocks, thighs and calves, and stretching your stomach and neck. Again, no jerking or overdoing it. You'll need a mat, pillow or a soft carpet on which to do these.

OK, grab a mat or pillow and lie on your tummy. Anyone who has a bad or weak back should fold the end of the mat, and place the fold under the lower stomach for this first exercise. If you don't have a mat, use a cushion or pillow.

Keep both your feet on the ground, legs wide apart throughout and feet pointed hard (flexed if you go into cramp).

Clasp your hands behind your back by entwining your fingers, tighten legs and buttocks and pull up, blowing the air out as you come up for 8 continuous counts.
Repeat: *3 sets of 8.*

ON STOMACH WITH HANDS FLAT EITHER SIDE OF CHEST

Legs still apart, but feet flexed, rest the insides of your feet on the floor. Don't dig your toes in.

Put hands on either side of your chest, palms flat, nice and wide, and push upper body up.

Arch your back, keeping your pubic bone on the floor. Head right back, eyes open, mouth open wide, arms straight and keep shoulders well away from ears.

Slide your hands away from your body – your shoulders are scrunched to your ears until they are as far away as possible from your ears. Now push your shoulders back and down, opening up the chest. Really concentrate on pushing against the floor, with your hands. Stretch your stomach.

Keep your legs fully stretched especially at the knees, and hold it. Release.
Repeat: *3 times.*

ON STOMACH, LEGS APART

Fold a mat or pillow under your pelvis and pubic bone. Head to one side, resting on your cheek, arms by your side, or wherever is most comfortable. Both legs apart.

Dig the toes of both feet into the floor, tighten the backs of your knees and buttocks and lift both legs up and push for 8 counts.

Hold it – keep your knees straight and release.

Take a deep breath into your stomach, and pull your legs up slowly and hold them in that position for another count of 8. Release. Make sure you don't ever bend at the knee. Your leg height is irrelevant. Just flex your feet. It is hard to get a straight knee.
Repeat: *2 sets, holding for the count of 8.*

*D*on't jerk the body; stretch through, feeling the muscles opening up.

ON STOMACH, RAISING BOTH LEGS TOGETHER

If your mat is folded or you are using a pillow, slide your body so that the middle of your stomach is resting on the fold. Keep your legs wide apart and point your feet, keeping them firmly on the ground throughout this exercise. Grab hold of your elbows.

Bum and legs tight, blow *out the air as you lift your elbows and chest off the ground. Pull up and lift for the count of 8. Push up from the front of your thighs and pelvis.*
Repeat: *2 sets, pushing for the count of 8.*
Remember to use your breathing as you push up.

ON STOMACH, ARMS STRAIGHT

Arms stretched out in front of your body, forehead lightly leaning on the floor, legs apart, feet pointed.

Gently lift legs, arms and head together and hold for 8 counts. Keep knees straight all the time. Lift from the stomach and pull up for the count of 8. Remember to keep breathing in and out slowly and fully.
Repeat: *Twice more.*

THE HIP JOINTS

We are now going to work on an area that I personally hated when I started – the hip joints. The reason I used to hate it was probably because I couldn't get into the correct positions, let alone do the exercise. It was even worse for Sylvia as she suffers from arthritis of the joints. However, now we both find these exercises much easier. Pay special attention to moving your hands to the most comfortable position whilst doing the exercises.

These exercises are very tough at first, but you will be surprised how soon this area of your body will open up completely. Just keep going and you will break through your barriers. Be careful not to collapse your posture during these exercises.

These exercises are to increase your flexibility and circulation in your hip joints and to tone up the surrounding muscles.

KNEE LIFTED AND BENT. PUSH FORWARD AND BACK

Kneel down, knees together with hands in front of you, flat on the floor. You should have your hands far enough from your knees so that your shoulders relax completely away from your ears. Contract your back slightly.

Keep your arms straight at the elbows at all times and keep your head up. Let your back arch naturally, don't hunch.

Lift your right leg up to the side, knee higher than the foot. Point foot and bring knee back and forth holding the same position of leg right the way through.

When you go into the exercise, adjust your hands according to what is most comfortable for you, and arch your back as you bring the knee back. This will help to stop you collapsing your elbows and head.
Repeat: *2 sets of 8.*
Now ease that out: sit with your bottom back towards your right foot and stretch back flat towards your left knee, easing out the muscles.
Now do exactly the same on the other side and finish by easing that out.
Bottom back towards the left foot and stretch your back flat towards your right knee.
Do ease this out between each exercise.
Repeat: *8 times.*
Now try getting into the same position and lifting the knee up and down instead of forward and back. Repeat on both sides, easing out between each.
Last but not least, take right leg out to the side, quickly get hands and back into the most comfortable position and lift leg up and down, gently without touching the floor, for the count of 8. Keep knees and elbows straight.
Ease that out.
Repeat: *1 set and do the same on the other side.*

HIPS FORWARD, RELEASE BACK

Now let's work on easing out the hips a little bit more. Sit with your feet on either side of your bottom, knees apart, feet touching your bottom and hold your ankles.

You may have to lift your bottom off the floor at first, but you will be able to ease it down little by little. Now push your pelvis forward and then push your pelvis right back, arching your back as you do so.

Keep doing this gently, taking your knees wide apart and your bottom nearer to the floor.

Now begin to push one hip forward, and then the other. Release back slowly, gently bouncing or pushing your thighs and pelvis to ease the muscles along the front of your thighs, hips and the base of spine.

Only go to where you can, and slowly work through until you are lying (if you can) on the floor. Again, this

may take months – go only to where you can. Some people only ever bend one knee at a time, with the other knee straight in front, and then they alternate legs. That is fine to do if you are at that stage.

Breathe deeply and slowly at the same time as lifting and pushing the pelvis, to release any tension. As soon as you can, lie still with knees wide.

Gently sit up and go back to the beginning.
Repeat: 2 times.

Release legs and go back into the first kneeling exercise we did to show you the improvement by simply concentrating thoroughly and correctly on one area.

STOMACH EXERCISES

Throughout these exercises you have used your stomach constantly in one way or another: This next section is going to concentrate specifically on strengthening your stomach and back muscles. These are closely linked. Each exercise has a special ingredient for this area, and your posture and the flexibility of your back, pelvis and groin are the keys to being able to perform these exercises to their full potential.

This takes time but the benefits are more than just a hit-and-miss stomach smacker.

PELVIS AND GROIN TIGHTENERS

Lie on your back, feet wide apart on either side of your mat, close to your bottom. Beginners: put your hands behind your head. Advanced people: put your fingertips on the side of your forehead.

Elbows kept pushed out either side. Squeeze your pelvis tight, keep knees wide apart, squeeze chin down on to chest and squeeze your stomach hard, enabling you to lift your shoulder blades off the floor.

Breathe deeply and continuously and hold this position for 4 counts and gently release.

Repeat: 4 times, holding for the count of 4.

STRETCH BODY OUT TO RELAX

Let's stretch that out. Arms by your sides, feet pointed and bum tight, stretch one side longer than the other.

Then bring the knees into the chest and pull them in, easing out the lower back.

CENTRE OF STOMACH TIGHTENER AND BACK STRAIGHTENER

Lie on the floor. Beginners: put your hands behind your head. Advanced people: your fingertips should be on the side of your forehead.

Lift your feet up and cross them at the ankles, keep the knees bent and apart, and feet pointed so the legs are in an L-shape.

Beginners and people with any injury or weakness in lower back: rest in between each lift. Everyone else: keep the legs bent, and ankles crossed throughout the exercise.

Gently squeeze up, chin pulled down to your chest, keep breathing. Don't bring knees into the chest, keep them facing up to the ceiling and slowly release.

Don't drop the position of your legs.

Repeat: 10 times.

Now cradle your knees into your chest, and stretch arms and legs as before.

LIE BACK, KNEES BENT, SIT UP, PUSH SIDEWAYS TO ANKLES

Lie down, arms by your side, feet either side of your mat, and away from your bottom. Knees should be as wide as your feet, with your head and chin pulled forward and down to your chest.

Lift arms and shoulders off the floor, and take left hand to left heel and bring body back to the middle.

Repeat: 10 times on either side.

Relax back and then do both sides together.

Repeat: 10 times.

Stretch arms and legs as before. Breathe deeply in and out of your stomach to release tension in between all exercises.

STRETCH OUT BODY

Bring both knees into the chest, feet pointed and arms by your sides. Straighten one leg and lower for the count of 8. Keep the middle of your spine touching the floor the whole time. If your back begins to ache or arch, move leg back to where it feels comfortable.

Hold the leg just off the floor, keeping knee straight, and lift head and shoulders off the floor and push towards your leg for 8 counts. Make sure your movement comes from the stomach and not your head, neck and shoulders. Bring in knee and repeat on other side.

Repeat: 2 times to the count of 8.

SIT UPS (C)

We are going to end this section with sit ups that concentrate on the stomach and spine. No pumping or going down, or coming up with flat or arched backs and landing with a bump! No finishing off with hunched shoulders and bent backs, no feet coming off the floor with knees straightening.

Learning to relax is as important to the shape and feel of your body as exercise.

Your main movement comes from the pelvis. Your feet stay flat on the floor, knees bent as you roll, and I mean roll, back. As soon as you feel your back start to straighten or arch, or your knees straining to remain bent, and your feet leaving the floor, stop. Only go back to where your body can comfortably go, without breaking the rules. That is your breaking point.

Hold the position with your stomach, and then come up with a rounded back.

As you sit up, straighten your back, opening the rib cage and chest, shoulders down and back. Beginners: have your arms out in front, keep your elbows straight and don't swing your arms around to do the sit up for you. Intermediate people: cross your arms and keep them touching your body at every point of the exercise. Advanced people: put your fingertips on your forehead.

Repeat: 20 times.

Then cradle your knees into the chest, stretch that all up and slowly sit up.

ALL-OVER STRETCHING

In order to shape and open up the whole body, your groin, hips and legs need to work constantly in unison. You have done this individually throughout the different sections, and now you are going to put the whole lot together to unleash as much tension and stiffness as possible.

To finish off, we are going to do some exercises that concentrate on stretching out your legs in different directions, paying particular attention to your pelvis and groin, the base of the spine and the backs of your knees and legs.

PELVIC, GROIN AND THIGH STRETCH AND STRAIGHTENER

Lie on the floor, knees bent and feet flat on the floor close to your bottom – eighteen inches apart. Arms by your side, push the pelvis as high as it will go towards the ceiling. Push for 2 counts of 8.

(Don't let your bottom touch the floor.) Hold it there and bring your knees in and out without letting your bottom dip to the floor. Do another 2 counts of 8.

Release that and breathe. Repeat the exact same sequence on half point. Move your feet closer to your bottom so you can really arch your feet.

LIE ON THE FLOOR, LEFT KNEE BENT, LEFT FOOT FLAT ON THE FLOOR, BRING RIGHT KNEE INTO CHEST

Lie down on the floor, left foot flat on the floor and knee bent; bring your right knee into your chest and cradle your knee with your arms.

Put your left hand through the inside of the back of your calf, and hook your right arm around the back of your thigh. Now pull your knee back to your underarm or chest, and let your leg straighten slightly until you feel a slight pull on the back of your thigh.

Then, gently push, bringing your head forward to your chest, if it feels more comfortable.

Now gently push, easing and opening the hamstring (at the back of your leg). Keep your left hand on your calf, and bring your right hand and rest it just above the front of your knee. You can therefore push on the thigh and pull on the calf to get a really straight knee.

For people who are very stiff in the knees and at the base of the spine: please sit up and do this so that you don't strain your muscles.

Now, pulling on your calf and pushing on your leg, above the knee, straighten your leg completely if possible, especially at the knee.

Bend the knee, pulling the leg into the first position.

Repeat: 6 to 8 times, and do the same on the other leg.

Breathe in on the bend, breathe out on the stretch.

If something hurts, breathe and release into it. Then think about the pain. Is it just stiffness? Muscles that haven't been used for many years? Or is there something wrong? If you ever feel sharp or recurring pain, see an osteopath immediately.

SAME EXERCISE, EXCEPT THAT LEGS ARE TO THE SIDE/APART

Now for leg stretches, concentrating on the inner thigh muscles, groin and hip joints.

Lying down, bend your knees into your chest and push your knees out to sides, feet off the floor.

Rest your hands on the inside of your knees and gently bounce the knees to warm up the groin and hip joints.

Keep your left hand and knee in this position, and slip your right fingers and palm through the inside and around the back of your right knee. Straighten your leg out to the side and slightly back, being careful to straighten the knee. Lift your head off the floor, if it makes it easier. Don't keel over to one side – maintain a V-shape. Bend your knee to the first position and continue.

Repeat: 6 to 8 times, and then do the same, only the other side.

Now try both legs together, relaxing your legs whenever you want.

Well done. I know this area is a tough one, but if consistently done, you will feel and see a great difference.

We will now work the same areas of the body in a different position.

EXTEND FORWARD ON TO LEGS

Sit up with your legs together, out in front of you. Place your bottom as far backwards as possible so that your chest is tilted forwards. This is hard at first – due to sitting all day, bad posture and injuries, most of us do not have a great deal of mobility in the lower back and leg area.

If this is not possible, fold your mat or pillow to lift your bottom off the floor, and slide yourself down to the edge of the fold so that your body is thrown automatically into this position. This will also take the strain off the base of your spine.

Bend your left knee and bring your left foot up to the inside of your thigh. Don't slide your foot under your leg to make it easier. Make sure your right leg is not veering off to the right, but is straight in front of you.

You are going to drop your head down to your knee, and stretch your leg to make sure you straighten your knee properly.

I want you to put your hands one on top of the other under your knee, calf or ankle, and when you pull forward, bend your elbows and tighten your leg, flexing your foot to maximize on straightening your leg and getting your body as far forward and as close to your leg as possible. Concentrate on a rounded back and relaxed head. Gently push from the chest or rib cage.

Push for 8.

Hold the position for a few minutes on each go, shaking your legs.

Bend and stretch the knee. Repeat this on the other side. Both legs together. Remember to shake them when you want.

Rock on your bottom from side to side as you are stretching. Bend and straighten legs alternately, and push out with a relaxed but straight back and head.

Repeat: 1 more time.

SITTING, LEGS WIDE APART, PUSH THE KNEES DOWN
INTO THE FLOOR, THEN GO FORWARD ON TO THAT
LEG AND STRETCH

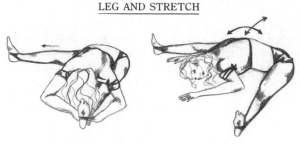

Legs wide apart, use your mat or pillow under your bottom if you want. Shake your legs to ease out the muscles, and move your pelvis back and forward.

Turn your body to the right, as far as you can, hands under your knee, calf or ankle, and drop down, relaxing your head and neck to your right knee.

Gently push forward, using your chest and torso, and now, if you can, release and straighten the leg. Rock from side to side.

If you want to ease and massage your muscles, slowly roll up to the centre and repeat on the other side. Now, slowly roll up to the centre again, and ease yourself forward to the middle, relaxing your head and neck, and very gently pushing, bending and straightening your knees, as well as pushing with a rounded back.

Come up to the point where you can straighten your head and back, and push forward, using your chest and rib cage to ease and work the base of your spine.

Don't roll your feet inwards. Now push – with a straight, then a rounded back.

Roll up slowly and bring your legs together.

Repeat: as many times as you can. The onus is on staying in ach position for a long time, and relaxing and stretching in each position.

Note: *Just bending the knee slightly, or keeping it straight for the whole time in exercise is incorrect. That is why you do a mixture of the two in Holistix exercise. You also straighten out the knee to work the muscles, and increase the circulation in the backs of the thighs and calves, and in the base of the spine.*

RELAXATION

Learning to relax is as important to the shape and feel of your body as exercising is. You will notice how after a massage your facial features and body skin appear smoother and younger. Relaxation also does this, as well as improving your ability to breathe correctly. Through this, your ability to counteract stress, insomnia, tension, headaches and so on, is increased.

Turn the lights down or off and lie down on the floor. We will end the exercise programme with a relaxation exercise.

If you like, you can record this sequence on to a cassette – or ask a friend who has a soothing voice to do it for you. Play your favourite relaxing music in the background.

Lie down on your back with your eyes closed, legs uncrossed and palms resting on the floor. Just relax every muscle.

Squeeze your toes hard . . . and release. Flex your feet hard up to the ceiling . . . and release. Now isolate and contract the calf muscles tight . . . and release. Squeeze your thigh muscles tight . . . and release. Next push your pelvis forward, so that the small of your back touches the floor. Hold it . . . and release.

Now for some deep breathing: breathe in fully through your nose, filling each area, and concentrate on exhaling all the stale air through your mouth. First, take a slow deep breath in, filling your stomach and pelvis . . . hold it . . . and breathe out again. Now for the waist and chest, breathe in deeply . . . hold it . . . and slowly release. Concentrate on the base of your spine, along each vertebrae of the back, into the tension area of your shoulders, neck and head. Breathe in deeply and hold it . . . hold it . . . hold it and release. Finally, concentrate on the whole of your diaphragm and rib cage. Take a deep breath in . . . hold it . . . and release.

Now breathe away quietly. Clench your hands into tight fists . . . and release. Bend your hands at the wrist up towards the ceiling . . . and release. Then bend your arms at the elbow up towards the ceiling . . . and release. Shrug your shoulders hard up to your ears . . . and release. Shrug your shoulders across your chest . . . and release.

Swallow hard, releasing your throat and relax your lips and tongue. Relax your cheek bones, ears and nose. Blink hard, and release your eyes. Frown hard, and release your eyebrows, forehead and skull. Relax throughout your whole body, letting it sink more and more into the floor.

Now you're going to visualize being on your favourite beach, so metaphorically shake out your towel and place it on the sand, lie down and close your eyes. Take a deep breath, right into your body, filling your stomach and back. And release. And another deep breath – in through your nose and out through your mouth, then breathe gently, normally. Start to release and sink down: 1–2–3–4–5.

Squeeze your eyes tight and release, feeling all the tension seep away from you into the sand. Release across your eyebrows, right into the temples, and feel yourself sinking down, down, down, deeper and deeper.

Release over your forehead and release right through the scalp, all the way over your head. Feel all the tension seeping away, right away from you and into the sand.

Feel the warmth of the sun on your body and feel the power of relaxation releasing you. Hear the sounds of the water lapping on the beach, the air warm, soft and gentle – refreshing.

Sink down even deeper: 1–2–3–4–5. Down, down, down, deeper, deeper, concentrating on the muscles of the neck and shoulders.

Allow the muscles and tissues of your neck to release and go soft and limp.

Now concentrate on the thick shoulder muscles that hold so much into your body and release. Breathe normally and gently, and on the count of 1, open your eyes.

5–4–3–2–1.

Lie quietly, listening to your breathing for a few minutes before you slowly get up.

Feel refreshed? Soothed? That is the way all exercise programmes should end. All our bottled-up energy having been released, and our muscles worked and stretched, and then relaxed.

After doing this exercise for a couple of weeks, you will find your strength, breathing and flexibility will increase; you will find that performing the exercises will become a relaxing form of releasing physical tension, as opposed to a great feat of strength.

Whether this is your first or twenty-fifth run through these exercises, you'll find your body constantly changing, both in terms of mobility and strength, and, later on, in terms of your shape.

Remember: as you get better you can do more repetitions, get wider positions on pliés, etc. Play with your body once you have really got to know the exercises and you will find advanced ways to do everything.

HOW OFTEN TO EXERCISE

This question could be answered differently for every one of us, depending upon how we feel after exercising, how much time we have on our hands, how effectively we exercise and our state of physical fitness.

If you are thorough in the first three to four weeks of exercising, we would suggest a minimum of three times a week. The following will help you to set up a system that works for you.

YOUR FIRST TIME

Concentrate on your posture and breathing, going through these exercises until you know them by rote. As we said earlier, it is important to remember and employ these exercises in your everyday life. In times of tension, stress, anxiety

---

Holistix works to balance, strengthen and reshape the body. The exercises do require hard work, but they are never exhausting if you do only what you can, and slowly build up. Instead of feeling tired or weak afterwards, you will feel invigorated and refreshed. Most importantly, however, you will notice the benefits after just a couple of sessions if you follow the instructions carefully.

Annie

Generally speaking, Annie was just feeling under the weather when she came to see us. She suffered from constant headaches and lower-back problems. Her energy level was low and she felt generally dissatisfied.

Her main problem was stress. She ran a busy company and spent most of her time in meetings, working late, dashing all over the country and so on.

It was obvious from her first class that Annie would need special help. Her posture was appalling – she was a slouch-shoulders, bum-sticking-out type. We explained to her that the position of her shoulders would inevitably lead to tension in that area, and that because her pelvis tipped backwards, it would cause her the backache. So we set to work.

We spent a long time working on her posture, getting her used to pushing her pelvis forward, and opening up her chest and ribcage. The slouching shoulders were the easiest problem to remedy, and after a few weeks she was much more open in that area, which in turn reduced the tension she suffered there. The headaches began to disappear.

Working on her breathing also helped enormously with this. She was one of those people who breathed very shallowly into her chest, bringing her shoulders right up towards her ears each time she breathed in. No wonder she's suffered from tension in her neck and shoulders.

Her back took more time, but was a slow but sure process. We did special 'back' classes for her and people with similar problems, gently easing the area out. We also worked very much on strengthening and

straightening the back of the knees, because these two areas directly correlate in terms of mobility.

Eventually, she could tilt her pelvis forward and keep her knees straight. Then she had to learn to do this quite naturally. Over the coming months we drilled and badgered her until, with each class, she needed to be reminded less and less of her posture.

Because her body had now opened up to such a degree, her circulation improved no end and other changes began to take place. Cellulite, which she had always had, began to disappear, and excess weight fell away.

Through consistently working her body in a particular way, she can hardly believe the changes. She looks taller and more confident, and now moves smoothly and gracefully, comfortable in her body rather than at odds with it.

---

or depression, *breathe, stand up straight, realign your back* and *concentrate on our relaxation therapy.*

After your breathing and posture work, practise opening your chest and diaphragm, systemically going through the exercises until you feel confident you have mastered them, and have not suffered any strain or pain.

Your barre work should take between twenty to thirty minutes, and make sure you do every exercise slowly, and concentrate on your breathing. Finish your exercises with the relaxation programme if you wish. Not only will it loosen your muscles after their work-out, but it will also leave you feeling relaxed and refreshed, a bit of inspiration to keep you going.

THE FIRST WEEK

Try doing only what you attempted in the first class, paying special attention to the notes above. If you want to try all of the exercises, go ahead, but beware of straining rusty muscles. It is actually easier to use only this basic foundation of exercises in the first week. It will make the next

lot much easier. Again, always take time to relax.

THE SECOND WEEK

Try the rest of the exercises, but start off with the chest and diaphragm sequence, going through it three complete times before you begin to move on.

THE THIRD AND FOURTH WEEKS

Choose any combination of the exercises that you particularly enjoy, or that you feel work for you. Do continue to incorporate breathing, posture and relaxation into your individual programme.

Alternatively, you can choose to do a full sequence of exercises from a particular body-area grouping. For instance, one day you might like to focus solely on the stomach, and the next, on the hip joints. Don't just whiz through the exercises in any section. Really concentrate on the part of the body you are working on, and complete all of the recommended repetitions. Too little work on an area will certainly undermine your overall effort.

YOUR EXERCISE PROGRAMME FOR LIFE

Take into consideration the work you have done throughout the first four weeks. Choose a sequence that interests and inspires you. Focus one day on a particular part of your body, and the next, on your body as a whole. Some days you will feel energetic, and with time on your hands you might wish to complete the entire sequence, from beginning to end or speed it up by using different tempos of music. But play it by ear. Only ever do what you feel up to, and remember to relax, breathe and monitor your posture.

Exercise is like good nutrition. It needs to be consistent, constantly monitored and updated, and full of self-appraisal. Learn when to push and when not to. If you feel you need a break, don't exercise at all. Be flexible, and create a programme with variety. The minute you get bored with the exercises, you'll become bored with your body. Start off with breathing and posture exercises before you play squash, or go swimming. Incorporate the exercises into your regular fitness regime. And if you don't have one, try extending the Holistix exercises to incorporate other forms of sport. After a few weeks of carefully following the programme, you'll have more energy and stamina to tackle sport, or traditional exercise. When you have energy, sport is definitely a lot more fun.

When exercising, always remember that if something hurts, breathe into it. Allow yourself to release, and to open the muscle. We cannot stress often enough: *Breathe in on the easiest part of the exercise, breathe out on the hardest part. Always breathe into pain then breathe out fully.*

Beware of sharp or consistent pain. Is it just stiffness? Muscles that haven't been used for many years? Or is it something more? If you suspect that something is wrong, please see an osteopath at once. People are funny – we worry if we don't feel something, and yet, when we do, we worry that something might be wrong. The more you get used to the exercises, the more confident and relaxed you will feel. Soon you will know exactly how far to take it. Every one of us feels the effects of exercise in different ways.

If you are consistent in the beginning, no matter how hard you find the exercises, you will begin to see and feel a difference every time you do them. *Especially* after the first three classes, when you then go into a 'honeymoon period'. At some point after that, you may feel like you have gone backwards. However, it is just your body's way of letting you know that you are through to the next step on the ladder.

If you look in the mirror when doing a couple of the exercises, you will notice that your performance has taken a leap forward. For example, you can now lie your stomach on your leg with a flat back, instead of a rounded one. So you are bound to feel something.

Don't let your Commentator get in the way. You will keep hitting plateaus throughout your exercise programme. This is natural. All you have to do is know when to take it easier with your body, and when to push. If you are getting bored, push a little harder. Try a new sequence of exercises. Increase your repetitions. Do not continue to repeat the same exercises over and over, with no respite.

Breathing is vital. Whether you are learning, or well into your individual programme, you must continue to concentrate on your breathing. If you hit a plateau there is a tendency to become slack.

Some people feel tearful and angry when exercising. This is perfectly normal. On a daily basis you build up tension and stress, at home and at work, without being aware of your body's capacity to retain the impact. Breathing and exercise can sometimes bring it to the surface, by releasing the tension that kept it in.

Grace, flexibility, excellent posture, a trim figure, stamina, strength and a sleek body, with no swelling or puffiness, are the results of a sensible and successful exercise plan. If you do not have each and every one of these qualities, your exercise programme is insufficient, or simply wrong for you.

Do not let your breathing, posture or relaxation exercises lapse. By breathing properly, your body will respond better to both exercise and to stress. And through that, your body will acquire more grace and quiet, vital strength.

Whenever you experience any negative situations or emotions in your life, take special care to relax in the exercises. And if you just don't feel up to exercising at all, try the relaxation therapy on its own. *Never bash out emotion on your body.*

You can choose virtually any time of the day to exercise, as long as you do not have a full – or empty – stomach. Eat a light snack before exercising, or wait for a couple of hours after a meal. Exercising on a full stomach will cause cramps, and possibly nausea. The energy which your body needs to digest a meal will be expended elsewhere, and you will feel tired quickly, and probably suffer some stomach pain. Exercising on an empty stomach can lead to fainting, undue weakness and also a chance of nausea. Your body will have to draw from stores of energy it may not have.

I did each of these exercises on and off for about a year, and was able to go from having a totally rounded back and head when trying to reach my legs in the stretching exercises, to eventually being able to lie my stomach flat and head flat on my legs.

My hips went from eighty-five per cent immobility to total mobility – and whereas I couldn't complete a full sit up, I can do hundreds on end.

The change in my shape was extraordinary and, even more important, I had got rid of my ever-present nagging pain in my lower spine.

Once you have mastered the instructions, alternate your back movements when stretching, from a rounded, relaxed back to pushing from the base of the spine and rib cage with a flat back.

The exercises you choose – and when you choose them – will change daily. Think about how you are feeling before you plan your daily programme. Every day you will have different needs, moods and levels of energy. Develop your programmes around those daily factors.

Holistix has eight-week courses, with a week's break in between. This is mental time off – a well-deserved rest from concerted effort. At the end of that week, most of our clients are raring to go again, their bodies refreshed and relaxed after the break. Why not try the same thing with your own programme? Time off for good behaviour, so to speak.

Now it's up to you. The decision is yours – you either follow our guidelines faithfully, create your own programme based on these guidelines, or develop a programme that envelopes or incorporates various sequences from our guidelines. And from that, coupled with correct nutrition, you will begin to feel healthier, more dynamic, full of energy, relaxed, free of headaches, backaches, stomach troubles, lethargy and poor circulation, and you will look as good as you feel.

Or you can skip it altogether and find a friend who will be sympathetic to your health complaints.

I know what I'd do.

EIGHT

Looking After Yourself

ARE YOU ONE of those people who collapses in a heap at the end of the day, throwing the nearest available fast food down your throat, watching television in a semi-conscious state until you can't keep your eyes open any longer, shoving your clothes into a corner and crawling into bed feeling too apathetic to have a bath?

Do you wake up in the morning feeling and looking as though you could sleep for another three hours, drag yourself out of bed at the last minute, ignore the mess from last night, have a quick bath or shower, bypass the kitchen and skip breakfast, and then leave the whole, horrible mess to ferment for yet another day?

Not only is this not a very good way to finish or start a day, it is a very poor way to organize your life; it will do nothing to help you look or feel better; and, it is, in fact, detrimental to your health.

The purpose of the first part of this chapter is to encourage you to establish an environment that is conducive to supporting your general wellbeing on a daily basis.

Personal organization in the home is the one area I feel strongly enough about to stick my neck out and say: 'There is no choice. You have to get organized.'

When working with people in business, and women who ran busy households, I realized just how much they neglected themselves. While they worked efficiently and productively during the day, getting every job, subordinate, goal,

manager and child handled, they were ready to collapse in a heap at the end of the evening.

Although everybody is aware fundamentally of the importance of being clean and tidy, I often receive comments like the following:

'I'm too busy';

'I'm too lazy'; and

'I know it's important but I don't quite see its relevance to my health and wellbeing'.

We are probably all guilty of letting things around the house slip, whether it's due to pressure of work, untidy flatmates, feeling unhappy about the place in which we live, laziness, or because we always leave things to the last minute. The reasons are endless.

Yet, most of us feel great when we have a big clear-out, or stay in a hotel, or even have a bath at somebody else's home. It can be a real treat and a relief.

The most important thing to remember is that your home should always be lovely to return to, a retreat from the outside world. Coming back to a house that's always warm, clean and tidy, with a well-stocked kitchen and an organized bathroom, is the foundation block for other jobs, such as finding time to exercise, improving your eating habits and combating stress.

When you become organized you will find that so many aspects of your life are easier. For example:

○ Your social life can improve. You will no longer feel embarrassed about having friends round, and when they do come they will find your home an environment that is easy to relax in;

○ You won't lose, break or forget so many things. Frustration and slovenly habits do lead to forgetfulness and clumsiness;

○ Living in chaos can take its toll on your sex life. Why not give yours a chance.

○ There will be fewer arguments with the rest of the household;

○ You will feel more cheerful. When your home is a mess you may wind up feeling moody and uncommunicative – although you may not have realized that this is one reason why;

○ You will be better able to let go of tension;

○ You will be more likely to make time to buy in the right food and to prepare it in an appealing manner. You will not resort so heavily to eating rubbish;

○ You will have more inclination to begin to organize other areas of your life that are important, such as personal finances and planning; and

○ Other domestic chores will be easier to handle, such as washing, cleaning, mending and tidying.

Whether or not you like your home, you must make the most of it, otherwise the situation will only deteriorate. You deserve to have as pleasant and enjoyable an environment as possible. Creating a warm and intimate atmosphere is vital to your wellbeing.

If you have problems with the people you live with, don't remain silent and resentful, dropping the odd sarcastic or indirect comment. Don't be afraid of hurting their feelings or of losing their approval. Make a list of *everything* that is unsatisfactory, sit them down and tell them directly what upsets you about the state of the place, and what you want done by each one of you on a daily and weekly basis.

CREATING A HEALTHY ENVIRONMENT

When I first went through the process of changing my home so that it could remain clean and tidy, a few people asked me if I would make a checklist of the parts that seemed the hardest.

Easy, I thought. Well, it was quite a long, tough task. In the end, however, a sensible organization and cleaning plan was developed. Most importantly, it works. For a top-to-bottom, any-season clean, try the following.

ESSENTIAL TOOLS

Big, strong bin liners, Sponges, Disinfectant, Bio-degradable household cleaners, Paper towels, Dishcloths, Non-aerosol furniture polish, Dusters, Dust sheets, Bucket, Hoover, Dustbuster, Dustpan and brush, Scrub brush, Floor polish, Vinegar and water (to wash the windows)

Make a list of everything that needs attention – both cleaning and organization. I started with the bedroom:

1. Go through your wardrobe and divide your clothes into sections – dresses, trousers, blouses, jackets, outfits, sweaters, T-shirts, dancewear, underwear, tights, shoes, boots, and accessories.

2. Take a careful look at each section and decide what you:
   ○ Want to give away;
   ○ Want to sell;
   ○ Want to throw out;
   ○ Need to wash;
   ○ Need to have dry-cleaned; and
   ○ Need to mend.

Put these clothes into separate bin liners, and put the filled bags straight into the car or out of the way. Clean your cupboards with disinfectant and dry them, and put everything back in its section. Shoe boxes are an ideal place to hold underwear and tights, and help me to maintain order.

Sort through your make-up and dressing table, discarding any products that are past their date. Bookshelves and drawers are the next job to tackle. Organize your stationery, household accounts and books in an easy-reference order. And give those shelves and drawers a good clean. There are several new scented drawer liners on the market, available at chemists or giftshops, and they make a nice finishing touch to newly cleaned and tidied drawers.

Go through the whole room, cleaning

When starting any kind of health programme, making time to relax and to refuel, and looking after your hair, facial and body skin is of utmost importance. By paying attention to improving your appearance, and by relaxing more, you will have more incentive and more staying power to tackle the tougher processes you are dealing with, such as losing weight.

everywhere – radiators, window sills, under the bed, door frames and the top of your wardrobe.

In the kitchen, throw out all the tins and cans that have been stored forever, creating order out of chaos, and clean everything in and out of sight. Make a list of cooking utensils, food and storage jars that you need to buy, and then do the same in the bathroom.

The next step is to organize yourself to maintain this. Set aside a day every three to four weeks to shop for items that can be bought in bulk: still mineral water in two-litre bottles (purchased in boxes of six to store at home and at work); cleaning products; toilet paper; frozen goods (providing you have a good-sized freezer); and baking goods, etc.

Note: In some areas it is now possible to have mineral water delivered directly to your home.

Next, arrange for all the windows, curtains and carpets to be cleaned, and take the time to get on with the washing, ironing and mending.

With the essential cleaning complete, you might want to approach your partner or flatmate about devising a system to keep it that way. I sat down with my flatmate and told her that I would arrange for a cleaner to come in once a week for

four hours, at a cost of £10 each. That went down fine. I then ventured to tell her that I wanted both of us to clean the bath and sink after every use, and to ensure the bathroom always looked perfect. She baulked a bit at this until I suggested two things: people who visit are offended when your home is messy or unhygienic, and it would mean that bathing and relaxing would seem more like a treat than a chore. She got the message and agreed.

Having completed a top-to-bottom clean and clear-out, it is really important to maintain a consistent standard, especially when you are feeling negative about any area of your life. With your surroundings in pristine condition, you'll find the upkeep is far easier. And that allows you a little more time for yourself.

CARING FOR YOUR SKIN AND HAIR

When starting any kind of health programme, making time to relax and to refuel, and looking after your hair, facial and body skin is of the utmost importance. You will find that by paying attention to improving your appearance, and by relaxing more you will have more incentive and more staying power to tackle the tougher processes you are dealing with, such as losing weight.

Good health, happiness and calmness shows in the condition of your skin and hair. When your skin glows, your hair shines and feels good to touch, and you dress more carefully, your outlook and behaviour immediately improve, while your energy increases.

I have seen many men and women who are busy coping with a home and/or business life who do not take or make time to care for themselves. Yet, if they did, they would get so much more out of their day-to-day situations.

In my work I have come across every type of skin. Amongst the many things I have noticed is the interesting fact that there are very few people who make the most of the skin on their face and body. Many people, it seems, are unaware of the impact that a dull complexion or a problem skin has on their overall presentation, and they have very little knowledge of how to improve it. I have also noticed other factors that are important for you to think about:

○ Many women concentrate on covering up their face with make-up, rather than working to improve the texture and natural glow of their complexions. And some men still tend to think that skin care is for women only!

○ Many people have very little perception of how enjoyable having a good skin can be, both personally and to the opposite sex. There is great pleasure in the touch and smell of soft, clean, fresh skin.

○ Many people do not bathe or shower daily, and do not see the importance of this.

○ Some people do not know how to wash their private parts properly, and are unaware of the odour that this can cause.

○ Many people have a constant odour that secretes from the pores due to the build-up of toxins. We also secrete this odour in abundance when we are emotionally upset, scared or angry.

○ Improperly washed or dried clothes can affect your smell. Damp or dirty cupboards will worsen the situation.

FACIAL SKIN

We have already established the crucial role of good nutrition in determining the condition of your skin, and that blocked bowels and other internal problems and weaknesses are the main source of poor or unhealthy skin. There are a number of points on skin functioning that will help you to understand better how to take care of your skin, and will help you when talking to a beauty therapist about specific treatments:

1. Your skin is a living organism that renews itself constantly. Its most important functions are to protect us, to maintain an even body temperature, and to excrete toxins and waste through perspiration. These functions are affected by our circulatory systems.

2. If your skin is dull or problematic, it usually means that the kidneys and the lungs are overloaded and unable to cope with the toxins. It also indicates that stress is getting the better of you, as stress affects the nervous system and the production of hormones.

3. When toxins are left in the tissues of the skin, premature ageing can occur.

4. For the skin to function properly, it has to be free of dead surface cells. Promoting healthy cell turnover is important.

5. The flow of your lymph system – the body's main drainage system, which runs parallel to the circulatory system – is directly linked to the health of the skin.

6. Your skin is affected greatly by environmental factors.

Stress and fatigue: Both stress and fatigue have a major effect on the condition of your skin. Lack of sleep slows down your circulation and denies your skin the required amount of time to restore and nourish itself. Tension and emotional upset interfere with the digestion of food, and affect the nervous system and hormones, which in turn affects the complexion. Therefore, making time to relax is crucial.

Smoking and alcohol: Many of the toxic elements in cigarette smoke are oxidants, generators of toxic oxygen forms that can cause tissue and cell damage. Smoking also interferes with respiration, and rids the body of essential vitamins and minerals. The destructive oxygen toxins and deficiencies which develop have been proven to cause premature ageing of the skin, which leads to the development of lines, wrinkles and dry, flakey skin.

Alcohol has a similar effect, as it removes important nutrients from our digestive system and bloodstream when it passes through. Alcohol also weakens the capillaries, the liver and kidneys, whose blood-cleansing role is essential to life. All of this damage will manifest itself in the skin, in the form of premature ageing, spots (the body's attempt to rid itself of toxins), visibly broken blood veins and pallor.

Both alcohol and smoking remove moisture from the skin, making it dry and less elastic.

Environment and the skin: Your face is exposed to five main environmental elements,

most of which can be controlled to a certain
degree. They are:

○ Sunlight;
○ The wind;
○ The cold;
○ Central-heating and air-conditioning; and
○ Pollution.

Sunlight: The sun's ultraviolet rays are the prime
cause of wrinkling and premature ageing of the
skin. UVB rays are responsible for burning and
skin damage, and UVA rays, which are weaker
but penetrate deeper into the skin, are believed
to be responsible for much of the visible skin
ageing.

While most of us still love to get a tan, the
best advice now is to use high-protection
sunscreens and never to burn. It is especially

important to protect children from the sun; as few as two sunburns in childhood are linked to dramatically increased risks of skin cancer and other skin problems in later life.

It is important to remember, however, that sunlight is the most natural source of Vitamin D. The sunlight's ultraviolet rays work on the skin's oils to produce the vitamin, which is then absorbed. Ensure that you do get enough sunlight, but avoid burning.

Always protect your face, neck and decolleté in the sun, and if you want to tan, minimize the tan on these areas, which show the signs of premature ageing so clearly. Always wear sunglasses or sun goggles to protect your eyes and the tender skin around them. Excessive exposure to the sun on these areas can cause noticeable wrinkles and broken capillaries to develop.

Some cosmetic houses now incorporate sun protection factors in moisturizers for year-round wear, to protect against the ultraviolet light that constantly surrounds us. RX is one of the best suntan ranges on the market.

The wind and the cold: Harsh winds strip the skin of moisture and greatly increase the dehydrating effect of heat and cold on the skin. Be sure that you always apply adequate moisturizer to the eye and cheek area before going outside.

Extremes of temperature can lead to broken capillaries. Moisturizer can provide a barrier – but never go in to roast in front of an open fire when you have been in very cold temperatures outside. If you have a rosy complexion, your blood vessels lie very close to the surface and will be irritated by all the environmental factors mentioned. Blotchiness, itchiness and broken capillaries can be protected against with a rich moisturizer. Remember to apply sparingly, to avoid clogging the pores. It is the moisturizer's richness, not its quantity, which will best protect your skin.

Central-heating and air-conditioning: Centrally heated rooms can be drier than the Sahara desert. This type of atmosphere will steal moisture from your skin, as it does any other

moisture in the air. If you can see many fine lines on the surface of your skin, or if your face feels tight, use a high-powered moisturizer daily. Air-conditioning will increase the effects of central-heating. If you have central-heating or an air-conditioner, use humidifiers or place bowls of water around the room. Some aromatherapy oils are suitable for vapourizers – therefore, not only would you have an increased moisture level in the air, but also a soothing or invigorating therapy to complement it. See pages 174–176 for details of aromatherapy oils suitable for vapourizer use.

Pollution: The air is full of pollutants, which leave a film of toxic chemicals and dust clinging to your skin's surface, clogging the pores and making the skin dull and grey. We also breathe in these pollutants, which can hamper the blood's ability to supply nutrients to the skin cells. Take care to clean your skin carefully each day, and it might be a good idea to invest in an air purifier for your home. These can be purchased with disposable filters, and they will clear the air of pollen, dust, cigarette smoke and ordinary atmospheric pollution.

Drinking plenty of fresh water will also give your body a chance to cleanse itself of the toxic pollutants which can build up in the bloodstream. Anti-oxidant vitamins will build up your body's defence to these pollutants; these include Vitamins A, C and E, and the mineral selenium. See pages 123–125 for details of the foods in which these are naturally present.

Special tips to remember: Women, men and children have different requirements in terms of acquiring and taking care of healthy skin. Most of us cause problems for ourselves by unknowingly blocking pores, or by allowing our skin to go unprotected to environmental factors. Some of these notes may help.

Women: You make yourself look older by covering up a poor-condition skin with heavy make-up. If you decide to clean up your eating habits and to take a couple of months, giving your face special attention every night, you must also decide to forego wearing mask-like make-up. Use only what is recommended in **Presentation** (chapter nine). Be sure to make your priority a glowing, clear skin. Again, it is a question of getting yourself to drop the habit and at first you will feel quite naked. The rewards, however, are well worth it.

If you smoke or drink you should ensure that you are drinking plenty of fresh water, and making the anti-oxidant vitamins an essential part of your nutritional plan.

Women in menopause will notice big changes in the texture of their skin. The protective effects of oestrogen are no longer present, and ageing can set in quite quickly. Dryness and sensitivity are the most common problems. Being immaculate, gentle and patient while cleansing your skin is vital. You will need to nourish and protect it more. Treat your face and body skin with moisturizer twice a day, and try adding some of the essential oils to your bath water! See pages 123–126. Many women find natural HRT (Hormone Replacement Therapy) the ideal way to re-introduce oestrogen to the body, to continue its protective role.

Men: Given how hard you work, it is important to learn how relaxing and refreshing it can be to do more than just throw cold water over your face, or use soap, which can be harsh and drying to the skin. Many men suffer from spots and ingrowing hairs – the result of shaving – so softening the skin by removing dead skin cells is very important. All the advice and procedures in this chapter about skin apply to you as well as to women. So try them – you never know, you might like it! Better still, get your partner to treat you to a pamper once she's got the hang of it herself. I shan't name them, but all the male clients of Holistix revel in this stuff!

Children and teenagers: Children in particular need to be treated with care and taught how and why to look after themselves. By the time they reach puberty they will be able to deal with the problems that are often inherent at that age.

It's never too early to protect the skin from sunlight, and to begin using moisturizers. There are a number of light products specially formulated for children's skin, and, contrary to rumour, spots are *not* caused by these products.

RECOMMENDED SKINCARE PRODUCTS

I particularly like the Dead Sea Discovery (DSD) range of products because the results I, and many Holistix clients, have had with them have been, well, miraculous – from improving fairly 'normal' skins, through to effectively treating problems such as acne, psoriasis and eczema.

I have been experimenting with products on myself and others since I was eleven, and this is the first range that I have found that corresponds with the body's needs. The high concentrations of minerals in the products are particularly beneficial to the skin. Many ranges – which commonly contain plant, herb or cell extracts – can contain properties that are not produced naturally by the body, and as they are organically based, they start to lose their potency as soon as they are exposed to oxygen. Minerals are inorganic and therefore longer lasting.

Some people with sensitivity problems may find that the DSD products are too powerful for them. When trying any new product on a sensitive skin, always do a patch test first by applying a small amount of the products to the inside of one forearm overnight.

Homoeopathic skincare ranges are very good for sensitive or allergic skins. A very good range is produced by the homoeopathic company Weleda. In particular, I like the products that treat burns, bruising, and aches and pains. Weleda products are available from most chemists and healthfood shops.

Helena Harnik produce an excellent range of special preparations to treat unsightly red veins and open pores. Their astringents, face masks and spot healers are also worth having in your bathroom cabinet. These products are available worldwide by mail order, and come with an information pack.

Noxzema skin cream is the most versatile of the lot. It is a greaseless, medicated cream which contains camphor, phenol, clove oil, eucalyptus oil and menthol. It softens hard skin and dries out spots; it soothes and cools sore, bruised and sunburned skin. I like to use it when my eyes are tired, by smoothing a thick layer over the eye area and lying down with my eyes shut for fifteen minutes. It doesn't sting!

For dry skin, burns and after sunbathing, try Elizabeth Arden's Eight-Hour Cream. Particularly beneficial to older skins, it really does work. Use it overnight to smooth, nourish and heal.

Simple's excellent products are for any skin type, especially allergic and sensitive skins. They can be used on the face and body.

Blisteze ointment, commonly used for cold sores, is excellent for use on red infected spots or acne. The ointment cools, soothes and anaesthetizes the area, bringing the infection and swelling right down.

LOOKING AFTER YOUR FACE

CLEANSERS:

Before you go to bed, make sure you cleanse your face thoroughly. Women should remove eye make-up first. One excellent way of removing it easily (as well as the rest of your make-up) is to wet a piece of cotton wool with warm water, squeeze it out so that it is just damp, and sweep it over the eyes. Then apply a small amount of baby oil, wheatgerm oil or glycerine mixed with rosewater to one side of the cotton wool and gently wipe over one eye in circular motions. Then use other side, without oil, to remove any excess. Repeat on other eye and the rest of the face if you like. Wetting the skin and the cotton wool prevents the oil from sinking into the skin.

For men and women, choosing a cleanser is important. It must be light, so that it doesn't cling to the skin and block the pores; it must remove make-up and excess oils efficiently; and it should be as simple in its formulation as possible. Many cleansers are perfumed, rich and fussy in content, and can irritate the skin.

Wipe-off cleansers work well on normal to dry skins; wash-off cleansers are good for oily and combination skins. Do not use soap, which upsets the skins acid mantle and can lead to excessive dryness and irritation.

Two excellent wipe-off brands are Simple and Dead Sea Discovery. Use only a minimal amount and massage gently, using light circular movements in an upwards direction. Massaging will loosen debris and dead cells, and increase the circulation. Wipe off with a piece of muslin or, even better, a round flat facial sponge. Remember: if you have oily or spotty patches, use an astringent after your cleanser. This will deep-cleanse excess oils. Helena Harnik is the best we've found so far.

TONERS

If you use a wipe-off cleanser, use a toner to remove any excess. Again, Simple or DSD are highly recommended. Do not use toners that contain alcohol, even on oily skins – alcohol will dry unnecessarily the outer layers of the skin. Always work in a circular, upward motion (against the pull of gravity), to cleanse entirely. Never use tissues, which can imbed tiny splinters into the skin. Cotton wadding or muslin is the best cleansing tool.

MOISTURIZERS

Moisturizing the skin is vital. Avoid applying too much moisturizer, as working in the moisturizer in a heavy-handed way can irritate the skin and cause itching and rashes. Wearing too heavy a moisturizer can prevent the skin from adequately producing its own natural oils. It also encourages the pores to enlarge and become slack. If your

If your skin is dull or problematic, it usually means that the kidneys and the lungs are overloaded and unable to cope with the toxins. It also indicates that stress is getting the better of you, as stress affects the nervous system and the production of hormones.

skin is normal to problem, you need only the minimum of moisturizer – be especially sparing on the greasy areas of the face like the forehead, nose and chin. You may wish to leave these areas free of moisturizer from time to time. Applying moisturizer once a day can be enough for some skins, otherwise touch up your skin whenever it feels dry.

If you have dry skin, eczema or psoriasis you should use specialist creams. DSD Energizing Day and Night Creams are excellent. If these are too strong for you, there are homoeopathic equivalents. Some people find wheatgerm, almond or lavender oils a natural and soothing option for dry skins.

EYES

Eye creams, gels or ointments are a good investment for this delicate area. Avoid putting your regular moisturizer around the eyes or anything that contains lanolin – it may irritate them, and if the product is rich it could make the skin swell. An eye gel or ointment applied in the morning with light tapping movements will refresh the eyes and ease any puffiness. Always apply eye cream in the evening, giving your skin the night to absorb its goodness.

Never rub your eyes, as the tender tissue and skin lacks the elasticity of the rest of the facial skin, and can be irreparably damaged. Delicate, feather-stroke motions will cleanse and apply moisturizer to the eye area with the minimum of pulling.

Don't wear waterproof mascara every day, as it dries the lashes and is more difficult to remove than water-soluble mascara. Try one of the new mascaras available, with added moisturizer and collagen.

For tired, red or itching eyes, try wedges of cucumber, pressed gently over closed eyelids. The coolness of the cucumber, and its high water content will relieve the discomfort. Similarly, Optrex or Evian water soaked into a cotton ball and laid across the eyes will soothe them.

Helena Harnik eye creams, gels and ointments are excellent for overnight and day wear. And Optrex eye masks cool and soothe tired, red eyes.

EXFOLIATORS

In addition to daily cleansing, your skin will benefit from the regular use of an exfoliating treatment in order to get rid of dead skin cells and enable the skin to excrete toxins fully.

I recommend using a peeling mask on your face, and prefer this to scrubs with grains, which can be too harsh and can quite easily mark the skin and cause broken capillaries. The best peel I have come across is the DSD peel by Finders, as it is completely smooth in texture and mineral based. The mineral properties go deep into the skin and are able to create an equilibrium more effectively than some products with plant or animal extracts. The peel is best done at night, after removing make-up and before toning.

There is one scrub which I would recommend you use once a week, or once every couple of weeks – Clinique's Face Scrub (available in the women's range and in Clinique's Skin Supplies for Men). Instead of the emphasis being on the scrubbing action, smooth the cream over damp skin, and then leave the scrub on, like a mask, for five to ten minutes. Rinse off and you will find that your skin feels really tingly. Be careful to avoid the eye area when using a peel or scrub.

Normal and problem skins can use a peel every day or every other day; remove it by rubbing gently with small circular movements, supporting the skin with the opposite hand as you do so. Sensitive and older skins can use peels daily, but must take the peel off with a damp face cloth or sponge. This softens the peel sufficiently not to irritate the skin but still allow the dead cells to come away from the surface. Use cleanser and toner afterwards to remove any residue.

MASKS

Once a week, or whenever you feel run-down, use a face pack. Always keep different types to hand, as it is very rare that your face will be restricted to one specific type. Your skin actually needs different treatments at different times; it can change from day to day, with some areas becoming greasier or drier.

Clay and mud masks: These are good for

problem and greasy skins, and for drawing out impurities on the centre panel. The DSD Dermabalance Stabilizing and Black Mud Masks and the Helena Harnik Chalk and Water mask, are the most effective. Other mud and clay masks are equally good; avoid masks with alcohol. Boots produce a line of excellent masks, in various strengths and consistencies.

Moisturizing masks: These don't dry on the skin, and the best ones are usually of a creamy consistency. Use them on drier areas, such as the cheeks and under the eyes, whilst you have a mud pack on the oily areas. The DSD Energizing Mask for dry and older skins, Simple for ultra-sensitive skins, and any homoeopathic mask of your choice, will do the trick. Use a moisturizing mask once or twice weekly.

Refreshing and revitalizing masks: These are like exercise for the face. They bring out the tone and colour, and stimulate the circulation. A mask like this usually has a thick consistency and may smell of eucalyptus or camphor. Try these masks once a week – or whenever your skin appears to take on a greyish pallor. The scent has the double effect of uplifting the senses as well. Try Rose Laird's various masks.

If you want to go the whole hog after using either a clay, mud or moisturizing mask, you can finish off with a revitalizing mask. But check that your skin isn't sensitive first, and reduce the amount of time that you keep both masks on the skin the first couple of times you use them. Some skin tends to react to too much attention when it's not used to it! Others can respond miraculously well to experimentation.

BODIES AND BATHING

Whatever time you get in from work or from socializing, you must bathe or shower before you go to bed. Even if you are ill in bed, or just sleeping all day, you must bathe at the end of every day. No matter how clean you think you are, your body is excreting waste products, not only in your stools and urine, but all day long in your sweat. Your body also accumulates tension and strain. All this has to be washed away in

order for you to wind down, have a satisfying sleep and allow your body to repair. Relaxing in this way benefits your circulation and digestion.

Bath or showertime, whatever is going on in your life or around you, is the one time when you can lie back, collect your thoughts, let go of the day and prepare for the next. Overnight, the acids and oils in your body rise to the surface of the skin and these should be washed away by showering or bathing in the morning and lotioning your body afterwards.

After carrying out this routine for some time most people notice that their energy is higher during the day, their skin is more youthful and its quality and condition vastly improved, they find it easier to sleep, and their rest is more refreshing. This is particularly useful if you are suffering from any depressive illness, recurring physical illness, fatigue, PMS or menstruation, or emotional upset.

When washing, avoid soap, which is difficult to rinse off and drying to the skin and to the body's natural secretions. Look for body shampoos instead which are kinder to the body's private areas. The Body Shop's herbal body shampoo leaves a lovely fresh smell. Wash and rinse your private parts especially carefully.

To look after your breasts, it's a good idea to splash your bust with cold water after showering or bathing, in order to stimulate the circulation. Apply firming and toning lotions afterwards. It's a little messy, but wheatgerm oil is an excellent choice to prevent ageing and stretchmarks. When you are applying cleansers, moisturizers or massage lotions to the face always move in an upwards direction, and on the body, move towards the heart. To get the lymphatic system moving, use firm movements, especially around the groin area.

BATHTIME BLISS

There is a way of feeling very luxurious and relaxed at the end of the day, by using certain substances and materials on your skin. Whether your skin is smooth, dry, spotty or rough, follow this routine and it will improve rapidly.

To start off with, run a bath, hot but not scalding, add something to soften the water. (My

Wearing too heavy a moisturizer can prevent the skin from adequately producing its own natural oils. It also encourages the pores to enlarge and become slack.

favourite is the DSD mineral bath gel, as it helps to break down the toxins in my body, is unperfumed and has no allergic effects on ultra-sensitive skin.)

Whilst the water is running, take a good exfoliating cream (Clinique and DSD are excellent, as they have the finest grains and the deepest cleanse), and rub it all over your body. Most people exfoliate on a wet skin, but try this with completely dry hands on a dry body. (If you have sensitive or allergic skin, make sure you test on a sensitive area of the body.)

The easiest way to work is from the feet upwards, section by section, stimulating the circulation by massaging cream thoroughly into each section, until the cream has disappeared and you are left only with the grit. When that is done step into the bath and rinse off the grit with water and a Body Shop sponge or Body Shop body cloth, and relax for as little or as long as you like. Then take your sponge or cloth and apply a body shampoo of your choice. (DSD Bath and Shower Gel is perfect to use, if you like it, or use a herbal body shampoo.)

Have a really good scrub all over, rinse and get out of the bath. After you have dried off, apply body lotion again. DSD Body Lotion is excellent for skin and circulation, especially in the morning, or when you go out, as it does not put grease on your clothes. If you want something richer, especially at night, see if you can get hold of pure almond oil, or DSD massage cream, wheatgerm or apricot kernel oils. This routine may seem long, as you're exfoliating, but it should be carried out once a week.

If you have cellulite, or want to relax, aromatherapy and cellulite body oils are excellent on your body or in your bath at night. Micheline Arcier's are some of the finest essential and aromatherapy products for face, hair and body. The Tisserand range is also excellent – and has been tried and tested for years. Note: If you are pregnant, there are a number of aromatherapy products which are dangerous. See pages 174–177 for details of essential oils.

Some of the cellulite massage creams and soaps can be incorporated into your bathing routine.

The Mineral Salt Bath: It's an excellent idea to finish your exfoliating routine by having a DSD Salt Bath. This concentrates on pulling out toxins and increasing circulation to the body. Epsom salts in huge amounts in the bath are also excellent for stripping toxins. You actually feel physical lighter after these routines and your skin tone and texture are immediately improved. For your Dead Sea Salt Bath, dissolve half a bag of Dead Sea salts into a body-temperature bath and soak for thirty to forty minutes once a week – twice a week for extreme cases of eczema, psoriasis, arthritis, rheumatism, insomnia, bad circulation, cellulite or any skin or weight disorder. Make sure the bath is body temperature once you have warmed up, and continue to put cold water in your bath until the temperature is comfortable enough for you to soak.

Make bathtime a treat: ensure that everything else is taken care of in the house, so you don't have any chores to deal with afterwards. For example, outstanding phone calls, correspondence, bills, personal accounts, cleaning and washing should be taken care of, with your food, clothes and papers ready for the next day.

This whole routine is a must for eczema and psoriasis sufferers, but do add a cupful of DSD salts to your bath every night, soak for ten to fifteen minutes, and make sure you use the DSD Life product range – both in and out of the bath – on your face and body, alongside the DSD

Energizing range for the face. Take special care both nutritionally and in terms of relaxation – you will have to become skilled and consistent in all areas.

These above-mentioned products can be used by everyone except for those who suffer from a very greasy or spotty skin. For you the salts, bath gels, body shampoos and light body lotions are sufficient to keep and increase your body's suppleness and tone.

Use DSD spot treatment for spots, boils, or any other erosions on every part of the body. (see page 181 for more information on dealing with spots.) And as an extra boost, a DSD Black Body Mud can be applied to pull out the toxins and inject minerals to kill off the poisons, just before you exfoliate and soak in the bath.

HEALTHY HAIRCARE

Keeping your hair in good condition is vital. Most products on the market, whether they say so or not (especially the 'mild' frequent-wash shampoos), are full of detergent (that's the ingredient that causes shampoo to lather), which weakens the hair considerably.

For years, I researched and tried all sorts of products and methods for different types of hair. I found little difference from one to the other. You know what it's like – great for a while, then that particular product ceases to have an effect.

Not very long ago I came across a product range called J.F. Lazartigue. These people test the hair and then concentrate on separately treating the scalp and root from the rest of the hair. When you think about it, that makes perfect sense – like your skin, your hair can also change.

It's no wonder that those of you, like me, who have dry, curly hair, put on treatment after treatment, only to notice a greasiness in the scalp, development of lacklustre hair, or suddenly finding it difficult to style or to grow.

Likewise, those with greasy hair use products for a greasy scalp, which often leads to overdrying and split ends on the rest of the hair, making it flyaway and unmanageable.

Many of Lazartigue's shampoos don't lather, which feels strange at first, but when you come to style your hair, you notice an immediate improvement in its texture. Six months after prescribed action you get it checked out again, and probably change products.

This is just to give you an example of what a hair product should give you. You may find that when you choose products, you can formulate your own way of treating your scalp and hair separately. Again, experiment by looking at natural homoeopathic and organic products in your local healthshops, and play around with the numerous products available.

TEN TIPS FOR HEALTHY HAIR

○ If you are an every-day hair washer, see if you can have a break once or more a month, by leaving a treatment on your hair for a couple of days, and using the treatment to style your hair in a slicked back way. This way you will give the scalp a well-deserved rest.

○ When treating your hair, dry, greasy, normal, eczema-prone or otherwise, leave the treatment on overnight to benefit fully. Tuck a towel over your pillow to protect it from the treatments.

○ For flaky scalps of any sort, use specific treatments from DSD, Lazartigue or homoeopathic ranges, as they are by far the most effective.

○ Don't continually run your fingers through your hair, as this irritates any condition;

Tania

Tania was covered with psoriasis from head to toe when we met her. Obviously, we had to deal with the nutritional and psychological side of it, which helped greatly; however, we also had to clear up her body physically. We put her on Finder's Energizing, Life and DSD Salt products. Within six weeks the whole lot had cleared up. It was remarkable. There were a few little scars left on her elbows and knees, but that was it! She looked and felt terrific.

greasy hair constantly falling into your eyes leads to nasty spots on your forehead.

○ Get a brush that doesn't tear your hair; bristle brushes can do this. Mason-Pearson, or wide-toothed brushes are better. Never overbrush your hair. Brush up to the knots. Stop and then brush from the knot, gently, to the head.

○ When your hair is wet, don't brush it, but use a wide-toothed comb instead. Start detangling by combing from the ends first, then work up to the roots. Saw cut combs are the best choice.

○ Get a haircut or trim every six to eight weeks, to prevent split ends, and give hair back its bounce.

○ When washing your hair, concentrate on the scalp, as the scrubbing action increases the blood supply to the scalp, thereby nourishing the hair. And concentrate your conditioner on the ends of your hair – normally the driest part.

○ Avoid mousses and hairsprays with alcohol – they can damage hair irreparably.

○ Try a homemade conditioner: mix a little mayonnaise with a quarter of a teaspoon of olive oil. Let it soak into your hair for thirty to forty-five minutes. Rinse and wash as normal.

HANDS, NAILS AND FEET

These are such simple areas to take care of, and many people do not bother to take the time. By applying body lotion to your hands and feet on a daily basis, you can easily care for both the skin, cuticles and nails. Just make sure you massage hands, feet and cuticles thoroughly, and apply an alcohol-free cuticle softener, three times a week. When you massage cream into your hands, spend time working it into your wrist area firmly and slowly; this area governs a large part of the whole body's circulation. Furthermore, wrists tend to age very quickly, with the bending, stretching and exposure to elements they undergo. A little moisturizer, applied daily, will help slow down this process.

This is a part of physical maintenance that both men and women neglect. If you are lazy or

You must bath or shower before you go to bed; you must bathe at the end of every day. No matter how clean you think you are, your body is excreting waste products, not only in your stools and urine, but all day long in your sweat. Your body also accumulates tension and strain; it is important psychologically, as well as physically, to wash this off at the end of every day – to wind down, have a satisfying sleep and allow your body to repair.

don't know how to look after these areas fully, treat yourself to a professional treatment.

TEN TIPS FOR HEALTHY NAILS

○ Try a paraffin wax treatment, which you can do yourself. The warmth of the wax acts to stimulate the circulation to the nails, thereby enhancing growth. Warm the wax in a saucepan, let it cool until it's comfortable to touch. Place one hand on a piece of cling film or tinfoil, and paint on several layers of wax (five or more) with a brush. Wrap your hand in silver foil and then relax for twenty minutes. The wax will peel easily. Repeat on the other hand.

○ Sweet almond oil, combined with a little salt, and rubbed into the nails and cuticles, will strengthen weak or broken nails and provide nourishment to dry and flaking cuticles.

○ Massage the cuticles and nails with cod liver oil – paying particular attention to the

white moon at the base of the nails –
nourishes, and stimulates growth.

○ Always use alcohol-free nail polish
removers; standard removers strip nails of
their sheen, and dry them out, causing
peeling and breakage.

○ Try rubbing a rich hand cream or
petroleum jelly into your hands and nails,
then covering with an old pair of cotton
gloves. Keep the gloves on overnight,
allowing the heat of your hands to work
with the moisturizer to provide a 'hot-oil'
style treatment. Try the same treatment
on your feet, wearing cotton socks.

○ Healthy skin, hair and nails is promoted by
Vitamin B2 (Riboflavin); ensure that you
are getting sufficient quantities in your
diet. See page 124 for details of foods
which contain Riboflavin.

○ Zinc and calcium help get rid of white spots
on nails, and iron helps strengthen brittle
nails. These minerals should be an
essential part of your nutritional
programme. Check the list on pages 123–
124 to see if you are getting enough.

○ If you suffer from splits in your nails or
skin, or some sort of dermatitis, wear a
pair of cotton gloves beneath the rubber
ones you wear when washing up. This will
absorb perspiration and prevent re-
infection, as well as protecting your hands
from detergents.

○ There are several excellent homoeopathic
strengtheners available – both in external
and internal forms. Pay a visit to your local
healthshop or chemist to see what's
available. We recommend Weleda products.

○ Any stimulation of the nails will encourage
growth. Massage the base of your nails
whenever you can; and remember that
typing, piano playing or any other exercise
which requires substantial finger
movement will increase the blood supply
to the fingertips.

DENTAL CARE

If we are to look at the body holistically, we
cannot discuss body health without including the
health of the mouth – for the health of one
reflects the health of the other. How many times
have you seen a girl with a very pretty face?
Then she smiles and reveals mis-shapen,
discoloured teeth which spoil her looks. And how
many times have you longed to have teeth like
those of the fashion models in glossy magazines?

Dentistry has progressed a long way over the
past ten years. And the excuses we give
ourselves for not having healthy mouths: if only I
were younger; if only I were more wealthy; if
only I had a decent dentist, can no longer apply.
Good dentistry and healthy mouths are available
for all of us at any age, and whatever our financial
status. We can view this from two aspects – the
work and commitment we require from the
dentist and, secondly, and probably most
importantly, the care we have to provide on a
daily basis for ourselves.

Take a large mirror, put on a strong light, or
preferably daylight, and take a good look at your
mouth. Are you happy with the colour of your
teeth? With the shape? With the alignment?
Make a note of all the things you find. Then
discuss them with your dentist.

Colour of the teeth can be improved with
veneers, bonding (or bleaching). Shape of the
teeth can be improved with crowns and bonding.
Alignment of the teeth can be improved at any
age with orthodontics. The colour and texture of
the gums can be improved by a scale, polish and
instruction in self-care. And what if your dentist
won't do it? Then find one that will. Go on the
recommendation of friends – it's usually the most
reliable way.

Worried about payment? Ask to be treated
under the National Health; join a dental insurance
scheme; or, ask your dentist if he will arrange a
series of monthly payments.

TEN TIPS FOR HEALTHY TEETH

The most sophisticated dentistry will do you no
good if you pay little heed to the daily cleaning
routines: getting rid of the plaque that sticks to
our teeth.

○ Choose a nylon toothbrush with a small
head and chunky handle which you can grip
properly. Replace the brush every two months.

○ Use any fluoride toothpaste, apart from smokers' pastes, which are too abrasive, but only use a small amount (about the size of a pearl). Then work in a circular pattern around your mouth. Brush all the way round the outsides of the bottom teeth, and back round the insides. Do the same with the top teeth, and finish by cleaning the chewing surfaces of all the back teeth.

○ Always angle the brush into the gums so that the nylon bristles work on the area where tooth meets gum.)

○ Use either short back and forth strokes for back and side teeth, top and bottom, and small circles for front teeth. You will find that it takes about two and a half to three minutes to do this routine effectively. Choose the time of day that you feel is the most appropriate to spend that long on brushing. You may feel that the brushing you do first thing in the morning and last thing at night is purely a social clean because you have no time for anything else. As long as one brushing per day is for two and a half to three minutes, it really doesn't matter when you do it.

○ Finish by using dental tape between the teeth to remove the plaque which the toothbrush has been unable to reach.

○ Your diet will also be reflected in the health of your teeth and gums. Too many sweet/sticky foods will make plaque stickier and harder to remove. Constant snacking will make your teeth decay more quickly. Try Endekay dental gum, which can be chewed after eating and drinking, to neutralize the plaque acids when you can't get to your toothbrush.

○ Healthy teeth and bones are the result of adequate calcium consumption – make sure you're eating enough. See page 123 for details of calcium-rich foods.

○ The acid in fizzy drinks can strip the enamel from your teeth – and rob your body of the vitamins and minerals necessary to healthy and strong white teeth. If your teeth become transparent-looking, cut down immediately.

○ An excellent home bleach for teeth can be prepared by mixing ¼ teaspoon of hydrogen peroxide (available at the chemist) with 2½ tablespoons of bicarbonate of soda (baking soda) and ¼ teaspoon of water. Carefully press this paste along your teeth, brushing gently. Try to avoid touching this paste to your lips or gums, which could lead to blistering.

○ There are a number of homoeopathic toothpastes and tinctures on the market. If you suffer from bleeding gums, rinse your mouth with a solution of warm water and sea salt, then rub your gums with hyperal tincture (available at the chemist). Bleeding gums is a sign of Vitamin C deficiency. Make sure you are getting enough.

BEAUTY TREATMENTS

When you go to a salon for a treatment, there are several factors that it is advisable for you to check:

1. When choosing a therapist, check the training they have received, particularly if you are having treatment of a more serious nature, such as electrolysis, waxing or permanent eye-lining. It is well worth being informed about the treatments, so that you can talk in a knowledgeable way to the therapist.

2. Don't ever sign up for a course of treatments without:
   a) Finding out the pros and cons and limitations of the treatment. Insist on having a proper consultation first (this should be at no extra cost), and always try one session before agreeing to a complete course;
   b) Enquiring what you can do on a nutritional level, or any level, to back up the treatment; and
   c) Discussing your expectations of the treatment so that the therapist can verify them.

3. If you feel a treatment or product was a 'rip-off', rather than complain to friends and colleagues about it, go straight back to the salon. You may be able to get some sort of compensation.

The important thing with beauty treatments is that you don't simply hope for the best – you could be left cynical and demoralized. You must become involved in what is going on. Don't feel guilty or shy about doing this. The creator of the DSD products, and of many very effective treatments, Bharti Vyas, taught me that a beautician's job is to increase her client's knowledge of his or her body in as many ways as she is qualified to do. A beauty therapist should always take into account that, on a treatment level, everybody is completely different, even if the actual products are the same. It is especially important that they check for contra-indications; for instance, if you are pregnant or suffer from high blood pressure or varicose veins, certain treatments will not be suitable for you.

Before using beauty treatments it is important that you are eating correctly and consistently, and looking after your face and body daily, or no treatment or course of treatments has a hope of being beneficial. So use the treatments in conjunction with your own day-to-day routines to speed up the process of attaining your desired results.

The treatments I have chosen to outline are those that concentrate on relaxation, and which continue to work on a deep level to clear out toxins, to open up blocked energy paths, and to increase the circulation.

TURKISH BATHS

Also called steam rooms, these are better than taking a sauna because they do not dry the skin to such a degree, and are more pleasant to use, as breathing is easier. You should not use a Turkish bath if you are pregnant, have high blood pressure, a heart condition or psoriasis. If in doubt, check with your doctor.

Stay in the steam for as long as you feel comfortable, and then, ideally, step into the cold plunge pool, or take a cold shower. Try to repeat this three times and you'll find that you feel completely different and remarkably relaxed afterwards. I massage an aromatherapy oil, in a base oil, on to my body after two steam/plunge sessions so that it can be deeply absorbed into the skin and inhaled deep into the body. See **Essential oils**, pages 174–177, for the oils that are suitable for this process.

If you are taking a Turkish bath for the first time, take a warm shower first and then switch to cool water, before steaming for five minutes. Then take a cool shower (not a plunge) and return for five to seven minutes. Repeat once more if you wish.

Up to one-third of the body's waste products, which would normally be disposed of via the kidneys, can be sweated out in a Turkish bath. The alternation of the hot and cold temperatures is excellent for stimulating the circulation, which will help to nourish, and release, tight muscles.

Drink plenty of fresh water afterwards to replace body fluids, and relax in a warm, quiet place for half an hour.

JACUZZIS AND HYDRO BATHS

Both of these are very relaxing, and are best used in conjunction with mineral-salts. Jacuzzis and hydro baths are an excellent relaxant and circulation stimulant, before having a body wrap or massage. The hydro bath is more powerful than a jacuzzi, but both are ideal for stimulating circulation, for relaxing stiff muscles and joints, and for producing a state of total mental and physical wellbeing. Both are generally filled with hot water; make sure it is not too hot, or its beneficial effects will be lost. Jacuzzis and hydro baths are not recommended for pregnant women, as the movement and heat of the water may lead to contractions.

You can quite cheaply fit a jacuzzi system in your bath at home, and it is an excellent way to combine your bathing routine with a type of water massage. If you have one in your home, why not experiment with some aromatherapy oils – they really work.

MASSAGE

If it were possible I would have a daily massage! I believe that massage is invaluable in reducing stress. When being massaged it is important that you breathe deeply: breathe out completely – especially when the masseur/euse hits the sensitive points. Remember, in chapter five, we learned that pain control is easier when you breathe *into* the pain; i.e., exhaling deeply instead of inhaling – our body's natural reaction.

Splash your breasts with cold water after showering or bathing in order to stimulate circulation and muscle tone.

Be prepared to relax into the treatment; in order to release tension completely, you need to find a massage expert you feel at ease with. There are so many different methods and many good therapists; everyone has a favourite, so ask around. It is a good idea to shower first, if possible, and ideally to have a heat treatment, such as a Turkish bath or a short session in a jacuzzi to relax you beforehand.

Massage should never be used to relieve pain caused by injury; in fact, stimulation of and pressure on inflamed joints and muscles can cause enormous damage. If you are injured, contact a registered osteopath.

Deep massage, such as G5 or over-zealous skin brushing on the legs can be lethal on skin that is prone to broken veins. If your circulation is poor below the waist, and you know that your muscle tone is not good, of if you have cellulite or are overweight, you are best advised to use lymphatic drainage or aromatherapy, along with any body wraps you may like to try. Only when you have either lost weight and maintained the weight loss, or you notice that your skin has become a good, even colour should you have G5 or other forms of deep massage. When you do have these treatments, check your skin immediately after the treatment, and for the following three days to see that broken veins have not developed on the legs.

BODY WRAPS

Body wraps use either mud, seaweed or paraffin to achieve a number of things:
- They can produce inch loss by flushing out excess fluid;
- They can feed, soften and moisturize the skin more effectively than a regular moisturizer or body lotion can (especially paraffin wax);
- They stimulate circulation, improve cell metabolism and improve skin tone;
- They detoxify the skin; and
- They reduce the effects of stress, and relax tense muscles.

I find the DSD mud wrap the most effective for inch loss, softer skin, weight and toxin reduction and the pleasant sensation of having toxins leeched from the body.

Have a body wrap once a week for the first four weeks of your new health regime; then once every other week for the following month. After that, continue for as long as you want.

As with any therapy, you must remember to aim to improve all areas of your life before you will be able to see visible results. Nutrition is particularly important under these circumstances. For your body to release toxins successfully, you must supplement the therapies with internal cleansers, and that means plenty of fresh water, herbal teas, fresh fruit and vegetables, and avoiding caffeine, alcohol and tobacco. Seer **Nutrition**, chapter six, for details.

LYMPHATIC DRAINAGE

The lymphatic system plays a vital role in the transportation of toxins, and in protection against disease. The lymph is moved by the pumping action of the muscles. Most conditions that involve poor lymphatic drainage are the result of a poor circulatory system or insufficient activity. Manual massage to key points can increase lymphatic drainage.

There are also beauty treatments (developed in hospitals to treat severe cases of oedema, or fluid retention), which improve the functioning of the lymphatic system. The Normaform system uses inflatable leg 'boots' to create pressure, which pushes the lymph along. As well as having health benefits, it is useful in conjunction with a mud wrap to treat cellulite. You should have the lymphatic treatments regularly and close together – twice a week, ideally – to get the full benefit.

Some aromatherapy products, for instance

rosewood and geranium, will encourage the lymphatic flow. Furthermore, a healthy diet which stimulates circulation – avoiding the sluggish flow of blood caused by toxins – will also benefit your lymphatic system. A healthy lymphatic flow will wash away cysts, which could otherwise have led to cancerous growths. Any sort of stress due to fatigue, emotions or worry can result in the breakdown of the lymphatic system.

AROMATHERAPY

As we discovered in Chapter Five, one of the greatest pleasures of the more medicinal kind is the field of aromatherapy. The essential oils have a healing effect on the body, penetrating the skin, and having beneficial effects on the emotions when they are inhaled.

Essential oils can effectively ease and treat many problems: sleep, stress, nervous tension, excitement, fatigue and depression, for example. They can be used to invigorate and stimulate, or to relax the system. Many oils have anti-viral and antiseptic properties.

You should use the highest-quality oils you can find. As a rule of thumb, the pure essential oils are expensive, as the cheaper versions are synthesized. Aromatherapy is the one instance where we recommend buying the most expensive products.

Essential oils can be used in a number of ways:

1. *In the bath:* Add six to ten drops to the running water and swill them round before you get in. Close the bathroom door so that you can make the most of the vapour.
2. *For massage:* Generally speaking, the oils should *not* be applied neat to the skin, but should be diluted first. Use two drops of your chosen oil to two teaspoons of a carrier oil – or a mixture of carrier oils – such as almond, wheatgerm or sunflower oils. Many essential oils are beneficial for the complexion. Don't rub into the face – just smooth the oil on.
3. *Inhalation:* Place six to ten drops in a basin of hot water. Then place a towel over your head and the basin. Inhale the perfume for five to ten minutes. Or place a drop in a plant spray bottle filled with water, and spray into the atmosphere.

You can add a few drops of one oil, or a blend of oils, to a little water and place on a source of heat, such as a radiator. Special vapourizers are very effective, and are available from some healthfood shops and aromatherapy oil suppliers (see page 177 for details). You can also try placing a drop on to your pillow before you go to bed, or in a handkerchief.

4. *As a compress:* Add two drops to approximately one half pint of water. Skim a flannel over the top of the water, wring it out and place it over the affected area. Cover with a towel, and leave for ten minutes. Use cold compresses for sprains and headaches, and hot compresses for menstrual pain, boils, earaches, etc.
5. *As a cosmetic scent:* You can certainly use the oils as a perfume, blending with a little carrier oil first, or if you prefer a lighter scent, with a blend of oil and fresh water. Remember that some aromatherapy oils can stain clothing.

Note: *Never* take essential oils internally, their effects are purely on an external basis.

ESSENTIAL OILS AND HOW TO USE THEM

The following guide to some of the essential oils outlines some of the best ways to use them. There are, of course, numerous other beneficial effects; consult an aromatherapist for a complete list (see page 177 for details).

The abbreviations denote the following:

B	Bath	S	Skincare
C	Compress	V	Vapourizer
I	Inhalation	X	Do not use during
M	Massage		pregnancy
P	Perfume		

Bergamot: Revives your spirits. Good for balancing out oily skin, and for treating acne and cold sores. Useful when suffering from cystitis. Never use bergamot when you are going to be exposed to ultraviolet light; for instance, when sunbathing. B C M P S V

Chamomile: Very calming for emotional upset,

and for soothing the skin. Use on dry, irritated or inflamed skin. An excellent relaxant: ideal for insomnia, stress and tension relief. Sitting in a chamomile bath, along with drinking chamomile tea, will bring relief from thrush. B C M S V

Camphor: Antiseptic, this oil is used for treating coughs and colds by inhalation. Use with caution, and avoid if you have sensitive skin. I V

Cedarwood: Soothing and astringent, it is good for oily skin and acne, and can be inhaled if you have catarrh or a cough. It will also repel insects. B M I S

Clary sage: This uplifting oil is warming and soothing, and can be massaged on to muscular aches, and during painful menstruation. It has sensual properties, and gives you a sense of wellbeing. B C M P V X

Cypress: This refreshes and revitalizes. It is good for oily skin, and can be massaged on to the stomach during painful periods. Particularly useful for fighting cellulite and fluid retention. B C I M S V

Fennel: With its distinctive aniseed aroma, it is used to treat cellulite and fluid retention, and for the digestive system, particularly aiding nausea. Be careful with it, if you have sensitive skin. M V X

Frankincense: Restores tone to mature skin. It soothes and aids meditation, and will ease colds, catarrh and coughs. B I M S V

Geranium: This oil has a balancing effect on the mind and body. It is astringent and good for oily skin, and for fluid retention. B M P S V

Jasmine: With an exotic aroma, this sensual oil will uplift you, and relax tense muscles. It is very good for hot, dry skin, and for swelling. Excellent in pregnancy. B M P S V

Juniper berry: Tones, stimulates and purifies the skin and body, and is good for fluid retention and the breaking down of cellulite. B I M V X

Lavender: This popular oil relaxes, restores and balances the body. It is excellent for muscle aches and pains, headaches and aching feet, nausea, fatigue and general depression. Add a few drops to your pillow to aid restful sleep. *Can* be used neat on minor burns, headaches, insect bites and cuts. It is also an insect repellent. Lavender is particularly useful for preventing

stretchmarks, when mixed with neroli and a carrier oil. B C I M S P V

Lemon: Astringent, cooling and cleansing, a lemon oil facial massage is good for oily skin. Can be used neat on corns, verrucas and warts. Beware if you have sensitive skin, and do not use if you may be exposed to strong sunlight. B C M V

Lemongrass: A refreshing and cooling oil. Do not use if you may be sunbathing, and avoid on sensitive skin. An excellent tonic for fatigue and nausea in pregnancy. B M V

Mandarine: You can add this to lavender and neroli to help avoid stretchmarks during pregnancy. It is also good for the digestive system. B M S V

Sweet Marjoram: Wonderful for tense, tight muscles, and for massaging the stomach during painful periods. Very soothing at night. B C I M V X

Melissa: Known as 'lemon balm', this soothes both body and mind, and revives your spirits. You can inhale it if you have a cough. Avoid on sensitive skin. B I M V

Myrrh: This is good for chapped skin, to treat athletes foot, and when suffering from colds, a sore throat or catarrh. B I S V X

Neroli: This beautiful, sensual oil soothes, calms and revives you. It is very relaxing at night, and is good for dry, mature or sensitive skin and on scars. B M P S V

Orange: A revitalizer and soother, this warming oil is good for winter-time baths. B M V

Patchouli: With its musky aroma, this is useful for dry, mature and irritated skins, and for treating acne. It is also spiritually uplifting. B M P S V

Peppermint: Cooling and uplifting, it is good for the digestive system, tired feet and headaches. It can help clear thinking. This oil is one exception to the external-use-only rule. A drop of peppermint oil on a sugar cube, taken first thing in the morning helps prevent morning sickness in pregnancy. B C I M V

Pine needle: A powerful antiseptic, this oil stimulates and cleanses. Useful in inhalations for colds, catarrh, sinusitis and sore throats. B C I V

When washing your hair, concentrate on the scalp, as the scrubbing action increases the blood supply, thereby nourishing the hair and stimulating growth. And concentrate your conditioner on the ends of your hair – the driest part.

Rose: A soothing and uplifting aromatherapy oil that can increase your confidence. It is widely used for dry, mature and sensitive skins, and it can reduce the appearance of thread veins. B M P S V

Rosemary: Revives and clears the mind, helping concentration. It is good for muscular aches and when inhaled, for colds and catarrh. You can add it to water and use it as a final rinse on your hair for extra shine. B C I M S V X

Sandalwood: This musky aromatic oil relaxes and calms you. It is good for dry or oily skin and for acne. It also soothes sore throats. B I M P S V

Tea tree: This powerful antiseptic oil can be used to treat acne, and *can* be applied neat on to spots, verrucas, warts, white spots on skin and insect bites. It is good for coughs and colds, and when suffering from thrush. Avoid using on sensitive skins. B C I M S V

Vetivert: An exotic oil that calms and relaxes you; it can be successfully blended with sandalwood or jasmine. Excellent for deep sleep. B M P V

Ylang-ylang: This sweet, exotic scent calms and soothes, especially at night. Use of this oil provides a sensual massage. B M P S V

TEN TIPS FOR AROMATHERAPY

These are some of our favourite oils and treatments, and you can probably learn to blend your own. Don't be afraid to experiment.

○ Rose oil (the most expensive of the essential oils) is excellent for dry and ageing skin. Blended with a little jasmine in a base oil, and gently massaged into the face and neck, is healing, soothing and rejuvenating.

○ Soak in lavender oil in your bath for five to twenty minutes. It is healing and relaxing for tight muscles and tired bodies, and will aid insomnia.

○ If you are under stress, or want to relax and have a good night's sleep, our favourite aromatic remedy is to place a few drops of vetivert in a little carrier oil and massage into the palms of the hands, the soles of the feet and then anti-clockwise on the solar plexus, just before you go to sleep. Sylvia, who was an insomniac, found this amazingly effective – which is saying a lot. She had tried every known trick in the book, until she found this method worked.

○ Use essential oils of lavender, chamomile and rose, singly or blended, as a massage oil to ease nausea, faintness, low blood pressure and headaches.

○ Rosewood, geranium and palmarosa oils have bacteria-killing and healing properties, and can be used to treat cystic mastitis and to encourage the lymphatic flow. These same oils are used to fight fear and depression. Use them in the bath together, or separately, or in a vapourizer.

○ Full-body massage with an individual blend of essential oils, like rosemary and lavender, may increase intestinal movement and relieve constipation.

○ Massage with bergamot, sandalwood, geranium and lavender helps to prevent infection and to enhance the healing process following an operation, thus lessening pain and discomfort. Speak to your doctor about when it will be safe to bathe fully, with these oils in your bathwater. Until then, use a vapourizer or a few drops on your pillow.

○ Massage and bathing in clary sage and rosemary can help prevent infertility in women, by increasing cervical mucus and acting directly on the hypophiso-ovarian axis. Full-body massage is an excellent prelude to intercourse, and a number of these oils will prevent stress, now known to be a major cause of infertility. Rose oil for men, in the bath or a vapourizer, can help to increase sperm production.

○ Gentle massage of the abdomen with geranium, rose or cypress helps to lessen heavy menstrual flow and flooding. Clary sage can help regulate your menstrual cycle.

○ Daily scalp massage with a blend of lavender, rosemary or chamomile in apricot kernel oil increases scalp circulation and nourishes your hair follicles.

Note: These tips are printed as guidelines only; don't be surprised if you are prescribed something entirely different. All aromatherapists prepare blends of oils to suit individual requirements, taking into consideration mental and physical characteristics and complaints.

We have found that one of the best centres for the real Mccoy of aromatherapy treatments is the Micheline Arcier salon in London. Her oils are available by mail order and can be sent worldwide. Her combination oils include circularome, coldarome, sleeparome and vigarome – which helps you fight depression and fatigue. Contact: Micheline Arcier Aromatherapy, 7 William Street, London SW1 (071-235 3545), for a catalogue, or to arrange an appointment.

Robert Tisserand, also one of the most respected aromatherapists, sells his oils, and base oils, through healthfood shops, and by mail order. They are of the highest quality. See page 68, in **Staying Healthy**, for details.

Danièle Ryman's and Bodytreats' oils are also widely available and are very good. Danielle Ryman's products are available from the Park Lane Hotel, on Piccadilly in London; or call 071-753 6707 for details. Bodytreats Limited is situated at 15 Approach Road, London SW20; or call them on 081-543 7633.

COMMON COMPLAINTS AND CURES

Like those internal ailments, which we discussed in Chapter Five, there are numerous cosmetic and external problems which can be dealt with by making dietary changes, and by taking care of our bodies. Most importantly, however, cosmetic complaints *can* be cured, or altered, with the various methods available today. The following is a list of causes and preventative measures for those niggling skin and body problems which plague us all.

BODY HAIR

Waxing is one choice. Another choice for the legs is the new gadgets that have spinning wire wheels which pluck out the hairs at high speed – worth investment (unless you are very sensitive to pain), as you do not have to wait for the substantial amount of regrowth necessary for waxing. You do have to grin and bear the pain (especially around the ankles and knees), but the system is quick and efficient. You should not use these epilators on the bikini line, on the face or under the arms.

If you occasionally have ingrown hairs, which occur particularly on the face, the groin and the legs, gently exfoliate the area every day. There is a very good lotion by a French marine-based cosmetics company Thalgo, which is called Biodepyl. This soothes the skin after waxing, threading or shaving and helps to prevent ingrown hairs.

Creams and old-fashioned shaving are other options, but for long-term smoothness, and the least-damaging process, we suggest the above, or electrolysis.

When you massage cream into your hands, take time to work it firmly and slowly into your wrist. This area governs a large part of the whole body's circulation.

There is a new type of electrolysis, combining two theories. The first type of electrolysis was called Galvanic and involved a chemical reaction, resulting in the fluid in the hair follicle turning into a slightly caustic substance, and thus killing the hair.

The second type of electrolysis was called Diathermie, and basically cauterized the hair cells. This new type is a combination of the two, and is very simply called The Blend. It is much quicker and more gentle, and regrowth is noticeably slower.

CELLULITE

So how do you know whether you have got cellulite in the first place? One of the main features is dimpling, which you will see if you stand up. Flabby or fat skin does not necessarily have this. Another factor is that areas of cellulite feel cold to the touch because the circulation is poor in these areas. The skin may be lighter or darker, too, and difficult to tan.

If you pinch an area with cellulite, you will find that it stays up for longer than, for instance, skin on the forearm. This indicates that the fat cells are waterlogged. In the early stages, it is soft, but if it is allowed to accumulate, it becomes hard and grainy feeling. The harder cellulite is, the more difficult it becomes to get rid of, although it is never impossible.

Cellulite has nothing to do with being overweight. You can be slim or skinny and still have cellulite deposits. Alternatively, you can be extremely fat and not have any cellulite at all.

If you do have cellulite, you should do all you can to get rid of it. It indicates that your body is in a toxic condition. If the cellulite is left untreated, the toxicity could lead to more serious conditions, such as arthritis or permanent water retention. The presence of cellulite is a warning that your body needs a thorough cleanse and detoxification.

There is plenty of evidence to suggest that it is caused by poor nutrition, stress, intake of drugs, lack of exercise, tea and coffee and alcohol, cigarettes, poor circulation and a sluggish lymphatic system.

Cellulite is not a problem confined to older women. The condition can appear as early as twelve or thirteen, and then remain for life if left untreated.

In fact, it is thought that the condition is caused above all by the presence of oestrogen. The more oestrogen there is in a woman's body, the more likely she is to develop cellulite. The danger times for developing cellulite are puberty, overwork, lack of sleep, pregnancy and menopause, the greatest time of hormonal fluctuation.

The reason most of us don't feel ill when we have a cellulite problem is that the body has been successful in sending the rubbish far away from vital organs. With men, the rubbish is retained nearer the centre, which is why they are far more likely to suffer from heart, circulatory and blood pressure problems, and beer bellies.

There is very little we can do about the amount of oestrogen circulating in our bodies. However, oestrogen will not send rubbish to outlying areas unless there is rubbish to send. So, the first thing to understand about cellulite is that it is caused mainly by leading an unhealthy lifestyle. The body does all it can to neutralize the effect of those substances which it does not need, and which may actually have a harmful effect.

Lifestyle: Women who are very active, eat a wholefood diet, and abstain from alcohol, cigarettes and caffeine, will rarely get cellulite. These days, many women have sedentary jobs. Prolonged inactivity of this kind can slow down the circulation. When treating cellulite, therapists often notice that cellulite deposits are at their worst where the legs meet the chair edge, the place where circulation is cut off the most.

Dry skin brushing: You have to use the right kind of brush. An ordinary loofah or bath mitt won't do, nor will those patent self-massages advertised at high prices. The only kind of brush which does an effective job of helping to cleanse the lymphatic system is a long-handled wooden brush made from natural fibres. At first, this kind of brushing will feel strange and rough but most people find it invigorating and beneficial in a short period of time.

If you suffer from splits in your nails or skin, or some sort of dermatitis, wear a pair of cotton gloves beneath the rubber ones you wear when washing up. This will absorb perspiration and prevent re-infection, as well as protecting your hands from detergents.

Brush by using long, firm and brisk strokes – starting at the feet and working up the legs, and over the thighs and buttocks. But take care if your cellulite is bad or you may cause broken veins.

You have to begin skin brushing at the same time as starting to correct your diet. Together, the two work wonders to get rid of cellulite that has been long held in body cells, and will encourage it to disperse. However, as cellulite is often very hard, you may need the help of aromatherapy and massage as well. See pages 174 to 176 for details of the oils which encourage lymphatic drainage and circulation.

On the nutrition front, cut out wheat, yeast, alcohol, coffee, tea, red meat, and cut down on acidic foods.

ECZEMA AND PSORIASIS

Eczema: The symptoms of eczema are often an itchy red rash, raw skin and blistering. Atopic eczema, which often develops in very young children, is due to a defect in the immune system which causes the skin to react to a number of different substances. People with atopic eczema are frequently prone to asthma and hayfever. A wide range of allergens – foods (particularly cow's milk and dairy produce), household dust, feathers, animal hairs and pollens, for instance – can lead to it.

Eczema, although similar in appearance, differs from an allergic skin reaction, where a person, once sensitized to an allergen, will always react to any amount of that substance; and it is different to contact dermatitis, which is the result of concentrated or long-term application of an irritant and which does not necessarily recur.

Treatment: Because the skin looks the same in these three cases, it can be very difficult to pinpoint the cause. All allergic and irritant skin reactions are itchy. Avoid the use of soap and water, which will dry the skin and use a non-fragranced bath cleanser such as E45 Bath Oil. E45 Cream, used on the skin, will also soothe it. Avoid using corticosteroid creams, if possible, which are prescribed for the condition. They cause thinning and reddening of the skin by damaging the collagen. In addition, the skin can become 'hooked' on these corticosteroids and a rebound effect may occur. Evening primrose oil supplements, although expensive, are useful. Take 500 mg a day.

DSD products, as described on page 167, are also excellent.

Psoriasis: The red, flaky patches that indicate psoriasis most commonly affect the scalp, elbows, shoulders, lower back and knees. The precise cause is unknown at present; it is the result of the cells turning over too quickly and it can be triggered by stress, shock, fatigue and depression. The condition is frequently hereditary.

Treatment: Alternative therapies, such as acupuncture and homoeopathy, can prove helpful. Bathing in mineral salts is recognized as a potent remedy. DSD produce a tar shampoo which, although thick and strong-smelling, helps many people. DSD Life and Energizing products, as explained on page 167, are essential to relieve the problem.

FACIAL HAIR

The four methods we have tried are waxing, bleaching, electrolysis and threading.

Waxing: This is fast and effective. We prefer to go to a beauty therapist rather than do it ourselves, as the skin on the face is so delicate. Waxing also tends to be good for the skin, acting as a moisturizer and rejuvenator.

Bleaching: On light growth this is a good option. Make sure you go to a competent beautician, however, Badly bleached facial hair can look patchy, and the sensitive skin can be burned.

Electrolysis: This destroys the hair in the follicle. However, it is a long process as the therapist has to catch each hair in its growing cycle, and if she overworks the area (which more often than not is the case), it will quite rapidly wrinkle and scar at a later stage. Although it is a permanent solution we feel that the risks are very high.

Threading: The Chinese art of threading is by far the least painful and most effective I have come across. It takes two years for a therapist to master the technique properly. Using simply cotton thread, wound around the fingers, the therapist can remove the hair from the whole area in one session. The regrowth is definitely weaker. For ninety-five per cent of people, scarring is non-existent and, at worst, minimal. As with anything else, the pain factor depends on how sensitive that area of skin is for you.

Avoid having a waxing or threading treatment just before your period, when the skin is more sensitive.

MOLES

You should keep a close eye on moles, and look in particular for any changes in shape or colour. If you notice a change, you must have it checked by your doctor immediately, as early treatment is vital in cases of potential malignancy. If there are any moles you are uncertain about, even if they have not changed, do consult your GP.

Moles, if you consider them unsightly, can be surgically removed. Remember that even the tiniest moles can cause scarring when removed. Be careful to check on the pros and cons of removal.

PIGMENTATION MARKS

This is a condition where the skin on the face and body develops a marked difference from the natural skin colour, and blotchy patches – which may be lighter or darker than the normal skin colour. The main causes are the contraceptive Pill and over-exposure to the sun. Smoking and drinking coffee and tea can also contribute.

The best thing to use is a daily peeling mask, and then at night apply an ointment of salicylic acid and sulphur ointment BPC. Please check with your doctor first, as he/she will be able to give you a prescription for this. Always wear high-factor sunscreens (ideally a 'sunblock') when sunbathing, particularly on your face.

Black-skinned men and women are particularly susceptible to changes in pigmentation, and should not have electrolysis, or use facial scrubs.

Pantothenic acid, taken internally as a vitamin/mineral supplement can retard and remove age spots, and extremely varied pigmentation. Natural dietary sources include eggs, wholegrain cereals and organic meats, or if you aren't getting enough, try taking 100mg daily (although the dosage may be increased to 600mg for severe cases; you *must* consult your doctor before taking such measures).

RASHES

Common causes of rashes are reactions to toiletries or cosmetics, reactions to household or industrial chemicals (contact dermatitis), and a

---

The acid in fizzy drinks can strip the enamel from your teeth and rob your body of vitamins and minerals necessary to strong and healthy white teeth. If your teeth become transparent, give up fizzy drinks at once.

reaction to food that you have eaten. If the rash concerns you, you should consult your practitioner. Try to avoid putting anything at all on the area until the rash has subsided, and try to identify the source of the problem. Drink plenty of water to cool down the blood, and stay off all other fluids, except perhaps nettle and limeflower teas, which have an astringent and antiseptic effect.

Prickly heat rash is usually spotty, occurring when the sweat glands become blocked, mostly on the chest, arms and back. If you know that you are prone to it, take the following measures to avoid it:

○ Avoid excess heat and sweating, and take cooling dips or showers frequently. Gently pat the skin dry afterwards;

○ Avoid strong sunlight, especially between eleven a.m. and three p.m.; and

○ Wear a high-protection sunscreen. Piz Buin's Allergy Lotion was formulated with prickly heat sufferers in mind, and provides good protection against the UVA rays.

If you do develop prickly heat, stay cool, out of the sun, until it goes away completely. Apply calamine lotion and wear loose clothing with natural fibres. I have also tried TCP lotion on someone with severe prickly heat and, although it is very strong, it did give instant relief and cleared up very quickly. You should test a small area first, and take it from there. When you go back into the sun, build up very slowly and try to stay cool.

For rashes in general, wear cotton clothing to allow your skin to breathe. An oatmeal wash (six ounces of oatmeal, tied in a muslin or linen cloth) will sooth itching. Chickweed ointment, available from some chemists is soothing and relieves the itching.

SPOTS AND BUMPS

Spots and bumps start to appear from puberty as a result of hormonal changes in the body. 'Adult acne', as it is known, is also very common, and can last into your thirties or longer; this is often linked to stress, lack of sleep and a history of poor nutrition (sugar and carbohydrate orientated). The chin and neck are common sites for stress-related break-outs. The contraceptive Pill, iodine and very humid atmospheres are some of the conditions that can aggravate inflammation for some people.

Squeezing spots can spread the infection within the tissues, and lead to bruising and scarring. Leave them alone until you know you can remove the infection cleanly. *Don't* use abrasive scrubs on inflamed skin, or harsh cleansing products which strip the skin of oils, as they will irritate it and dry the surface of the skin. Duller, yellow skins scar easily, so although this is a rule for everybody, *don't pick* if this is your skin colour. Picking and squeezing also encourages unequal pigmentation. Learn to emulsify any blockage with a spot treatment.

Stay away from using cream cleansers. Use a mild astringent to cleanse instead. Keep some TCP in your cupboard, and sparingly treat the spots with it during the day and night. It's quite harsh and can sting, but it will dry out excess oils and toxins. Make sure you only dab it on the affected area, or it will dry your skin unnecessarily. Lightly apply DSD Mud Mask to infected areas overnight. However, if you have a blind spot (you know, the ones under the skin that really hurt and have no head) apply Magnesium Sulphate paste BP, which is available from chemists; it will draw it out.

One timeless product to have, that you can get from practically any chemist, is Noxzema. It is soothing and healing, and relieves bruising and soreness more quickly than anything else I have tried. If it's an evening or weekend, and you are relaxing around the house, keep applying Noxzema to the area, covering it completely every time the cream dries. Alternatively, use Germoline, which is non-greasy, soothing and antiseptic.

During the day, treatments which also help to disguise spots are a good option. Two of the best ones are the Helena Harnik spot healer (very good for healing scars), and the DSD spot treatment.

If you suffer from constant break-outs of spots or severe problem skin, regular salon facials will make a big difference. The

Cathiodermie facial by René Guinot has been used for well over twenty years for problem skins, and can greatly ease the problem, reducing the risk of permanent scarring. It deep-cleanses and sterilizes the skin.

Vitamin C from fruits and vegetables is a natural detoxifier, and helps to prevent the formation of blemishes. Drinking hot water and lemon juice, or rosehip tea helps too. Any vitamin deficiency could lead to problem skin; remember to keep your diet balanced, it will be reflected in virtually every aspect of your appearance.

One important point to note on sunbathing and spots is that although the sun dries out spots and temporarily improves the situation, you may well find when you return from holiday that your skin becomes oilier and more problematic than before.

Drink plenty of fresh water, and eat fresh, unprocessed foods with a high water content. The more water your body has to work on, the easier its job. And one of the first places a toxin-free body manifests its health is the skin!

STRETCHMARKS

Caused by rapid changes in weight, and by the presence of the hormone oestrogen, stretchmarks often appear after pregnancy or dieting. Stretchmarks also often appear at puberty and as a result of taking steriods. Prevention is the key: don't crash diet. But in pregnancy there is only so much you can do to avoid them. Once stretchmarks have formed they cannot be removed, although they will fade with time. It is interesting that many men develop stretchmarks, too, as a result of hormonal changes.

Fine, delicate, very pale and sensitive skins are especially susceptible to stretchmarks, and women with these skin types should watch their weight from an early age. You must wear a supportive bra when the breasts become heavy during pregnancy – or if you have heavy breasts naturally. Cotton bras are much better than synthetic bras, which can lead to perspiration, clogging pores and eventually weakening the skin.

In pregnancy, from day one, you should gently massage an oil (pre-natal oils are available from most good chemists or try Vichy's anti-stretchmark lotion which has shown good results) into the breasts, stomach and thighs twice a day. An excellent prevention oil can be prepared by mixing one and a half ounces of wheatgerm oil (rich in Vitamin E) with fifteen drops of lavender oil and twelve drops of neroli. Massage this into the skin daily. This blend can be used by anyone with burgeoning stretchmarks or while dieting, as well as throughout pregnancy.

Vitamin E oil (pure and undiluted) can be applied daily to the affected areas to prevent scarring and tissue damage.

A slightly higher protein diet, combined with 25 mg of pantothenic acid, and 400 IU of Vitamin E per day increases elasticity. This combination has been proven to eradicate stretchmarks from former pregnancies and growth/weight spurts.

Moist, healthy skin contains a great deal of elasticity. By taking care of your skin, the potential for stretchmarks decreases dramatically.

RED VEINS

Broken capillaries often manifest themselves as unsightly, enlarged red veins on the face and legs. To prevent this from happening, it is important to keep your capillaries strong and healthy, and that means ensuring you are getting sufficient quantities of bioflavonoids (found in bright-coloured fruit and vegetables; for instance, spinach, mango, canteloupe), which will also prevent bruising.

There is a new treatment, using the Diathermie process, which involves draining the blood from the dilated part of the artery, and then cauterizing both ends of the same artery at either side of the dilated area, to cut off the supply of blood. This process is excellent on surface veins and on the face, chest and arms.

Aromatherapy, with circulation-stimulating oils, will help. (See pages 174–177, for details.)

IT'S UP TO YOU

Looking after yourself is the one part of your regime that you can enjoy. It involves all the pleasurable aspects of health: good food, fresh water, comforting baths, fresh, clean-smelling skin, shining hair and strong white teeth. A clean environment and an organized lifestyle are all essential to feeling and looking great, and before you begin to pamper and properly care for your body, you must get that part of your life in order. Then watch your life, attitude and appearance change. Gone are the spots, fatigue, cellulite, excess weight and dull, lifeless skin and hair. The healthy new you will have energy and bounce, freedom from worry and strain, and a healthy, positive outlook.

This is especially important when you hit life's rough spots. Instead of becoming introspective and reflecting on their effects on your appearance and lifestyle, turn that energy around and be extra careful to take care of yourself. Consider all the treatments in this chapter, undertake the ones that make you look and feel your best, then bulldoze through those problems.

Marilynne

When Marilynne first came to see us she looked quite terrifying. She was extremely uptight and nervous, and her manner was sullen and withdrawn. Physically, her face was pinched and drawn, she was very pale and much too thin. Overall, she appeared to be listless and lethargic.

We established that she was grossly constipated, and had been since the age of sixteen, and that she had an anorexic outlook, in that she was terrified of putting on weight and, consequently, could go for days without eating. At best, her eating habits were erratic – she never ate breakfast, lunch was diet biscuits, and dinner was a few vegetables. In the meantime, however, she would constantly snack.

Her history had been one of bullying at school, parents who divorced when she was young, a feeling of never being quite good enough, and a good deal of trauma and upset.

We decided that the first areas to be addressed should be her physical symptoms, on the basis that once her body was functioning properly and she felt healthier, her outlook on life could change considerably. The main objective was to get Marilynne to eat three meals a day, and so we spent a great deal of time going through ideas for meals, ideas for snacks, what to eat in a restaurant, and how to organize her domestic arrangements and kitchen, in order for it to be really easy to eat good, nutritious food, regularly. She agreed to do a complete clear-out of her kitchen and then go shopping for all her food and to arrange for someone to come in and batch cook for her (which she would then freeze). Muesli was to be a staple diet for breakfast, using our own wheat- and sugar-free recipe, and if she really wanted a snack or dessert, we suggested another bowl, in order to get her bowels moving again.

After that, we took her through a very detailed Pamper, encouraging her to really enjoy the treat of looking after her skin and body properly. We gave her ideas of products, tips on how to deal with her very dry skin and then, because by this point she seemed to have opened up to all sorts of ideas and possibilities, we were able to recommend that she have her hair done and suggest a good hairdresser. We also said we'd go with her, if she liked.

She went away looking like a new person. She was animated and excited, and already her energy was lifted.

In the course of the next few weeks, she really did bring about the changes, and the effect was immediate. Initially, simply because she had made some decisions about her life, she immediately looked more alive and felt more energetic – her face became more open and her eyes brightened.

Then things really changed. To her delight, her bowels started to work daily, her skin and hair lost the dry and listless look, and her energy just kept improving. Through consistently attending class, her body remained slim, even though she gained a few much-needed pounds, but became strong, firm and more streamlined.

Throughout the course, she kept us up to date on how she was doing, and we were able to constantly throw new ideas at her about nutrition, relaxation, presentation, etc, so that she could maintain her enthusiasm and optimism and, therefore, her results.

To my mind, the most delightful side-effect of all this was that because she looked so much more open and alive, her impact on the people around was entirely different, and consequently, her confidence level increased along with her self-esteem. I believe she's actually rather fond of herself now.

NINE

Presentation

THE WAY IN which we present ourselves to the world is of vital importance. It says much to others about how we feel about ourselves, and it shapes their opinions of us. Changing our appearance can also dramatically affect our confidence and energy levels.

Most people think that buying new clothing, or changing the way they style their hair or apply their make-up, should be left until after they have achieved a physical change – most commonly, that they should lose weight first. I would recommend the exact opposite to this. By changing your appearance you can look – and feel – completely different within the space of twenty-four hours.

Although most people dress in only one or two styles, you would be surprised at how many different looks suit you. When choosing clothes, try on styles to suit your different moods. This way you won't become bored and will develop a strong personal sense of style and charisma.

START AT THE TOP

When somebody is feeling rundown, is under- or overweight, or under stress, you will find that in most cases their hair looks a mess. They simply don't take any time to care for or to style it.

If you have decided to go for change, start by changing your hairstyle or by having it cut and deep-conditioned. The following tips will help:

○ Spend a lot of time discussing what you want with your hairdresser. If you don't have a stylist with whom you have a good rapport or relationship, find somebody who you like and start by having a trim before you plunge in for a major change of style. That way, you'll both have time to get on each other's wavelengths;

○ Ask the hairdresser to experiment with your hair, after it has been cut, trying out different styles;

○ Never leave the salon until you know how to handle your new style yourself. Otherwise, you will spend the next six weeks – or until you visit the salon again – feeling that it is not looking its best;

○ Be wary of perms; so often a perm looks unnatural. Be very cautious about trying

such a dramatic change of style;

○ Don't try to grow your hair long if it is not thick enough and remember to consider the overall balance. If you are short, long hair may emphasize that. It is much better to have a shorter cut that enhances the condition and luxurious appearance of your hair than to have long, straggly hair and split ends.

○ If you want to colour your hair, never take it too far from the colour of your eyebrows. By going too blonde, you will bleach out your features. This may look great on a model but on many women it doesn't enhance their appearances. Just give your natural colour a bit of oomph.

MASTERING MAKE-UP

Simplicity and minimalism are the key factors for face-flattering make-up. Wearing heavy make-up, with foundation and powder, makes most women look older than they really are. I know it is difficult to break long-standing habits, but if you spend time improving the condition of your skin, you will find that the minimum of make-up will work best.

Try these tactics:

○ Use a concealer to cover dark shadows, blemishes and spots, and skip the foundation. This will give the skin a chance to breathe. Instead of applying concealer to the face direct from the stick, use a small, firm brush (buy a lip brush, for instance) in order to apply a very fine film over the area. Then set the concealer with a tiny amount of powder.

○ Powder can be used without foundation as a base, and will successfully prevent shine, evening out the texture of your skin. A transluscent loose powder is often the best choice, as it will give a featherweight coverage. Pat on firmly with a velour puff and then sweep off any excess using a large powder brush. Use pressed powder to retouch as necessary during the day. If possible, confine using powder only to the nose and leave the rest of your face natural. Most of the major cosmetic houses now produce powders which are very light in texture; Estée Lauder, for instance.

○ Leave your eyes free of eyeshadow, unless it's just on the outer edges of the eyes. Instead, use a pencil, if you like, on the outer corners, top and bottom. Grey and navy blue give a softer look than black. It is not advisable to outline the whole eye in pencil, as this can look very hard. A successful make-up should have no harsh lines and should always be carefully blended.

○ Keep blusher very soft and very natural-looking. You want your cheeks to look rosy, but not dark. Always apply as little as possible, and, when in doubt, opt for a lighter application. Cream and gel blushers are worth investigating as they give the cheeks a healthy glow. Guerlain's waterproof *Star Blush* is a long-lasting cream blusher, which is dispensed from a tube.

○ Choose a lipstick that enhances your natural colouring, never one that starkly contrasts to it. Look for sheer colours – most of the houses make these now – rather than lipsticks which are heavily pigmented. Always blot your lipstick after application; thick, glossy lipstick is not very attractive or comfortable. Blotting your lipstick will leave a healthy-looking stain of colour on your lips.

Aim to build up a set of make-up colours that follow the same colour themes, but with slightly different textures and shades, so that you can vary your look and adapt your make-up according to your moods and the time of day.

For those of you who don't wear any make-up, try the tips above, using the minimum of everything. You may be pleasantly surprised by the fact that doing this doesn't dramatically alter your appearance, but does give your face a fresh new look. Well-applied make-up shouldn't look like make-up. It is important that we change our appearance from time to time – use the element of surprise. In the evening, for instance, mascara

Always wear clothes and make-up that make you feel comfortable. Confidence in your appearance will allow you to relax, and we all know that posture, skin colour and breathing are affected by that. If you look happy, healthy and secure, you are certain to attract attention – of the best possible kind.

on its own will look great alongside your blusher and lipstick.

Healthy skin and hair are the essentials to looking good. See **Looking after yourself**, chapter 8, for details of products and regimes that will improve and enhance your natural good looks.

DRESS YOUR BEST

Our clothes speak for us, giving messages to those we are with about our lifestyle, our moods, our jobs and our interests. The golden rule of dressing is that you should *never* wear something in which you feel less than your best. This does not mean that clothes should be fussy, or that you should be overdressed. In fact, simplicity and classic cuts are some of the secrets of success.

Many of us – men especially – buy and wear clothes simply because we have to. We don't necessarily take pleasure in wearing them. Do allow enough time for clothes shopping. The following strategies will help you to make the right choices:

○ Before you go, go through your wardrobe and consider which of your clothes make you feel really fabulous. Consider which of the many looks you probably own are really you. Throw out or give away anything you don't wear, or that no longer suits you. Chapter Five, **Staying Healthy**, goes through the steps of organizing your wardrobe. When you know where everything is, and have decided what you can and cannot do without, co-ordination becomes that much easier.

○ Ask somebody whose sense of personal style you admire to come with you. They will probably encourage you to try on clothes you would never have thought of trying, and will make you more adventurous.

○ Look for sensual fabrics. Instead of buying the first white T-shirt you see, look around for a T-shirt in, say, a silky and more tactile fabric. Necklines are particularly important – look for tops with scooped necklines that reveal your shoulders and collarbones. Men, as well, should look for wider necklines and smaller or no collars.

○ Even when buying casual clothes, like jeans, buy them only if they are cut perfectly for you.

○ Get into the habit of buying complete outfits rather than separates. And concentrate on building a cohesive wardrobe, so that outfits can be added to and switched around. You do not want a wardrobe where clothes have to be thrown away and replaced. Avoid buying too many fashion fads.

○ Buy the best quality you can afford. Look at the cut and the top-stitching, especially on jackets. Change plastic buttons for metal ones.

○ Shoes can make or break an outfit. Boots can look great with many different outfits. The best advice is: Don't buy cheap-looking shoes or boots.

MEN

Dressing your best is just as important for you. Pay special attention to your suit – take time to find one that looks great on you, and invest in a good fabric. A good-quality, well-fitting suit will last for years.

Casual tops look best when worn slightly larger, as they will give the impression of a well-built chest (unless you are well-toned on top, when a tighter-fitting top works well). Men who do not have a defined waist are a difficult shape to dress and should always wear their tops slightly big to emphasize the shoulders.

Don't stick to plain black shoes. If you wear grey or brown, look for toning shoes, for instance. Try different shapes to find which one suits or looks best.

TEN TIPS FOR DRESSING TO SUIT YOUR SHAPE

Body shape is something which should be flattered to the greatest possible degree. Even if you are over- or underweight, there are looks that will enhance your natural shape, drawing attention away from the trouble spots to focus on an overall look.

Some of the following points are essential to remember, when co-ordinating a look, or even shopping for new clothes or accessories.

○ If you are short, try padding your shoulders to get a squared look. Lapels should be long and narrow. Garments worn on the upper and lower body should be of the same colour – as should your belt – to avoid 'cutting you in half'.

○ If you have a prominent stomach or bottom, wear loose, unstructured jackets, or a long cardigan over a dress and skirt. Try to avoid tight belts.

○ If your legs or ankles are heavy, avoid details on hemlines, as this will emphasize your worst point. Do not wear shoes that are too fancy, and avoid colour contrasts.

○ If your shoulders are broad, never wear large shoulder pads. Pay particular attention to jewellery: a brooch or an unusual, eye-catching pair of earrings will draw attention away from the shoulders.

○ If your bust is small, place emphasis on your shoulders or waist. Wear tops with gathered yokes, or a pocket on the bust area – all of which adds interest to the bustline.

○ If your hips are broad, avoid wearing gathered or pleated skirts, or tight-fitting trousers. It is far more flattering to play down that area by wearing tailored, well-fitting skirts and trousers that simply grace the hips and do not draw attention to that area. Avoid loud prints, large checks and unco-ordinated tops and bottoms.

○ If you are very tall and thin, break up your bodyline with a belt, contrasting tops and bottoms, and interesting shoes or boots. Draw attention to the mid-calf or bustline. Chest detail or pleats and gathers on a skirt will break up an overly long line.

○ If your arms are heavy, avoid shirts that cut off the armline; for example, mid-upperarm or forearm sleeves. Sleeveless shirts should cut in over the shoulder, adding length to the arm. Long sleeves should be tighter at the wrist, to draw attention to the slimmest part of the arm. Never wear wrist-length gloves; opt for full-length instead.

○ If your legs are short, avoid mid-length skirts and shorts. Short skirts, with matching tights will lengthen the leg. Or wear longer skirts, past the knee, with detail around the waist. An interesting belt could do the trick.

COLOUR CONSULTANTS

Having your colours analysed can make a remarkable difference to your appearance. When I worked for a marketing company, we arranged for 150 people to have consultations with colour experts, and were amazed at the results. Everyone looked alive and had more confidence.

Colour analysis works on the principle that we all have predominantly blue or yellow undertones to our skin. We can all wear practically every colour – for instance, we can all wear blue – but it is the *shade* of blue that counts.

Colour consultants will supply you with a palette of fabric colours, by which you can choose your clothes and make-up. Fair blondes, for instance, usually look better in warm, yellow reds than blue or purple reds. The same theory applies to every colour, and is designed individually for you.

Wearing the best colours for you instantly makes you look healthier. The right colours make your face light up, the wrong tones deaden your complexion and make it look dull.

Colours worn can often be an indication of problems that a person is facing. Clothes play an important role in making a person look and feel good, and can also be a crucial factor in winning or losing a job. Human reaction to colour is more important than people are aware. Almost all fields of human activity are finding that colour can influence their preferences, understanding and ability to communicate.

When you see some people in certain colours, you get that 'gut feeling'. Colour should *not* dominate to such a degree that it detracts from your face, one of your most important accessories. We can all wear colours – it is the shade and intensity which makes the difference.

The colours that suit you, and bring out your natural beauty, can give you confidence, help you to feel at ease, bring the most compliments from friends and, according to the latest findings of psychologists, colour also contributes to the whole person's development. And, as an added bonus, careful colour analysis can save money by creating a co-ordinated wardrobe.

Colour analysis is also a useful tool for tuning your eye into mixing colours together, and makes you more creative and adventurous in the way you dress. It also helps greatly in harmonizing your make-up.

Men benefit just as much as women from having their colours done.

Remember to update and review your appearance every couple of months. You don't have to spend a fortune doing so – just make subtle changes and add to what you already have.

Start taking delight in looking great – it will do a lot to increase your sense of wellbeing. Think how you feel when somebody you know walks into the office or into a room with a great new haircut and some wonderful new clothes – you rush over to compliment them, and you feel happy that they look so good. Why not do that favour for yourself?

Conclusion

SO THERE YOU have it – a pot pourri of ideas, facts, information and tips. But the most important element to take you towards complete wellbeing, satisfaction and total happiness is still missing. That element is you.

In order to change for the better, you must remember the following points:

- ○ It is entirely up to you – no one else. You can call upon friends and counsellors for support, but the only person who can change you is you. You have to want to change more than anything you have ever wanted before.
- ○ Your actions should be practical and, above all, logical. And that goes for nutrition, exercise, staying healthy and everything else we have discussed in this book.
- ○ You have to find patience, energy and commitment within yourself, or the job will only ever be half done.
- ○ Depending on how far you take it, you can completely turn around your entire life – if it needs changing to that degree. As you feel better and better with yourself, you might want to change more.

This is a little different from your usual diet book, or 'get-fit-quick' tape, I think. The ideas in this book are not flavours of the month, and are nothing out of the ordinary. Holistix is based on sound, practical and pleasurable theories, not fly-by-night or risky do-it-yourself programmes. In fact, you might have noticed throughout, how much the ideas confirmed a lot of what you believed, or thought you knew, anyway.

Each chapter of this book is equal in importance when it comes to the job of serving any one goal. The Staying Healthy and Presentation chapters are as important as Nutrition, when you want to lose weight. And the Exercise and Becoming Aware chapters are as important as the Looking After Yourself chapter, when you want to look and feel better. Keep this book close to you, and use it from time to time to wake you up, or as a reference book. Developing an accurate and objective knowledge of yourself is difficult. Most people who have attained what they want have had to learn some quite difficult lessons along the way.

Involve yourself with people who are caring and courageous, and above all, who have the ability to be honest with you at all times. Know that avoiding issues and uncomfortable situations is the most painful way to go about things.

Stop living your life in the gloom of thoughts of eternal failure. Start living and thinking in the present – think about things like your nutrition, hygiene, physique, relationships, health, welfare and lifestyle. Ask for help if you need it. These factors are of enormous importance.

And think about one more thing. When you find yourself in a situation where you are thinking too far ahead, worrying that circumstances should be different or better, becoming concerned that you are not learning or doing things fast enough, slow down. Imagine that your life is like a map, and where you are now is represented by a big red X. This is the most important point on the map, and the most perfect place for you to be. Everything you do at this point will come out of the X, which represents here and now. So start here and now, right where you are on your own personal map.

Just think about what it would be like if we were to put all the energy we spend talking about health, diet and happiness into doing something about it. That would keep us going for years! Don't just talk, act. And do it now.

When you are being true to yourself, doing something that you fully believe in, in all areas of your life, you will have authenticity and a reason to be. Authenticity is the greatest tool for getting what you want. Participating fully within your life, integrating both emotional and physical aspects is about staking your claim and being in charge of every aspect of yourself. Given half the chance, you'd want that, wouldn't you?

Well then – what are you waiting for?

Good luck.

CAROLE

Useful Addresses

Action Against Allergy
43 The Downs, London
SW20 8HG (081-947 5082)

Age Concern
60 Pitcairn Road, Mitcham,
Surrey CR4 3LL
(081-640 5431)

Al-Anon Family Groups
61 Great Dover Street, London
SE1 4YF (071-403 0888)
Support for families of anyone
with a drink problem; including
Alateen, support for young
people and teenagers who are
affected by drink in the family.

Alcohol Concern
305 Gray's Inn Road, London
WC1 (071-833 3471)

Alcoholics Anonymous
London: 071-352 3001
Scotland: 041-221 9027
Northern Ireland: 0232 373771
South-west Wales: 0222
   373771
West Wales: 0994 5282

Anorexic Aid
The Priory Centre, 11 Priory
Road, High Wycombe, Bucks
HP13 6SL

Micheline Arcier Aromatherapy
7 William Street, London SW1
(071-235 3545)

Bach Flower Remedies
Dr Edward Bach, Mount
Vernon, Sotwell, Wallingford,
Oxon OX10 0PZ

Bodytreats Limited
15 Approach Road, London
SW20 (081-543 7633)

British Acupuncture Register
and Directory
34 Alderney Street, London
SW1 4VE (071-834 1012)

British Association for
Counselling
37a Sheep Street, Rugby
CV21 3BX (0788 78323)

British Chiropractic Association
Premier House, 10 Greycoat
Place, London SW1P 1SD
(071-222 8866)

British Council for
Complementary and
Alternative Medicine
Suite One, 19a Cavendish
Square, London W1M 9AD
(071-409 1440)

British Dental Association
63 Wimpole Street, London W1
(071-935 0875)

British Homoeopathic
Association
27a Devonshire Street, London
W1N 1JR (071-935 2163)

British Medical Association
BMA House, Tavistock
Square, London WC1H 9JP
(071-387 4499)

British Society of Medical
Hypnosis
42 Links Road, Ashtead,
Surrey KT21 2HJ
(0372 273522)

Council of Acupuncture
Suite One, 19a Cavendish
Square, London W1M 9AD
(071-495 8153)

Cranial Osteopathic Association
478 Baker Street, Enfield,
Middlesex EN1 3QS
(081-367 5561)

DAWN (Drugs Alcohol Women
Now)
Omnibus Workspace, 39–41
North Road, London N7 9DP
(081-700 4653)

Dietary Therapy Society
33 Priory Gardens, London
N6 5QU (081-341 7260)

Drugline
9A Brockley Crescent,
Brockley, London SE4
(081-692 4975)

Drugs Release
169 Commercial Street,
London E1 3BW
(071-377 5905; 603 8654 –
24-hour emergency)

General Council and Register
of Osteopaths
56 London Street, Reading
RG1 4SQ (0734 576585)

Helena Harnik – Beauty
Products
19 Upper Berkeley Street,
London W1 (071-724 1518)

Helios Homoeopathic
Pharmacy
92 Camden Road, Tunbridge
Wells, Kent TN1 2QP
(0892 36393)
Homoeopathic mail-order
service.

Pamela Hornby – Colour
Consultant
6 Cannock Road, Aylesbury
HP20 2AN (0296 25365)

Institute for Complementary
Medicine
21 Portland Place, London
W1N 3AF (071-636 9543)

The Institute for Optimum
Nutrition
5 Jerdan Place, London
SW6 1BE (071-385 7984)

International Institute of
Reflexology
28 Hollyfield Avenue, London
N11 3BY (081-368 0865)

ISDD (Institute for the Study
of Drug Dependence)
1–4 Hatton Place, Hatton
Garden, London EC1N 8NP
(071-430 1991)

Lifeworks Centre for Natural
Healthcare and Remedies
11 Southampton Road, London
NW5 4JS (071-485 7122)

The Medical Council on
Alcoholism
1 St Andrew's Place, London
NW1 4LB (071-487 4445)

Middle Piccadilly Natural
Healing Centre
Holwell, Sherborne, Dorset
DT9 5LW (0963 23468)

National Institute of Medical
Herbalists
41 Hatherly Road, Winchester
Hants SO22 6RR (0962 68776)
PO Box 3, Winchester, Hants
SO23 8AA

National Osteoporosis Society
PO Box 10, Barton Meade
House, Radstock, Bath, Avon
BA3 3PY (0761 32472)

Natural Healing Centre
76 Berkely Road, Ruislip,
Middlesex HA4 6LF
(0895 675464)

Nature's Best
1 Lamberts Road, Freepost
PO Box 1, Tunbridge Wells,
Kent TN2 3EQ (0892 34143)
Mail-order health products –
send for free catalogue

Danielle Ryman Aromatherapy
Park Lane Hotel, Piccadilly,
London (071-753 6707)

Samaritans
17 Uxbridge Road, Slough,
Bucks (Slough 32713)

Denise Sedar – Nutritionist
349 Finchley Road, London
N11 (081-458 0785)

The Shen Tao Foundation
Middle Piccadilly Healing
Centre, Holwell, Sherborne,
Dorset DT9 5LW

Shiatsu Society
c/o Elaine Liechti, 19 Longside
Park, Kilbarchan,
Renfrewshire PA10 2EP
(05057 4657)

Society of Holistic Practitioners
Old Hall, East Bergholt,
Colchester CO7 6TG

Society of Homoeopaths
2 Artisan Road, Northampton
NN1 4HU (0604 21400)

Standing Conference on Drug
Abuse (SKODA)
1–4 Hatton Place, Hatton
Garden, London EC1N 8NP
(071-430 1991)

Terence Higgins Trust
52–54 Gray's Inn Road,
London WC1X 8JU (071-831
0330)

Tisserand Aromatherapy
Institute
10 Victoria Grove, Second
Avenue, Hove, East Sussex
BN3 2LJ (0273 206640)

Bharty Vyas — DSD Products
and Treatments
24 Chiltern Street, London W1
(071-935 5312)

Stephen Way – Professional
Hairdresser
109 New Bond Street, London
W1Y 99A (071-493 5304/5)

Yoga for Health Foundation
Ickwell Bury, Northill,
Biggleswade, Bedfordshire
SG18 9ED

Further Reading

Active Birth by Janet Balaskas (Sidgwick & Jackson)

Natural Pregnancy by Janet Balaskas (Sidgwick & Jackson)

Healing Without Harm by E.G. Bartlett (Eliot Right Way Books)

The Bates Method for Better Eyesight without Glasses by William H. Bates, MD

Minding the Body, Mending the Mind by Joan Borysenko, PhD

Hands of Light by Barbara Ann Brennan (Bantam)

Vegetarian Kitchen by Sarah Brown (BBC Books)

Eating Your Heart Out by Julia Buckroyd

An Introduction to Kinesiology by Brian Butler

The Foodwatch Alternative Cookbook by Honor J. Campbell (Ashgrove Press)

No Change by Wendy Cooper (Arrow)

Understanding Osteoporosis by Wendy Cooper (Arrow)

Nutritional Medicine by Dr Stephen Davies and Dr Alan Stewart (Pan)

Food, Facts and Figures by Jill Davies and John Dickerson

The Green Consumer Guide by John Elkington (Gollancz)

The Handbook of Alternative Medicine by Stephen Fulder (Coronet)

Food Combining for Health by Doris Grant and Jean Joice (Thorsons)

Wheat, Milk and Egg Free Cooking by Rita Greer (Thorsons)

You Can Heal Your Life by Louise L. Hay (Eden Grove Editions)

How to Banish Cellulite Forever by Liz Hodgkinson (Grafton)

The Alternative Health Guide by Brian Inglis and Ruth West (Michael Joseph)

Love is Letting Go of Fear by Gerald G. Jampolsky MD (Celestial Arts)

Raw Energy by Leslie and Susannah Kenton (Arrow)

Raw Energy Recipes by Leslie and Susannah Kenton (Arrow)

Alternatives in Healing by Simon Mills (Macmillan)

The Power of Myth by Joseph Campbell with Bill Moyers

Zest – Cosmopolitan Health and Beauty by Chrissie Painell

The Natural Food Catalogue by Vicki Peterson (MacDonald)

The Assertive Woman – a New Look by Stanlee Phelps and Nancy Austin

Journal of Alternative Medicine by Robert Tisserand

How to Use Plant Oils for Health and Beauty by Robert Tisserand

The Yeast Syndrome by John Parks Trowbridge and Merton Walker, MD, DPM (Bantam)

Candida Albicans by Richard Turner and Elizabeth Simonson (Thorsons)

Alternative Healthcare for Women by Patsy Westcott (Grapevine)

Index